New Perspectives on Keynes

New Perspectives on Keynes

Annual Supplement to Volume 27

History of Political Economy

**Edited by Allin F. Cottrell and
Michael S. Lawlor**

Duke University Press
Durham and London 1995

Contents

Introduction

Allin F. Cottrell and Michael S. Lawlor

Interest in Keynes seems to have reached a new highpoint in the last decade. This period has seen a burgeoning of the primary materials available to Keynes scholars. The steadily accumulating publication of Keynes's *Collected Writings* (CW) was completed in 1989 with the last volume, entitled *Bibliography and Index*. The *Writings* run to thirty volumes and 13,500 pages, yet, according to one of the editors (Moggridge 1992, xv), the concern of these volumes "was merely his professional life as an economist and his contributions to public affairs, and even then, they were selective." Predictably, plans are now under way to supplement the published papers in a number of ways. Rod O'Donnell plans an edition of Keynes's early philosophical papers in the near future. In addition, the unpublished Keynes papers, detailed in Jacky Cox's contribution to this volume, became more accessible to scholars once they were reunited in the King's College Modern Archive with the completion of the *Collected Writings* project. This whole collection is now available on microfilm for libraries willing to foot the bill.

Willing scholars have not been lacking to exploit this increased supply of the raw materials of their trade. The secondary literature on Keynes seems to have exploded pari passu. Whether this was a true supply-side phenomenon or demand driven is not clear, but the following few examples indicate the frenzy of activity involved. Three full-scale biographies were undertaken: two have appeared complete (Hession 1983; Moggridge 1992), and one is into a second volume (Skidelsky 1983; 1992). A journal devoted to post-Keynesian economics was launched and has sustained the interests of readers and contributors for over ten years. And quantities of papers, monographs, and conference volumes—too numerous to contemplate listing here—were published in this period. Any confirmed stalker of the library stacks will testify to the bulging of Keynesiana in the HB99 shelf.

Why, then, yet another volume? Our intention in selecting, and in some cases requesting, the papers collected here was to display and further promote one noteworthy aspect of the Keynes literature—an aspect that we believe holds considerable importance for the history of economics in general: namely, its emerging cross-disciplinary nature. We wished to gather around one table representatives of various communities that now claim a substantive interest in Keynes's life and works. Besides the expected economists and historians of economics, this now includes archivists, political, literary and social historians, political scientists, and philosophers, as well as a number of people who have been obliged to make of themselves some hybrid of these categories owing to the peculiar demands of the study of Keynes.

The result is the collection you now hold in your hands. We trust that this juxtaposition of varied views on Keynes—in many cases, with comments written by individuals from different sections of the academic community—will be enlightening and stimulating to the readers of *HOPE*. If the volume also stimulates further cross-fertilization of the disciplines—whether on the subject of Keynes or other aspects of the history of economics—we will be doubly glad.

Of the nine papers in the volume, six may be grouped under two broad themes, while the others are relatively sui generis. One theme is Keynes and philosophy. Following the seminal contributions of Anna Carabelli (1988) and Rod O'Donnell (1989), there is now a large and rapidly expanding literature on this topic, much of it concerned with the relationship between Keynes's *Treatise on Probability* ([1921] 1973, vol. 8 in the CW) and his later writings in economics. The topics treated here are rather different. Rod O'Donnell addresses the relatively neglected field of Keynes on aesthetics. He is able to show, drawing on several unpublished papers, that aesthetics was a subject that absorbed a good deal of the intellectual energy of the young Keynes: he further suggests that there are important connections between Keynes's writings on this topic and his ethical views, and that the study of this aspect of Keynes's work helps to illuminate his "philosophy of practice" more generally. Teddy Seidenfeld and Henry Kyburg both take up the theme of Keynes's theory of probability, but, as distinguished philosophers of probability themselves, they approach the subject from a somewhat different angle than most of the existing literature on Keynes and philosophy (largely written by economists). Seidenfeld is intrigued by the fact that both Harold Jeffreys and R. A. Fisher appealed to Keynes's ideas in the course of their debate over the status of inverse inference. While Jeffreys and Fisher agreed on the mathematical form of the answer to the problem at hand, each accused the other of committing· a foundational error in the explication of the mathematics, and both tried to coopt Keynes's theory in the service of their argument. Seidenfeld nonetheless concludes that Keynes would not have accepted either of their competing positions! Kyburg is interested in Keynes as a "serious logician," who sought to do for uncertain inference what Russell and Whitehead had done for deductive logic—namely, offer a consistent formalization of this domain of argument. While Keynes did not succeed in this, he did present and defend a theory of partially ordered probabilities that continues to interest philosophers, and Kyburg develops this theory, suggesting some variant interpretations of the axiomatization of Keynes due to algebraist B. O. Koopman.

A second theme is the investigation of the various mechanisms through which Keynesian ideas, initially heterodox, rather quickly became dominant and were assimilated into the orthodoxy of the economics profession. Donald Moggridge is concerned with the indices of the advancement of Keynesian thinking in economics journals and graduate programs in economics, as well as with the generational dynamics of the acceptance of the Keynesian "revolution." He finds that those involved in the early discussion, and acceptance, of the ideas in Keynes's *General Theory* were disproportionately drawn from the ranks of the most prestigious graduate programs of the time, contrary to Keynes's suggestion that it was "the young who have not been properly brought up" who would be most susceptible to his influence. Robert Dimand asks how it happened that the influence of Irving Fisher, the most cited macroeconomist during the 1920s, was so completely and decisively eclipsed by that of Keynes by 1940. He suggests that once the general Keynesian approach to macroeconomics—in terms of saving, investment, and effective demand—had become widely accepted, Fisher was left on the sidelines because, even though he clearly had a good deal to say about saving and investment, he had never managed to integrate these elements with his monetary theory of the level of economic activity. Kerry

Pearce and Kevin Hoover offer a detailed account of the emergence of "textbook Keynesianism," with particular emphasis on the domestication of the Keynesian revolution at the hands of Paul Samuelson in his best-selling *Economics*. Pearce and Hoover argue that the reduction of "revolutionary" ideas to a relatively simplified textbook orthodoxy is a general, and even a necessary, characteristic of "normal science" (in Thomas Kuhn's terms). The Samuelsonian presentation of Keynesian ideas as simply "modern macroeconomics" was, from this point of view, something of a rhetorical triumph.

The three papers that do not readily fall under the above headings each offer a distinctive new perspective on Keynes. Peter Groenewegen, viewing Keynes from his vantage point as a biographer of Alfred Marshall, is naturally concerned with Keynes's Marshallian heritage. He argues that there is more to be said on this matter than is offered in the recent biographies of Keynes by Skidelsky and Moggridge. Groenewegen is not so much concerned with tracing connections at the level of technical economic theory as with the broader themes of methodology, society, and politics. In this regard, he argues that Keynes's general attitudes toward capitalism and laissez-faire are very much in the Marshallian mold. Jacky Cox, as mentioned, gives an illuminating account of the Keynes archive at King's College. The archivist's perspective affords some interesting sidelights on, inter alia, Keynes's working methods and the broad range of scholars interested in consulting his writings. Cox suggests one relatively undeveloped angle that could be explored by reference to the archive: Keynes as a journalist, using both the quality and the popular press in efforts to persuade. Jim Tomlinson offers an analysis of the "unfortunate alliance" between Keynesian economics and Conservative government in postwar Britain. Keynes had written that if, via government action, the level of aggregate demand could be manipulated to achieve full employment, then the rest of economic decision making would best be left to the play of market forces. Tomlinson argues that once aggregate demand management by fiscal and/or monetary means had become an accepted lever of policy, this Keynesian conception fit well with the predilections of postwar British conservatism. It rationalized the neglect of industrial policy—a neglect that Tomlinson suggests must bear part of the blame for Britain's relative economic decline in this period.

Special thanks are due to Roy Weintraub, who first suggested the conference to us and then supported it with both enthusiasm and funds. Provost David Brown at Wake Forest also generously contributed to the staging of the conference (which took place at the Graylyn Conference Center of Wake Forest University on 1–2 April 1994). Beth Eastlick at *HOPE* handled the production details of the volume with great efficiency. Finally, to all the participants, we offer our congratulations on an enjoyable and a productive conference.

References

Carabelli, A. 1988. *On Keynes's Method*. New York: St. Martin's.

Hession, C. H. 1983. *John Maynard Keynes: A Personal Biography of the Man Who Revolutionized Capitalism and the Way We Live*. New York: Macmillan.

Keynes, J. M. [1921] 1973. *A Treatise on Probability*. Vol. 8 of *The Collected Writings of John Maynard Keynes*. 30 vols. Edited by D. E. Moggridge. London: Macmillan. (CW)

Moggridge, D. E. 1992. *Maynard Keynes: An Economist's Biography*. London and New York: Routledge.

O'Donnell, R. M. 1989. *Keynes: Philosophy, Economics and Politics*. New York: St. Martin's.

Skidelsky, R. 1983. *Hopes Betrayed, 1883–1920*. Vol. 1 of *John Maynard Keynes*. London: Macmillan.

———. 1992. *The Economist as Saviour 1920–1937*. Vol. 2 of *John Maynard Keynes*. London: Macmillan.

Keynes as a Philosopher

Henry E. Kyburg Jr.

Many people think of Keynes as standing for a certain kind of economic and political philosophy. As a political or social philosopher, Keynes was certainly controversial, and still is. I am not a student of these matters and have no informed opinion to share with you.

It is less well known that Keynes was a serious logician, and it is as a logician that he is discussed in this article. Many people know that he wrote a book on probability, but it is easy to think of that work as simply an outgrowth of his work in economics. After all, how can you do economics without probability and statistics?

A Treatise on Probability ([1921] 1973), however, was intended as a work on logic in a very traditional sense. A little background will illustrate how serious this intention was.

Keynes's father, John Neville Keynes, was an economist and a Cambridge don. He had also studied with John Venn, a distinguished nineteenth-century logician and probabilist (Venn 1865). He taught logic and wrote a well-known work on formal logic, *Studies and Exercises in Formal Logic* (1844). W. E. Johnson, a mentor of Keynes, planned a definitive four-volume work on logic. The first three volumes appeared (Johnson 1921), but the fourth, on "problematic inference" offered its author considerable difficulty. Keynes began work on the *Treatise* at a time when Johnson was still working on his own approach to what I shall call uncertain inference. Johnson was extremely helpful to Keynes. Keynes writes: "The result is that in its final form it is difficult to indicate the exact extent of my indebtedness to him. When the following pages were first in proof, there seemed little likelihood of the appearance of any work on probability from his own pen, and I do not now proceed to publication with so good a conscience, when he is announcing the approaching completion of a work on Logic which will include 'Problematic Inference'" (CW 8:116). In any event, the fourth volume of Johnson's work appeared only posthumously, in the British philosophical journal *Mind* in 1932, edited by R. B. Braithwaite.[1]

Keynes's years at Cambridge were rich years for logic. Bertrand Russell was there, and Russell and Alfred North Whitehead had published the monumental *Principia Mathematica* (1913) only a decade before in an attempt to demonstrate the reducibility of all of mathematics to logic. The process involved development of a new notation and a new approach to logic. Although this development was mirrored in various places in the world, it was the *Principia* of Russell and Whitehead that captured the interest of logicians and nonlogicians alike. G. E. Moore, also a member of Keynes's Cambridge circle, was not a logician, but his elegant work in analytical philosophy was consciously inspired by the work of Russell and Whitehead.

Keynes was an intimate of Russell (both were members of the famous "Apostles" of Cambridge), and he was strongly influenced by the success of the *Principia*. Keynes was not bowled over by the logical style developed by Russell:

> Those writers, who strain after exaggerated precision without going the whole hog with Mr. Russell, are sometimes merely pedantic. . . . It is possible under cover of a careful formalism, to make statements, which, if expressed in plain language, the mind would immediately repudiate. There is much to be said, therefore, in favour of understanding the substance of what you are saying *all the time*, and of never reducing the substantives of your argument to the mental status of an x or a y. (CW 8:19 n)

At the same time, he writes of "taking pains . . . to employ only such periphrases as could be translated, *if desired*, into perfectly exact language" (CW 8:19 n).

Keynes thus saw the logical precision of the *Principia* as an ideal, though one that was inappropriate to his own ends. There are neverthe-

---

1. This consisted of three long articles. The other three volumes of his work on logic appeared as *Logic*, published by Cambridge University Press in 1921, the same year in which Keynes's *Treatise on Probability* appeared.

less many logical formulas in the *Treatise*, and they deserve to be taken seriously and treated with respect. Not everybody thinks so, however. Frank Ramsey, also an intimate of both Keynes and Russell, thought the structure attributed by Keynes to probabilities was ill-conceived at the outset; Ramsey denied that there are any such objective logical probability relations as Keynes sought to explore in the *Treatise* and argued that one should be concerned rather with a numerical notion of rational belief. So far Ramsey has carried the day, and many writers would agree with Ramsey that "we do not regard it as belonging to formal logic to say what should be a man's expectation of drawing a white or a black ball from an urn; his original expectations may within the limits of consistence be any he likes" (1931, 189). I would like to give Keynes the chance to respond: "But if, knowing the proportion of white and black balls in the urn, his expectation differs from that proportion, we may expect from a rational man an account of the source of the difference." It seems to me clear that analysis of these reasons is exactly what Keynes wanted to introduce to formal logic.

Furthermore, the charge of excess precision can be made by both sides. Ramsey repudiates the idea that logic can constrain probabilities; in effect he acknowledges only the constraints of deductive logic (not those of "classical" deductive logic, but those embodied in the new logic of the *Principia Mathematica*). Keynes, on the other hand, repudiates the suggestion that probabilities are to be represented in all cases by real numbers—a suggestion to which Ramsey, as well as those modern personalists who adopt his Dutch book arguments, are committed.

In this article I would like to see what can be done for Keynes's view of the probability relation in a more modern style of logical inquiry. Is it possible that there is more to it than the psychologizers of probability are willing to see?

Keynes's Goal

Keynes sought to do for uncertain inference what Russell and Whitehead did for mathematical, or deductive, logic. How is that to be conceived? One difficulty in understanding both the goal and its execution is a difficulty that may be laid at the door of Russell and Whitehead. Sensitive in most other respects to the nuances of their mother tongue, Russell and Whitehead, in their formalization of mathematical logic, committed one horrendous blunder from which we are still suffering: confusion of the relation of implication with the operation of forming a conditional.[2] In oral English both may be expressed by the locution: "if . . . then—." In written English, a distinction is required by grammar: "If two angles of triangle A are equal to two angles of triangle B, then the third angle of triangle A is equal to the third angle of triangle B," is fine, but "two angles of triangle A are equal to two angles of triangle B *implies* the third angle of triangle A is equal to the third angle of triangle B" is simply ungrammatical. To make it grammatical, we must introduce quotation marks to render the terms of the relation substantives: "'Two angles of triangle A are equal to two angles of triangle B' implies 'The third angle of triangle A equals the third angle of triangle B.'" We can also do this orally by saying, "*That* two angles . . . implies *that* the third angle . . ."

Russell and Whitehead call the operation of forming a proposition from two others by truth functional "if . . . then—" connective "implication." In the context of mathematics, the distinction may not be so important: the conditionals that interest us are generally those that correspond to real implications. Given the reduction of mathematical to logical truths, which was the underlying goal of the work of Russell and Whitehead, the only *mathematical* statements of conditional form that are of interest are universally true—are *tautologies* in the idiom of the time.

But Keynes was concerned with inference from a body of knowledge. He recognizes that his concern with *inference* is distinct from "*implication*, as defined by Mr. Russell. This is a matter of very great importance. . . . [Russell] is not concerned with analysing the methods of valid reasoning which we actually employ" (CW 8:117–18). "Probability," he writes, "is concerned with *arguments*, that is to say, with the 'bearing' of one set of propositions on another set" (CW 8:117–18). The clearest statement of Keynes's concerns, I think, is to be found in the first two sentences of the *Treatise*: "Part of our knowledge we obtain direct; and part by argument. The Theory of Probability is concerned with that part which we obtain by argument, and it treats of the different degrees in which the results so obtained are conclusive or inconclusive" (CW 8:1).

For Keynes, then, the theory of probability is not a theory about beliefs, and not even, directly, about rational beliefs, but about logical import. It is certainly not, in his view, a theory about frequencies, though probabilities

2. This is particularly true in artificial intelligence, a field that is heavily indebted to formal logic.

are often related to frequencies. There is an indirect connection with rational belief since it is rational to apportion one's beliefs to the degrees to which the evidence supports those beliefs.

What is the role of formalization? Keynes says little about it. But I think the idea behind mathematical logic, and in the back of Keynes's mind, must be something like this: If we can formalize a kind of reasoning, we can be assured that we can come to agreement concerning any instance of it. This is not to say that we need present our arguments in formal detail, but that you and I can develop the formal detail of an argument to whatever degree is necessary to achieve agreement. Since the ultimate formalization completely mechanizes the steps of inference, we are assured of eventual agreement. I take it that Keynes was seeking to achieve the same kind of goal for uncertain argument—argument supporting that part of our knowledge we do not "obtain direct."

As regards this goal, one must admit that the *Treatise* was a complete failure. Two statisticians, two gamblers, or two economists who are willing to share the same evidence, but who have different opinions concerning an event, do not turn to Keynes's work to resolve their differences.

Note, though, that the idea that they should resolve their differences by getting more evidence *is* dealt with by Keynes, and he correctly observes that this is *not* a resolution of their differences. New evidence does not give them a more accurate idea of the old probability, but rather makes a new probability relevant (about which they might happen to agree more closely). This is a matter on which personalistic probabilists have been confused. Much is made of deFinetti's convergence theorem (under some circumstances the opinions of two agents will converge as they accumulate evidence), and in a recent book on the philosophy of science (Maher 1993) this same convergence phenomenon is applied directly to epistemic expectations to show that even if scientists do not share exactly the same cognitive values, they can be expected to converge toward acceptance of the same theories as evidence mounts. That's no help if we have to make a decision now; Keynes has already told us where we will be "in the long run."

The object is to systematize uncertain inference. This includes induction, scientific reasoning in general, arguments by analogy, and, of course, arguments that depend on or involve relative frequencies in the world. Let us dress Keynes's system in more modern clothes before looking at the question of whether the system lends itself to any such formalization.

Partially Ordered Probabilities

Since Keynes takes the theory of probability to be a theory of argument, he proudly introduces a new notation for probabilities: if h represents a body of knowledge, and a a proposition, the probability, the degree to which an argument from h supports the proposition a, is represented by the compound symbol a/h. We could think of a/h as the "degree of entailment" of a by h, since the term *argument* suggests nowadays a linguistic object—for example, a sequence of sentences related in certain ways. The word *degree* must be taken somewhat loosely, since probabilities are not linearly ordered.[3] Keynes argues that, while all probabilities are greater than or equal to 0 and less than or equal to 1, there are pairs of probabilities such that we can say neither than the first is greater than the second nor that the second is greater than the first, nor yet that they are equal. Probabilities, for Keynes, form only a partial order.

Ramsey takes the existence of only a partial order among probabilities to be a serious difficulty for Keynes, but there are a number of modern writers who also find a partial order among probabilities: I. J. Good (1962), C. A. B. Smith (1961), Patrick Suppes (1960), Isaac Levi (1974), myself (Kyburg 1961), and many others. Most of these writers had in mind the idea that probabilities could be measured by intervals. There are two ways to think of this. Good, Smith, and Suppes, for example, took the indefiniteness of probability to be a measurement problem. Thus, while degrees of belief are in principle point-valued, it may be that the closest we can come to evaluating that point is to enclose it in an interval. Levi's indeterminate probabilities derive from the assumption that the best representation of the credal state of an agent is by means of a convex set of classical point-valued probabilities. The result is that a given proposition has, for the agent, an upper and a lower bound. My view takes the value of the probability function always to be an interval (rarely, a degenerate interval). On my view, this may be taken to characterize rational belief, too. We cannot say of two beliefs, any more than of two probabilities, that one must be greater than, less than, or equal to the other.[4] From an abstract algebraic point of view, B. O. Koopman (1940a, 1940b, 1941) explored the structure of Keynesian probabilities.

---

3. Ramsey makes much of the fact that degrees of belief must be linearly ordered in order to be called "degrees" and uses this as an argument against Keynes's more general conception.

4. Ramsey (1931, 161) seems to take note of this possibility, but rejects it on the basis of his behavioristic view of belief.

The idea of partially ordered probabilities is thus not obviously absurd. Their identification with a measure of the degree of validity of an argument is another matter. Can we make sense of this? Some, among whom Ramsey may have been the first, simply expostulate that it is flatly absurd: "I do not see what these inconclusive logical relations can be or how they can justify partial beliefs. . . . The logical relation which justifies . . . inference is that the sense or import of the conclusion is contained in that of the premises. . . . [In] the case of inductive argument . . . [we] could accept the premises and utterly reject the conclusion without any sort of inconsistency or contradiction" (1931, 185–86).

We are in a better position now, perhaps, to make sense of this idea than we were when Ramsey wrote. Today we would not take the metaphor of containment ("the import of the conclusion is contained in that of the premises") to be at all clear or enlightening. We have learned since Alfred Tarski (1956) that truth can be defined for formalized languages and that for classical first-order languages the concept of validity can be expressed thus: an argument is valid if the conclusion is *true* in every model that makes the premises *true*. This way of characterizing validity removes us from the realm of metaphor and puts us squarely in the domain of semantics.

This suggests that we can indeed somewhat generalize the notion of logical validity. An inference is logically valid if the conclusion is true in every model of our language in which the premises are true. It is probabilistically valid, or near-valid, if it is true in almost all the models of our language in which the premises are true.

When we are talking of drawing conclusions of high probability, this seems to make reasonable sense; but Keynes's probabilities ranged from 0 to 1. What sense can we make in these terms of a probability close to 0? Keynes says that $a/h = 1$ represents certainty, and $a/h = 0$ represents impossibility (CW 8:134). The two notions are not quite opposites. The difficulty is that English has no word that bears the intended relation with "certainty." The best we can do is speak of the negation being certain: $a/h = 0$ represents an argument whose conclusion, given its premises, is certainly *false*. We could call such arguments "anticertain."

If we diagram relations of support, with anticertainty on the left, and certainty on the right, what we have so far looks like figure 1. The points on the line represent the strength of arguments that can be measured by real numbers; the other points represent other probability values; the

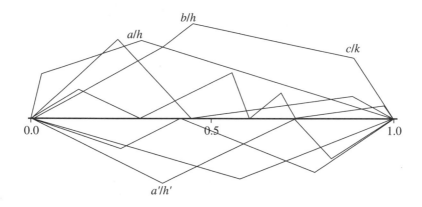

Figure 1   Relations between Certainty (*right*) and Anticertainty (*left*).

edges represent the possibility of comparison. There is, for example, no relation ($<$, $>$, $=$) between a/h and a'/h' in the diagram.

A natural interpretation of the partially ordered set of probabilities can be constructed as follows. Consider a/h. Let p be the largest real number such that there is argument of force p to which a/h can be compared, and q the smallest. These numbers (or their upper and lower bounds) exist, on Keynes's theory, since every argument can be compared to an argument characterized by certainty and also to an argument characterized by anticertainty.

Might there exist two probabilities, P and Q, such that they are distinct, yet bounded by the same real numbers? Keynes explicitly addresses this question: the answer is yes. There are "many cases in which . . . it is certain that it is not in our power to make the comparison. . . . In these cases the probabilities are, in fact, *not comparable*" (CW 8:112, italics in original). Every probability is bounded by 0 and 1; in the figure, the probabilities a/h and b/h are not comparable, though b/h and c/k are comparable. Thus we can say that c/k is greater than b/h, even though we cannot compare either with a/h. An immediate consequence of this fact is that probabilities do not form a lattice: two arguments may have upper bounds that are incomparable, so that there is no least upper bound.

If, inspired by William of Occam, we were to argue that probabilities should be identified with their bounds, then the way to a semantic representation of probability would be clear: we could identify the force of an argument with its upper and lower bounds, and we might take an argument to have force $[p, q]$ just in case its conclusion is true in from a fraction p to a fraction q of the models in which its premises are true. This fits nicely with the idea that an inference is characterized by a number near 1, just in case the conclusion is true in almost every model in which the premises are true. In addition, it makes sense in cases in which the conclusion is only rarely true when the premises are true. What it does not allow is that two probabilities can be comparable and one can be greater than the other when the numbers that bound them are the same.

It might be noted that this is an approach which is at least compatible with that of Glenn Shafer (see 1976, 1987), who takes an approach that relates uncertainty to certain canonical examples, usually related to games of chance, in which long-run frequencies are known precisely. We bound the force of our arguments by comparisons to arguments for which the degree of force is given numerically. From here there are two ways to go. One way, followed by Ramsey 1931 and Savage 1954, is to note that all we need is a well-balanced coin-tossing apparatus, and we can narrow down as much as we like the range within which a probability is known to lie. Thus we have no need for nonnumerical probabilities. But of course this presupposes exactly what Keynes is anxious to deny: that the force of any two arguments can be compared. The other way is to take Keynes seriously and to admit that often the numerical bounds are very coarse. For example, when it comes to the argument whose premises are our evidence concerning the weather and whose conclusion is that it will be sunny tomorrow, the force is more than that of an argument that a roll of a die will yield an even number and less than that of an argument that the die will yield any number other than 1—i.e., that it is bounded by 1/2 and 5/6. Is the force greater or less than 2/3? Answer: neither, nor is it identical to 2/3.

There are thus three positions to be distinguished.

(1) What I take to be Keynes's original position, which is that probabilities (the forces of arguments) can often be compared with each other, even when they can be compared with no arguments that admit of numerical measures of force.

(2) We can construct or imagine arguments that admit of n exclusive and exhaustive and equiprobable cases, and this allows us to bracket the force of a given argument as closely as we please by comparing it to the force of arguments that admit of numerical measure.

(3) The middle road: arguments can often be bounded by arguments admitting of numerical representation, but arguments having the same bounds need not be comparable.

What Is an Uncertain Conclusion?

There is one ambiguity left to resolve before we proceed to consider some of the technical consequences of this approach to uncertain argument. That is: What is the conclusion of such an argument? Is it a when a/h is high enough and h represents our total body of knowledge? Or is it that a *is probable*—namely, has a probability equal to a/h? The issue is put plainly by Carl Hempel (1965), who provides us with two schemata that show the distinction. Letting E play the role of the evidence for an uncertain inference and C the conclusion, we have either

$$\frac{E}{C} \text{, with high probability}$$

or we have

$$\frac{E}{\text{It is highly probable that } C}$$

Keynes never comes clean on this issue. He says that an "inductive argument affirms, not that a certain matter of fact *is* so, but that *relative to certain evidence* there is a probability in its favor" (CW 8:221). This suggests that the conclusion of our inductive argument is of the form "hypothesis a is highly probable, relative to the total evidence h." But only a dozen pages later Keynes says, "if our premises comprise the body of memory and tradition which has been originally derived from direct experience and the conclusion which we seek to establish is the Newtonian theory of the Solar System, our argument is one of Pure Induction insofar as we support the Newtonian theory by pointing to the great number of consequences which it has in common with the facts of experience" (CW 8:233). Here "the conclusion which we seek to establish is the Newtonian theory of the Solar System," *not* the proposition that the Newtonian theory of the solar system is probable relative to the total evidence.

This issue is very much a live one today. Serious Bayesian theorists, in artificial intelligence (Cheeseman 1988), philosophy (Earman 1992), and statistics (Lindley 1977) all take for granted that the conclusion of an uncertain inference is the assertion that a given proposition is probable. Non-Bayesians—Levi 1974, Popper 1959, traditional statisticians, myself, proponents in artificial intelligence of nonmonotonic logic—all take for granted that the conclusion of an uncertain inference is a categorical proposition, which, however, is accepted only tentatively and subject to further consideration.

Where does Keynes fit here? It seems clear, despite the reference to what an inductive logic affirms, that, given the purposes of his project, he wants us to be able to accept, within limits, as far as it goes, until further notice, *but nonetheless categorically*, the Newtonian theory of the solar system. Thus the schema he has implicitly in mind seems to be that of Hempel's first schema, rather than the second (1965). Let us now see if we can make semantic sense of this in line with the suggestion made above that a "probable" inference is one in which the conclusion is true in almost all models in which the premises are true.

Koopman's Axioms

First we must provide an interpretation for Keynes's symbolism according to which his definitions and axioms make sense and are true. To this end we turn to another scholar, B. O. Koopman, an algebraist. Here are Koopman's axioms (1940a) for Keynes's probability relation:

I.   Axiom of Implication
     If $a/h \succ k/k$, then $h \subset a$.
R.   Axiom of Reflexivity
     $a/h \prec a/h$
T.   Axiom of Transitivity
     If $a/h \prec b/k$ and $b/k \prec c/l$, then $a/h \prec c/l$.
A.   Axiom of Antisymmetry
     If $a/h \prec b/k$, then $\neg b/k \prec \neg a/h$.
C.   Axioms of Composition
     Let $a_1 b_1 h_1 \neq \emptyset$ and $a_2 b_2 h_2 \neq \emptyset$.
     If $a_1/h_1 \prec a_2/h_2$ and $b_1/a_1 h_1 \prec b_2/a_2 h_2$,
     then $a_1 b_1/h_1 \prec a_2 b_2/h_2$.
     If $a_1/h_1 \prec b_2/a_2 h$ and $b_1/a_1 h_1 \prec a_2/h_2$,
     then $a_1 b_1/h_1 \prec a_2 b_2/h_2$.

D. Axioms of Decomposition

   Let $a_1b_1h_1 \neq \emptyset$ and $a_2b_2h_2 \neq \emptyset$. Then if either of the eventualities (i) a_1/h_1, b_1/a_1h_1 has the supraprobable relation $\succ$ with either of (ii) b_1/h_1, a_1/b_1h_1, it will follow that the remaining case of (i) will have the infraprobable relation $\prec$ with the remaining case of (ii).

P. Axiom of Alternative Presumption

   If $a/bh \prec c/k$ and $a/\neg bh \prec c/k$, then $a/h \prec c/k$.

S. Axiom of Subdivision

   For any integer n, let the propositions $a_1, \ldots, a_n$ be such that $a_ia_j = b_ib_j = \emptyset \, (i \neq j) \, i, j = 1, \ldots, n; a = a_1 \vee \cdots \vee a_n \neq \emptyset; b = b_1 \vee \cdots \vee b_n \neq \emptyset; a_1/a \prec \cdots \prec a_n/a; b_1/b \prec \cdots \prec b_n/b; then $a_1/a \prec b_n/b$.

Koopman presents this system as an abstract algebra. He is not concerned with the details of interpretation, though he is explicit about trying to find a formal structure that answers to Keynes's system (1940a, 269 n.2). Once he has such a structure, however, he restricts his concerns mainly to "appraisable" probability relations—that is, those that can be measured by real numbers. Our concern, on the contrary, is to provide an understanding of the cases in which the probability relations are not "appraisable."

Take S to be a sample space. Let $\mathcal{A}_1, \mathcal{A}_2, \ldots$ be algebras of subsets of S containing S. For example, S might be the outcomes of rolling a die; some of the algebras might be those constructed from the following sets of atoms: {number up $= 1$, number up $\neq 1$}; {number up $= 3$, number up $= 2$, number up $\neq 3$ and $\neq 2$}; {number up $= 1$, number up $= 2$, number up $= 3$, number up > 3}.

We distinguish between a, b, etc., and h, k, etc.

Let the propositions h, k, etc. each give a convex set of distributions over one of the algebras of subsets of S—for example, the algebra generated by the six outcomes of the roll of the die. This algebra contains sixty-four elements (the set of disjunctive subsets of six outcomes, including S and the empty set). A distribution consists of an assignment of a real number to each of these six atomic outcomes in such a way as to satisfy the axioms for measure. Since the sum of these six parameters must be 1, we have five choices.

If we wish to represent *constraints* on these distributions, we have many more parameters to think about. We may stipulate that the measure of $\underline{1}$ lie in $[.1,.3]$ and that the measure of $\underline{2}$ lie in $[.1,.3]$, and still consistently require that the measure of $\underline{1} \cup \underline{2}$ lie in $[.25,.30]$. How many parameters may we consider? Two of the sixty-four subsets of S, $\emptyset$ and the set S itself, must have measure 0 and 1. The remaining sixty-two subsets may be divided into complementary pairs (thus $\underline{3} \cup \underline{5}$ is complementary to $\underline{1} \cup \underline{2} \cup \underline{4} \cup \underline{6}$). The set of pairs representing bounds on the distribution of the six-outcome set has thirty-one members, since we may impose tighter bounds on unions than are required by their components, but once we have bounds for a member of the algebra we have fixed the bounds for its complement. We represent h by the pair $\langle \mathcal{A}_i, \mathcal{M}_i \rangle$ where $\mathcal{M}_i$ represents a set of admissible distributions over $\mathcal{A}_i$.

Let s be a specific element of $\mathcal{S}$. Take the propositions a, b, etc. to be propositions asserting that s is in a specific member A, B, etc. of the algebra.

We require that no non-empty set be constrained to have the measure 0. It follows that no proper subset of S can be constrained to have measure 1.

The axioms contain terms consisting of the juxtaposition of symbols. We interpret ab to be the proposition asserting that s is in $A \cap B$. The symbol ah is to be interpreted as the set of distributions on the algebra of sets of the form $X \cap A$, where X is a set in the algebra for h and the distribution is derived from h—$m_{ah}(X \cap A) = m_h(X \cap A)/m_h(A)$— provided, of course that A is a set in the algebra of h so that $m_h(A)$ is defined. We represent the algebra of sets by $\mathcal{A}_i A$ and the set of measures by $\mathcal{M}_i A$: $\langle \mathcal{A}_i A, \mathcal{M}_i A \rangle$.

We interpret a/h as follows: it is the interval representing the measures according to h of the member A of the algebra that a asserts that s belongs to, provided that A is an element of that algebra. If not, we interpret a/h as $[0,1]$. Thus if our set of distributions h requires that the measure on $\underline{1} \cup \underline{2}$ lie in the set $[.25,.30]$, and a says that the element s of S belongs to $\underline{1} \cup \underline{2}$, the value of a/h is to be that same set $[.25,.30]$. We assume that the set of distributions in h is convex—that is, contains all its mixtures.

We interpret the relation $a/h \prec b/k$ as follows: it is to hold if and only if for every distribution m in h there is some distribution n in k such that $n(A) \leq m(B)$, and for every distribution n in k there is some distribution m in h such that $n(A) \leq m(B)$.

On this interpretation, the axioms given by Koopman turn out to be true. Axiom I is true if we interpret k to the left of the solidus as the assertion that s is in S. Then k/k must be $\{1\}$, and so to satisfy the relation the value of a/h must also be $\{1\}$, and that means that h implies

a, since we have not permitted contingent certainties or impossibilities in our distributions.

The axiom of reflexivity is obviously true; transitivity also follows easily. Antisymmetry makes use of the fact that if we assign the measure p to the element A of the algebra, we are forced to assign the measure $1 - p$ to its complement; for convex sets of measures if a/h is $[p,q]$, $\neg a/h$ is $[1 - q, 1 - p]$.

The axioms of composition present a little more difficulty. Where a_1 says that s is in A_1 and b_1 says that s is in B_1, the term $a_1 b_1 h$ represents a set of distributions on an algebra of sets of the form $A_1 \cap B_1 \cap X$, where X is in the algebra for which h represents a set of distributions. To say that $a_1 b_1 h$ is not empty is simply to say that $m_1(A_1 \cap B_1)$ is not identically 0 for all m_1 in $\mathcal{M}_1$, where $h_1 = \langle A_1, \mathcal{M}_1 \rangle$. Suppose that is the case. Every measure in $\mathcal{M}_1$ has the property that $m_{h1}(A_1 \cap B_1) = m_{h1}(A_1) m_{a1h1}(B_1) = m_{h1}(B_1) m_{b1h1}(A_1)$. Similarly let h_2 be $\langle A_2, \mathcal{M}_2 \rangle$. Every measure in the convex set of measures $\mathcal{M}_2$ has the property that $m_{h2}(A_2 \cap B_2) = m_{h2}(A_2) m_{a2h2}(B_1) = m_{h2}(B_1) m_{b2h2}(A_2)$. Assume that $a_1/h_1 \prec a_2/h_2$ and $b_1/a_1 h_1 \prec b_2/a_2 h_2$. We need to show $a_1 b_1/h_1 \prec a_2 b_2/h_2$. Let m_{h1} be a measure in $\mathcal{M}_1$. We need to show that there is a measure m_{h2} in $\mathcal{M}_2$, such that $m_{h1}(A_1 \cap B_1) \prec m_{h2}(A_2 \cap B_2)$. But $m_{h1}(A_1 \cap B_1) = m_{h1}(A_1) m_{a1h1}(B_1)$ and there is m_{h2} in $\mathcal{M}_2$ such that $m_{h2}(A_2 \cap B_2)/m_{h2}(A_2) \geq m_{h1}(A_1 \cap B_1)/m_{h1}(A_1)$, or $m_{h2}(A_2 \cap B_2) \geq m_{h1}(A_1 \cap B_1)[m_{h2}(A_2)/m_{h1}(A_1)]$. But since $m_{h2}(A_2) \geq m_{h1}(A_1)$ for every m_{h2} in $\mathcal{M}_2$, we must have $m_{h2}(A_2 \cap B_2) \geq m_{h1}(A_1 \cap B_1)$. In the same way, we can show that for every m_{h2} in $\mathcal{M}_2$, we can find a measure m_{h1} in $\mathcal{M}_1$ such that $m_{h2}(A_2 \cap B_2) \geq m_{h1}(A_1 \cap B_1)$.

Similar arguments will establish the other axiom of composition and the axioms of decomposition.

The axiom of alternative presumption can be established by observing that every measure in $\mathcal{M}_1$ can be represented as a mixture of measures on B and $\neg B$, and vice versa.

The axiom of subdivision, which is essential for connecting our intuitive assessments of probability to real numbers, is not in the form required by our interpretation, but we can easily put it in that form without changing its meaning:

$a_1/ah \prec \cdots \prec a_n/ah$ and $b_1/bh \prec \cdots \prec b_n h$ only if $a_1/ah \prec b_n/bh$.

In this form it admits of proof similar to that provided for the other axioms.

A Contrasting Interpretation

We have shown that Koopman's axioms have an interpretation in terms of our knowledge concerning frequencies that makes some sense and seem to correspond roughly to what Keynes had in mind. As expected, there are some cases in which neither $\prec$ nor $\succ$ holds. But is the correspondence we have suggested necessary? Might there not be other statistically based interpretations that fit what Keynes says?

First, we should note that this interpretation of the four-place "a is supported by h at least as much as b is supported by k" does not conform to the suggestion we made earlier. We suggested that a/h might be interpreted in terms of the proportion of models of h in which a is true, so that inductive acceptance could be made to correspond to "high probability." To see this, suppose the set of measures in h assigns measures ranging from .2 to .9 to A, and, correspondingly, from .1 to .8 to $\neg A$. A is clearly more "probable" than not, on this interpretation, but there is still a class of models—namely, those in which the true measure of A is .2—of which $s \in A$ is true only 20 percent of the time.

Let us consider the following weaker interpretation. Let the interpretation of a and h be as before, but let us take $a/h \prec b/k$ to mean that the interval generated by the measures of A in h lies entirely to the left of the interval generated by the measures of B in k or is identical to it. Thus if the bounds on measures of A in h are .3 and .5, and the bounds on the measures of B in k are .6 and .7, we would have $a/h \prec b/k$. It seems clear—we'll offer details shortly—that it is the *interval*, rather than the underlying distributions, that imposes constraints on the models and that we want to take account of in our decision theory.

Most of the axioms laid down by Koopman are also valid under this interpretation. The exceptions are particularly enlightening. The bounds of the measures of S in h are 1 and 1. Reflexivity is obvious. It is easy to show, by cases, that transitivity holds. Since the bounds on A in h are p and q only if the bounds on $\neg h$ are $1 - q$ and $1 - p$, antisymmetry holds. The axiom of alternative presumption no longer holds in general: let the bounds on the measure of c in k be r and s. We would need to show that if $a/bh \prec c/k$ and $a/\neg bh \prec c/k$, then $a/h \prec c/k$. Let m be any measure in h. Then $m(AB) = m(B)m_b(A)$, where $m_b(A)$ is the measure in bh corresponding to m, and similarly $m(A\neg B) = [1 - m(B)]m_{\neg b}(A)$. Case 1: the interval corresponding to a/bh and the interval corresponding to $a/\neg bh$ both lie to the left of the interval corresponding to c/k. Since for every measure m in h, $m(A)$ is a mixture of $m_b(A)$ and $m_{\neg b}(A)$, the interval corresponding to a/h also lies entirely to the left of that corresponding to c/k. The important and revealing case is Case 2: the interval corresponding to a/bh and that corresponding to $a/\neg bh$ are each identical to the interval corresponding to c/k. The measures in h may be quite precise about the measure of A without being precise about the measures of AB or of $A\neg B$. The measures associated with c/k may exactly reflect this imprecision.

Example Consider a box of dice, each of which is biased toward 1 or toward 2 by an amount d, with an exactly compensating bias against 2 or 1. Suppose there are half of each kind. Let k be a corresponding set of distributions concerning the measure of heads on tosses of a (heavily biased) coin—that is, the coin lands heads between $1/6 - d$ and $1/6 + d$ of the time. A is the set of rolls in which the die lands $\underline{1}$; B is the set of dice biased toward $\underline{1}$; C is the set of tosses on which the coin lands heads. Then we would have $a/bh = a/\neg bh = c/k = [1/6 - d, 1/6 + d]$, but $a/h = [1/6, 1/6]$. More simply, just consider a single die from the urn; though it is biased toward $\underline{2}$ or toward $\underline{1}$, it is clearly not at all biased with respect to $\underline{1} \vee \underline{2}$.[5]

As we will see later, if we divide the relation $\prec$ into its symmetric and asymmetric parts, the asymmetric part does satisfy the axiom of alternative presumption.

The axiom of division, surprisingly, does not fail. Assume the antecedents of the theorem. Let $[p_i, q_i]$ be the value of a_i/ah and $[r_i, s_i]$ be the value of b_i/bk. We show that $q_1 \le 1/n$ and $r_n \ge 1/n$. For consistency, we must have sequences $n_1 \le n_2 \le \cdots \le n_n$ and $m_1 \le m_2 \le \cdots m_n$ such that

$$\sum_{1}^{n} n_i = 1,$$

$$\sum_{1}^{n} m_i = 1,$$

5. This is the kind of case for which Shafer's belief functions seem to be designed. See Shafer 1976.

$$p_i \leq n_i \leq q_i, \text{ and}$$

$$r_i \leq m_i \leq s_i.$$

By the conditions of the theorem, $q_1 < 1/n$, unless we have identities throughout the whole chain, and $r_n > 1/n$, unless we have identities throughout. Thus $q_1 < r_n$ except in the case in which all the intervals are equal. In any event, we have the conclusion $a_1/ah \prec b_n/bk$.

If we separate out the identity part of $\prec$, we can satisfy all the axioms but those of composition and decomposition by the following interpretation on our quasi-statistical domain: one argument provides the same support as another, provided their bounds of statistical support are exactly the same—$[p,q] = a/h = b/k = [p,q]$—and one argument provides strictly greater support than another if the least bound of the first is at least as great as the greatest bound of the second: $a/h \prec b/k$ iff $a/h = [p,q]$, $b/k = [r,s]$, and $p > s$.

Semantics

There is very little difference between the view that the bounds on measures provide a measure of the support of an argument and the view that it is the set of measures itself. Keynes's writing provides little indication of his intent, other than the constant references to arguments, premises, and conclusions. These references at least suggest the interpretation we offered above in terms of relative numbers of models. Of course, we can only look at statistical models this way, but those at least are the sorts of things we can easily grasp, as opposed to the intuited strengths of arguments.

It is a short step from our informal interpretation to the characterization of a model in which (some) statistical arguments receive plausible weights.

Let us assume we have a first-order language, which we will take to be rather restricted for our purposes, though it is of sufficient power to express real number arithmetic. In addition, it contains one-place predicates (is blue, yields $\underline{1}$, is a toss of a die) and a single individual constant s. We suppose as axioms or meaning postulates general statements expressing relations among the predicates (for example, that a toss of a die has exactly one of the properties, yields $\underline{1}$, yields $\underline{6}$). Finally, we suppose that we have statistical statements whose truth is determined by the model we consider. It is quite clear that Keynes was happy to talk about frequencies in this sense. For example, in classifying the arguments with which he is concerned in part 5 of the *Treatise on Probability*, he speaks of purely inductive argument: "Given the frequency with which an event has occurred on a series of occasions, with what frequency may we probably expect it on a further series of occasions?" (CW 8:330). Keynes wants to focus on the probability with which we expect a certain frequency, but the form of the question indicates clearly that frequencies, even future frequencies, are to be distinguished from probabilities. So I think there is nothing improper about supposing as part of our probable knowledge statements alleging certain long-run frequencies.

We therefore include in our language syntax for doing this. Specifically, let us suppose that a sentence of the form "$\%(\phi(x), \varphi(x), p, q)$" means that the proportion of objects satisfying the formula $\varphi(x)$ that also satisfy the formula $\phi(x)$ lies between p and q. More specifically, this formula is true just in case the proportion of objects *in the model* that satisfy $\varphi(x)$ that also satisfy $\phi(x)$ lies between p and q.

Suppose we have a finite *empirical* domain **D** for our model (of course the domain over which real number variables range must be infinite) and that the interpretation function **I** tells us what objects in **D** satisfy what formulas makes $\%(\phi(x), \varphi(x), p, q)$ true. There is nothing more mysterious about this than the fact that the universal generalization "All *A*s and *B*s" is true in some models and false in other models, according to our interpretation function.

Now let us look again at the expression a/h. Our original informal stipulation was that h should contain assertions about the measures of a field of subsets of a subset of the universe S. Formally, this means that h should consist of sentences of the form $\%(\phi(x), \varphi(x), p, q)$, such that $\phi(x)$ belongs to an *algebra of formulas* based on $\varphi(x)$, and p and q are determined by a *set of classical measures* on that algebra of formulas.

$\mathcal{F}$ is an algebra of formulas based on $\varphi(x)$, denoted by $\mathcal{F}(\varphi)$, if φ itself belongs to $\mathcal{F}$, and if ϕ_1 and ϕ_2 belong to $\mathcal{F}$, so do $\neg\phi_1$ and $\phi_1 \vee \phi_2$.

A set of classical measures on the algebra $\mathcal{F}(\varphi)$, $\mathcal{M}(\mathcal{F}(\varphi))$, is a set of measures m such that if ϕ is in $\mathcal{F}(\varphi)$, $0 \leq m(\phi) \leq 1$, with the last relation being an identity only if ϕ is logically equivalent to φ, and if ϕ_1 and ϕ_2 are in $\mathcal{F}(\varphi)$ and are jointly inconsistent with the axioms of the language [i.e., the axioms entail $\neg(\phi_1 \wedge \phi_2)$], then $m(\phi_1 \vee \phi_2) = m(\phi_1) + m(\phi_2)$.

We can represent h by the pair $\mathcal{F}(\varphi), \mathcal{M}(\mathcal{F}(\varphi))$.

Example: Let φ be tosses of a die and the atoms of $\mathcal{F}(\varphi)$ be the six kinds of outcomes, $\underline{1}, \ldots, \underline{6}$. $\mathcal{F}(\varphi)$ is the algebra generated by disjunctions of one or more of these atoms, together with the empty set. Let us suppose that our evidence is that the die lands $\underline{1}, \underline{2}, \underline{3}$, and $\underline{4}$ exactly 15 percent of the time, and that it is loaded either to land $\underline{5}$ 10 percent of the time or to land $\underline{5}$ 30 percent of the time. Thus $\mathcal{M}(\mathcal{F}(\varphi)) = \{m : m(1) = m(2) = m(3) = m(4) = .15 \,\&\, (m(5) = .10 \vee m(5) = .30)\}$.

Let a, b, etc. be formulas of the form $\phi(s)$, where s is our single individual constant and ϕ is a formula in our original algebra.

Where $\phi(s)$ is a, and h is based on $\mathcal{F}(\varphi)$ and the set of measures $\mathcal{M}(\mathcal{F}(\varphi))$, let ah be the pair $\mathcal{F}(\varphi \wedge \phi)$, $\mathcal{M}(\mathcal{F}(\varphi \wedge \phi))$, where

$$
\mathcal{M}(\mathcal{F}(\varphi \wedge \phi)) = \left\{ m : (\exists n)\, (n \in \mathcal{M}(\varphi) \wedge n(\phi) > 0 \wedge (\forall y) \right.
$$
$$
\left. \times \left(y \in \mathcal{F}(\varphi \wedge \phi) \supset m(y) = \frac{n(y \wedge \phi)}{n(\phi)} \right) \right) \right\}.
$$

Finally, if h is based on $\mathcal{F}(\varphi)$, let h contain the sentence $\varphi(s)$.

We say that a conclusion a is supported by the premises h to the degree $[p, q]$ *in the semantic sense* if and only if, for every domain **D** and every interpretation **I**, the proportion of those models that make the premises h true that also make the conclusion a true lies between p and q. This is to be thought of as analogous to the standard claim: a conclusion a is entailed by premises h if and only if, for every domain **D** and every interpretation **I**, the conclusion is true in *every* model in which the premises are true.

Example: Suppose that h is the pair given as the previous die example, and that a is $\underline{1} \vee \underline{6}(s)$. Choose a domain **D** of cardinality K. We must assign an interpretation to φ and to the predicates $\underline{1}, \underline{2}, \ldots \underline{6}$ such that h and our linguistic assumptions (for example, that the predicates constitute a partition of φ) are true. The set of measures described has two members; according to both of them the proportion of the interpretation of φ—a subset of **D**—that are members of the interpretation of the predicate $\underline{1}$, **I**(1), is exactly .15, and the same for the interpretations of $\underline{2}, \underline{3}$, and $\underline{4}$. According to one, the proportion of members of the interpretation of φ that are members of $\underline{5}$ is .10, and according to the other, it is .30. We may easily calculate that the proportion of objects in the interpretation of φ that are also in the union of the interpretations of $\underline{1}$ and $\underline{6}$ must be either $.25$ and $.45$. (This also entails that K must be greater than 20.) How many models are there that make the premises h true? Given a value of K, we can actually calculate this. For large values of K, the calculations rapidly become a strain on the calculator. But this doesn't matter. *Whatever the interpretation of φ, we know that the proportion of objects that are in that interpretation that are also in the union of the interpretation of $\underline{1}$ and the interpretation of $\underline{6}$ must be either* $.25$ *or* $.45$.

Now let us consider the interpretation of the constant s. We may assign to s any object in the domain $\mathbf{D}$: $\mathbf{I}(s) \in \mathbf{D}$. In order for the premises h to be true, however, what we assign must also be one of the objects in the interpretation of φ. Suppose that the number of objects in the interpretation of φ is 20 J. There are thus 20 J premise-satisfying assignments we can make to the constant s. Since of these 20 J, either $0.25(20\,J)$ or $0.45(20\,J)$ will be in the union of $\mathbf{I}(\underline{1})$ and $\mathbf{I}(\underline{6})$, the proportion of *all* the models in which the premises are true, which are also such that $\underline{1} \vee \underline{6}$ is true, must be either 0.25 or 0.45.

Suppose now that our knowledge about the die is as before, except that the set of measures includes all those in which $0.10 \leq m(\underline{5}) \leq 0.30$. There is no difference in the support given by this set of premises and that in which only two measures were regarded as possible.

First, let us give an example in which the force of the argument may be regarded as very strong—strong enough to warrant acceptance of the conclusion in some contexts. Suppose we have two predicates in our language, A and B. Let us suppose that we have examined a large number n of Bs and found that, of them, m were also As. In every model of this language, there is some fraction r of the Bs that are also As. We can with only a little imagination put this situation in the previous framework: we can define a predicate B^n that holds of n-tuples of objects in the domain $\mathbf{D}$. We can define a predicate $Rep\,\delta$ that holds of n-tuples of Bs in a model just in case the difference between the sample ratio in the n-tuple and the proportion r of As among the Bs in the model is less than δ.

It is a standard exercise in probability theory to show that *whatever* be the value of r, almost all of the n-tuples of Bs will have the property $Rep\,\delta$. The proportion varies from a minimum of $1 - \varepsilon$, when $r = 1/2$, to 1.0, when r is 1.0 or 0.0.

The particular n-tuple that constitutes our sample corresponds to the individual s of the previous example. Let us consider the models of our premises, consisting of the report of the sample frequency. We may divide those models into equivalence classes according to the ratio r of As to Bs in the model. Some equivalence classes—for example, those in which

r is close to a half—are much larger than others. Nevertheless, in *every* equivalence class, the proportion of n-tuples of Bs that have the property *Rep* δ will lie between $1 - \varepsilon$ and 1. It follows that among the models in general the proportion of n-tuples of Bs that have the property *Rep* δ will lie between $1 - \varepsilon$ and 1.

Since in almost all (more than a fraction equal to $1 - \varepsilon$) of the models of our premises, the statement that our sample has the property *Rep* δ is true, we may take that statement to be highly supported by our evidence.

There is one gap to be filled in: Is it also true that "%$(A, B, m/n -$ $\delta, m/n + \delta)$" is highly supported? This is a small gap, since *Rep* $\delta(s)$ clearly has the same truth value, in every model of our premises, as the quoted statement. Thus they will each be true in the same proportion of models of our premises.

Thus, in a very special case, we have found not just a model of Keynes's probability relation but an inductive use to which it might be put. In the next section we will look at some of the cautions urged by Keynes.

Discussion

Keynes would have been quick to point out that the example just given is an instance of the "inversion" of Bernoulli's theorem and as such only holds when certain special conditions are met. He discusses these conditions in chapter 31 of the *Treatise on Probability*. The style of argument he mainly considers is that in which we argue from a prior probability that a statistical hypothesis is true, to a posterior probability that it is true, by Bayes's theorem. It is already clear that this is unacceptable for Keynes—the idea that one can obtain an exact probability for the result of a statistical induction is one that Keynes ridicules: "Nobody supposes that we can measure exactly the probability of an induction. Yet many persons seem to believe that in the weaker and much more difficult type of argument, where the association under examination has been in our experience, not invariable, but merely in a certain proportion, we can attribute a definite measure to our future expectations" (CW 8:388).

Does our example fly in the face of this good common sense? Not so. In the first place, we derive only a range of probability for the statistical inference. Far more important, in the second place, is the fact that our example is highly schematized and very primitive. Keynes himself was one of the first to insist that in inductive arguments we must take account of *all* the data we have, and not just a part of it. In the example I have supposed that our entire body of data consists in the statement that of *n* observed *B*s, *m* were *A*s. No realistic body of data could have this form. How were they collected? What other properties did they have? Which were *A*s and which were not? Especially, what *else* do we know about the world? Depending on the answers to these questions, the force of our argument from statistical data to a statistical conclusion may be completely undermined, or may be weakened, or, in fact, may be strengthened.[6] None of this, of course, undermines the positive suggestions that Keynes makes, nor the idea that support is only partially ordered, nor the idea that it can be measured by a ratio of cardinalities of models.

The form of the inverse argument that was prevalent at the time Keynes wrote was one in which prior probabilities were assigned to the statistical alternatives. Keynes believed that prior probabilities were needed for any form of inductive inference, and thus that statistics was no worse off—but also no better off—on this account than in any other form of induction. Two other assumptions, he claimed were required: an assumption regarding random sampling, and an assumption about the perfect analogy, with respect to the property *A*, among the *B*s examined.

Let us examine these three claims. The first claim, that prior probabilities are needed, seems clearly false for our model-theoretic approach. The prior probability in the example of statistical induction we gave, if it exists at all, must be reflected by the prior distribution of the ratio *r* among the models of our language, prior to the examination of a sample of the *B*s. Rudolf Carnap proposed a couple of these distributions, embodied in his measure functions c^* and $c^\dagger$, and then a continuum of them.[7] Both c^* and $c^\dagger$ have been rediscovered in the literature in artificial intelligence (Bacchus et al. 1992). But all this is irrelevant to our example: what we did there was to divide the models of our language into equivalence classes, and to show that the argument worked for each equivalence class. What the prior distribution of *r* gives us is information about the cardinality (or measure) of each of the equivalence classes. This measure varies according to the size of the domain of the model we are considering. *But that number did not enter into our argument.*

The second claim is more likely to be echoed by practicing statisticians of the present. (Of course if they are Bayesian statisticians, this

---

6. It can be strengthened if we have background knowledge that yields an empirical prior distribution for the parameter *r*, and this distribution is weighted (for example) toward 1.0.

7. The first two functions are defined in Carnap 1950; the continuum is introduced in Carnap 1952 and further ramified in Carnap 1980.

won't be so; Bayesian statisticians have a hard time explaining why a random sample is better than any other sample.) Surely, it will be said by classical statisticians, the grounds of our statistical inference require that the sample we have observed be a *random* sample.

But let us see what Keynes says about "random sampling," not on page 389 where he is talking about statistical inference, but on pages 290–91 in the chapter on objective chance and randomness. There he quotes C. S. Peirce as saying that "a random sample is . . . one taken according to a precept or method, which being applied over and over again indefinitely, would in the long run result in the drawing of any one set of instances as often as any other set of the same number."[8] As Keynes correctly notes, it is a fatal objection to this notion of randomness that (a) it is an empirical statistical hypothesis that itself needs evidential support, and (b) we often have good reason to think it false, even in the cases of statistical inference about which we feel most confident: objects in the population about which we want to make an inference that are far removed in space or time are very unlikely to be part of our sample. (For example, AIDS patients in the twenty-second century are unlikely to be part of a sample we employ now.)

Keynes proposes the following definition of "random selection": "a is taken at random from the class S for the purposes of the propositional function $S(x).\phi(x)$, relative to the evidence h, if 'x is a' is irrelevant to the probability $\phi(x)/S(x).h$" (CW 8:291). To us this may be less than lucid, but it points unambiguously to the fact that, logically, being a random sample is a four-termed relation: a sample s [first term] is a random member of a class B^n [second term], with respect to a property *Rep* δ (or membership in the class of representative samples) [third term], and relative to what we know—our total body of evidence h [fourth term].

All four of these terms are required. It is obvious that we need the first two. The third is needed: the sample s of our example is clearly *not* a random member of B^n with respect to the property of *containing m As*, nor with respect to the property of *having been selected by us*. But, so far as the example is concerned, it may well be a random member of B^n with respect to the property *Rep* δ. And the fourth is needed: to show this, we need merely add to the body of evidence h of our example: we might know that our sample came from a subset of B^n that was unusually

8. Quoted from C. S. Peirce "A Theory of Probable Inference," *Studies in Logic* (Baltimore: Johns Hopkins University Press), 152.

rich (or unusually poor) in As, or selected by a method—for example, the first n Bs to come to hand—that often, though not always, produces misleading samples: that is, a class of samples in which the frequency of $Rep\ \delta$ is lower than it is in general.

In the sense of randomness that follows from these considerations, it can be perfectly clear that a sample is "random" in the relevant sense when, for other instantiations of the third and fourth terms, it might not be. That a sample is drawn on Thursday is irrelevant, not because we know that Thursday's child is full of grace, but because we do *not* know, as part of h, that there is a relation between being a Thursday's child and drawing representative samples.

The third assumption, regarding perfect analogy, to which Keynes draws our attention is, nowadays, strange to us. We don't talk much of analogy, particularly in statistics. I *think* that what Keynes means is the following: When we have drawn our sample of $n\,B$s, and observed that m of them are As, we may find that not all the members of our sample that are As are As in the same way. That is, we may find that some are As simply in virtue of having been Bs, while others are As in virtue of something else—perhaps the way in which the Bs were selected. For example, we may be interested in what proportion of pots are cracked during a certain cooling process. If we take a sample of pots from the cooling oven, and drop ten of them on the way to the place where we will count them, those ten are not analogous to the others with respect to being cracked.

My feeling is that this question of analogy can be taken care of by the requirement of random sampling, construed as I have construed it. In the case at hand, it seems clear that those samples of which ten items were cracked by dropping are less likely to represent the true rate of cracking in the cooling oven than those samples that do not contain items cracked by dropping. I find it hard to think of an example that cannot be handled in some such way. Perhaps this merely reflects a paucity of imagination on my part.

In any case, I think Keynes has still a great deal to tell us about probability, and further that his discussion of statistical inference, while not entirely clear, contains a lot that we would do well to ponder.

References

Bacchus, F., A. J. Grove, J. Y. Halpern, and D. Koller. 1992. *From Statistics to Degrees of Belief.* AAAI–92, 602–8.

Carnap, Rudolf. 1950. *The Logical Foundations of Probability*. Chicago: University of Chicago Press.

———. 1952. *The Continuum of Inductive Methods*. Chicago: University of Chicago Press.

———. 1980. A Basic System of Inductive Logic, Part II. In *Studies in Inductive Logic and Probability II*. Edited by Richard Jeffrey. Chicago: Chicago University Press.

Cheeseman, Peter. 1988. Inquiry into Computer Understanding. *Computational Intelligence* 4:58–66.

Earman, John. 1992. *Bayes or Bust?* Cambridge: MIT Press.

Good, I. J. 1962. Subjective Probability as a Measure of Non-Measurable Set. In *Logic, Methodology and Philosophy of Science*. Edited by Ernest Nagel, Patrick Suppes, and Alfred Tarski. San Francisco: University of California Press.

Hempel, Carl J. 1965. Aspects of Scientific Explanation. In *Aspects of Scientific Explanation*. New York: Free Press.

Johnson, W. E. 1921. *Logic*. 3 vols. Cambridge: Cambridge University Press.

———. 1932. Probability. *Mind* 41:1–16, 281–96, 409–23. London: Macmillan.

Keynes, John Maynard. 1921. *A Treatise on Probability*. Vol. 8 of *The Collected Writings of John Maynard Keynes*. 30 vols. Edited by D. E. Moggridge. London: Macmillan. (CW)

Keynes, John Neville. 1844. *Studies and Exercises in Formal Logic*.

Koopman, Bernard O. 1940a. The Axioms and Algebra of Intuitive Probability. *Annals of Mathematics* 41:269–92.

———. 1940b. The Bases of Probability. *Bulletin of the American Mathematical Society* 46:763–74.

———. 1941. Intuitive Probabilities and Sequences. *Annals of Mathematics* 42:169–87.

Kyburg, Jr., Henry E. 1961. *Probability and the Logic of Rational Belief*. Middletown, Conn.: Wesleyan University Press.

Levi, Isaac. 1974. On Indeterminate Probabilities. *Journal of Philosophy* 71:391–418.

Lindley, Dennis V. 1977. The Distinction between Inference and Decision. *Synthese* 36:51–58.

Maher, Patrick. 1993. *Betting on Theories*. Cambridge: Cambridge University Press.

Popper, Karl. 1959. *The Logic of Scientific Discovery*. London: Hutchinson.

Ramsey, Frank P. 1931. *The Foundation of Mathematics and Other Essays*. New York: Humanities.

Russell, Bertrand, and Alfred North Whitehead. 1913. *Principia Mathematica*. 3 vols. Cambridge: Cambridge University Press.

Savage, L. J. 1954. *Foundations of Statistics*. New York: Wiley.

Shafer, Glenn. 1976. *A Mathematical Theory of Evidence*. Princeton: Princeton University Press.

———. 1987. Probability Judgment in Artificial Intelligence and Expert Systems. *Statistical Science* 2:3–44.

Smith, C. A. B. 1961. Consistency in Statistical Inference and Decision. *Journal of the Royal Statistical Society*, series B, 23:1–37.

Suppes, Patrick. 1960. Some Open Problems in the Foundations of Subjective Probability. In *Information and Decision Processes*, Edited by Robert E. Machol. New York: Wiley.

Tarski, Alfred. 1956. *Logic, Semantics, Metamathematics*. Oxford: Oxford University Press.

Venn, John. 1865. *The Logic of Chance*. London: Macmillan.

Comment

Jochen Runde

Professor Kyburg's paper is pleasing for the constructive spirit in which it is written. In a climate in which the subjectivist interpretation of probability is so dominant in economic theory, philosophy, and decision theory, it is refreshing to see a contribution that not only takes Keynesian intuitions seriously but also takes some positive steps toward fleshing them out. The organizers have asked me to say something about possible implications Kyburg's paper might have for economic theory. I shall concentrate on two central themes that emerge from it—his emphasis on the fact that Keynes's probabilities form only a partial order and his interpretation of the Keynesian probability relation.

Partially Ordered Probabilities

Kyburg agrees with Keynes that some of our beliefs are not comparable in terms of probability. Orthodox economic theory does not make much of this possibility, wedded as it is to Subjective Expected Utility Theory (SEUT) and the real-valued beliefs that go with it. That said, what Keynes and Kyburg have in mind is never far from the surface in the literature on Ellsberg's (1961) well-known counterexamples to SEUT. One of them goes like this. There is an opaque urn known to contain thirty red balls and sixty balls each of which may be either black or yellow. The decision maker is asked to choose between I and II, and then between III and IV below, the prize depending on the color of the first ball drawn (figure 1). It turns out that most people prefer I over II (I $\succ$ II) and IV

		Red	Black	Yellow
		30	60	
	I	$100	$0	$0
	II	$0	$100	$0
	III	$100	$0	$100
	IV	$0	$100	$100

Figure 1

over III (IV $\succ$ III). The challenge to SEUT is that there is no unique additive probability distribution consistent with this pattern of choices maximizing the expected value of some utility function. The assumption that these choices are based on a unique probability function $p(\cdot)$ leads to a contradiction, as I $\succ$ II implies that $p(\text{red}) > p(\text{black})$ and IV $\succ$ III implies that $p(\text{black}) > p(\text{red})$.

This does of course not mean that the decision maker necessarily fails to rank the events of drawing a red, black, or yellow ball in terms of their respective probabilities. The above pattern of choices is consistent even with real-valued beliefs if additivity is dropped (Gilboa 1987; Schmeidler 1989). But this move doesn't seem to capture the vagueness of our beliefs concerning the relative number of non-red balls. An alternative approach, one that has links with Kyburg's (1990) own, is to represent the decision maker's beliefs as consisting of not one but a set of classical probability distributions. In the above case, the statistical probability of red is $1/3$, whereas the probability of black (yellow) ranges in the interval $[0, 2/3]$. On this interpretation, the probability of drawing a black (yellow) ball is greater than drawing a red for some of the possible distributions, equally probable for one, and less so for the rest. The choice between I and II (III and IV) is then clearly also indeterminate with respect to expected utility.

The standard response to indeterminacies of this kind is to derive additional criteria by which options may be singled out as uniquely rational (Levi 1986 is an interesting exception who allows more than one option to be rationally choosable even though the decision maker may not be indifferent between them). One of the few formal analyses of economic implications of incompletely ordered beliefs is Bewley 1986. Bewley drops the completeness assumption of SEUT and assumes that agents have a convex set of probability distributions defined over a finite set of states. An option is then preferred to another only if it delivers a higher expected utility with respect to every one of the set of distributions in the convex set. (In terms of this theory, it is impossible to rank the options in either of the two choices given above.) Bewley's innovation is to introduce into the decision maker's action-set what he calls the "status quo," a privileged position that is chosen unless there is another action that is definitely preferred to it. The decision maker thus has the option of not taking an action if he or she feels unable to assign point probabilities.

I mention Bewley because he highlights an idea central to Keynes's writings on investment and liquidity preference decisions—that, in situations of uncertainty, people may wish to suspend judgment rather than commit themselves to particular courses of action. Indeed, it is often argued that this idea, that investors might "withdraw from the field" by moving into liquid assets, lies at the very heart of his theory of unemployment (e.g., Shackle 1972). What is interesting here is that actions motivated by a desire to remain flexible in the face of uncertainty cannot be pressed into the standard SEUT/point-probability schema. It is not possible to argue that decision makers' probabilities are implicit in their preferences if they refuse to take an action or if the choice of a liquid asset is interpreted as at least partially motivated by a desire to preserve flexibility. The very purpose of modern asset markets, moreover, is to provide such flexibility (which introduces a further disanalogy with SEUT as the interpretation of probability associated with it requires the possible consequences of actions to be fixed until one of them obtains— try to imagine a bookie offering bets that allow the bettor to negotiate the prize during the course of a horse race). So there is at least some support from an economic corner for the view that the standard assumption of real-valued beliefs may not always be appropriate and hence for the view that partially ordered beliefs "are not obviously absurd" (see also Hicks 1979, 103–22).

The Keynesian Probability Relation

Kyburg proposes to interpret Keynes's probability relation as a generalization of Tarski's notion of logical validity. This is an ingenious idea. But Kyburg's reconstruction seems to me too heavily colored by his own view of epistemic probability, as based on (but not identified with) a knowledge of relative frequencies or, more often, an interval of frequencies relative to some reference class (Kyburg 1983, 1990). I believe that Keynes would have it exactly the other way around: that relative frequencies are ultimately based on judgments of qualitative epistemic probability.

Keynes presents rational belief as arising out of the apprehension of a relation of partial implication (RPI) between some hypothesis a and the evidence h bearing on it. He treats the RPI as an indefinable that is not analyzable in terms of simpler ideas, and he devotes most of the *Treatise on Probability* to developing a logic of qualitative comparisons of *given* RPIs. While many RPIs are not comparable in terms of probability, according to Keynes, others are, and he shows how further comparisons of RPIs may be derived from comparisons of RPIs already given. Only under special circumstances do such comparisons translate into point probabilities—namely, when it is legitimate to apply the principle of indifference. Keynes's formulation of this principle provides criteria by which the alternatives to which numerical probabilities are to be assigned may be judged to be equiprobable and indivisible (i.e., not capable of being divided into subalternatives of the same form). Given that such equiprobable and indivisible alternatives are exhaustive and exclusive, the probability of any one of them is $1/n$ (where n is the total number of possible alternatives).

Keynes's interpretation of probability is often contrasted with the frequency interpretation. His own view, however, is that the frequency interpretation is a special case of his "logical" interpretation. Relative frequencies are truth-frequencies relative to some reference class, and the problem for the frequency theorist is to find the appropriate reference class. Keynes ([1921] 1973, 112–13) argues that the choice of reference class boils down to qualitative judgments of relevance and indifference. If this is so, relative frequencies are themselves ultimately based on judgments of comparative probability.

Whereas Kyburg's reconstruction of Keynes's system presupposes a knowledge of relative frequencies, Keynes begins with criteria for establishing the equiprobability of alternative hypotheses and builds up to relative frequencies. Kyburg acknowledges that we can only look at statistical models in the way he is proposing, but maintains that "those at least are the sorts of things we can easily grasp, as opposed to the intuited strengths of arguments." From the viewpoint of an economist interested in the theory of choice under uncertainty, however, it seems to me that Keynes's approach has three important advantages. First, it is more general in the sense that judgments of comparative probability seem among the most basic we can make, even if they are only of the form of "x is more probable than not-x." Second, it provides a theory of the choice of reference class, relative to which frequencies can then be defined. It is true that this theory is ultimately based on intuitive judgments, but it is hard to see how any theory could avoid this. Third, it makes it possible to retain the distinction between decision situations in which it is possible to make use of statistically based probabilities and ones in which it is not.

Although Keynes's notion of the intuited strength of an argument *is* a difficult one to get a grip on, this does not seem to me sufficient grounds for its abandonment. And whatever one's position on the "logical" status of Keynes's RPIs (I am skeptical about this myself), they are after all a primitive in the *Treatise*, serving the useful purpose of providing the set of objects over which his probability comparisons are defined and which permit him to develop his logic with having to become immersed in deeper questions of epistemology, psychology, and so on. Kyburg would presumably agree with this point, as he is providing an alternative interpretation of rather than questioning (Koopmans's version of) Keynes's axioms. Like any abstract formal system, however, Keynes's system admits of many possible interpretations. I would still hold out for one that begins with qualitative comparisons of probability (see Runde 1994), rather than one that assumes a knowledge of relative frequencies that must itself be accounted for.

References

Bewley, T. F. 1986. *Knightian Decision Theory Part I*. Cowles Foundation Discussion Paper no. 807.

Ellsberg, D. 1961. Risk, Ambiguity and the Savage Axioms. *Quarterly Journal of Economics* 75:528–56.

Gilboa, I. 1987. Expected Utility with Purely Subjective Non-Additive Probabilities. *Journal of Mathematical Economics* 16:65–88.

Hicks, J. 1979. *Causality in Economics*. Oxford: Basil Blackwell.

Keynes, J. M. [1921] 1973. *A Treatise on Probability*. Vol. 8 of *The Collected Writings of John Maynard Keynes*. 30 Vols. Edited by D. E. Moggridge. London: Macmillan. (CW)

Kyburg, H. E. 1983. Rational Belief. *The Behavioural and Brain Sciences* 6:231–73.

———. 1990. *Science and Reason*. New York: Oxford University Press.

Levi, I. 1986. The Paradoxes of Allais and Ellsberg. *Economics and Philosophy* 2:23–53.

Runde, J. H. 1994. Keynes after Ramsey: In Defence of *A Treaty on Probability*. *Studies in History and Philosophy of Science* 25:97–121.

Schmeidler, D. 1989. Subjective Probability and Expected Utility without Additivity. *Econometrica* 57:571–87.

Shackle, G. L. S. 1972. *Epistemics and Economics: A Critique of Economic Doctrines*. Cambridge: Cambridge University Press.

Jeffreys, Fisher, and Keynes: Predicting the Third Observation, Given the First Two

Teddy Seidenfeld

During three years, from 1932 through 1934, the *Proceedings of the Royal Society of London* was the setting for a stimulating, five-article exchange between Harold Jeffreys and Ronald Fisher about their differing views on the foundations of statistical inference. In what surely was a rare event in any debate with Fisher, Jeffreys got the first and the last word (Jeffreys 1932, 1933, 1934; Fisher 1933, 1934).[1] For our purposes at this conference on Keynes, I propose that we examine how, starting with Jeffreys's first rebuttal (1933) to Fisher, and continuing through Fisher's second reply (1934), and on to Jeffreys's final rebuttal (1934), each side used Keynes's 1921 *Treatise on Probability* to argue that the other was committing a foundational error.[2] To do that, first I review the statistical arguments Jeffreys and Fisher set out in their initial papers in this sequence. Then I examine how each side tried to co-opt Keynes's theory. Last I indicate some contemporary work that reflects, to my mind, how one aspect of the debate has evolved over sixty years.

I thank Rob Kass for some helpful comments on the material presented here.

1. However, just one year later, Fisher did not pass up the advantage of the "last reply" in his 1935 presentation and discussion, "The Logic of Inductive Inference," in the *Journal of the Royal Statistical Society*.

2. For a different perspective on this Jeffrey-Fisher exchange, see David Lane's stimulating essay from 1980.

Inverse Inference According to Jeffreys and to Fisher

In the 1930s, and even today, the foundational litmus test of a statistical theory is its solution to inverse inference: inference from "sample" to "population." A textbook case will serve as our heuristic. Let $(x_1, x_2, \ldots, x_n)$ be n i.i.d. $\mathbf{N}(\mu, \sigma^2)$ observations, where both parameters are unknown. What does your favorite statistical theory authorize may be inferred about the normal mean μ and variance σ^2 of the "population" from which the n observations have been independently sampled?

Harold Jeffreys was an advocate of Bayesian statistical inference, which solves inverse inference according to Bayes's rule:

$P(\text{Hypothesis} \mid \text{Data}) \propto P(\text{Data} \mid \text{Hypothesis}) \times P(\text{Hypothesis})$,

or,

Posterior probability $\propto$ Likelihood $\times$ Prior probability.

For our heuristic example, this becomes (in densities):

$p(\mu, \sigma \mid x_1, x_2, \ldots, x_n)$

$$\propto (\sigma^{-n}) \exp[-\{(n-1)s^2 + n(\bar{x} - \mu)^2\}/2\sigma^2]p(\mu, \sigma) \, d\mu \, d\sigma,$$

where the sample variance $s^2 = \sum_i (x_i - \bar{x})^2/(n-1)$ and the sample average $\bar{x} = \sum_i x_i/n$, are jointly sufficient. But what is the joint prior probability for the unknown parameters, μ and σ?

Jeffreys (1931), in *Scientific Inference*, had already argued that, in estimation, the appropriate probabilistic representation of ignorance about a parameter depends on how that parameter functions in a statistical model of the data to be acquired. That is, rather than using a Laplacean, uniform prior to depict prior ignorance about a parameter, Jeffreys argued by way of statistical symmetries what that ignorance prior should be. For inference about a location parameter—for example, for inference about the normal mean μ (given the variance, σ^2)—he argued that shift-invariance for the sample average justified the uniform (improper) prior density $d\mu$.[3] Likewise, for inference about a scale parameter—for example, for inference about the normal variance σ^2 (given the mean, μ)—he argued that invariance for powers justified the (improper) prior density, $d\sigma/\sigma$.[4]

---

3. Note that $\bar{x}$ is sufficient for μ, given σ^2.

4. Note that $\sum_i (x_i - \mu)^2$ is sufficient for σ^2, given μ.

However, Jeffreys found no compelling reason to mandate a joint ignorance prior for the two parameters (μ and σ) that is merely the product
of the separate ignorance priors, $p(\mu, \sigma) \propto 1/\sigma$.[5]

The first of the five papers, Jeffreys's 1932 essay, begins with a novel
argument for the improper joint density, $d\mu d\sigma/\sigma$. His reasoning is elegant. Let (x_1, x_2, x_3) be three (continuous) i.i.d. random quantities from
a statistical model. Let H be the hypothesis that x_3 lies (strictly) between
x_1 and x_2. *Prior to observing the data*, the probability of H is 1/3. (It
is immediate from the assumption the data are i.i.d. that all six orders
are equiprobable; hence, for two of six equiprobable cases H obtains.)
Suppose we observe two values (x_1, x_2) of three i.i.d. $\mathbf{N}(\mu, \sigma^2)$ variables. Jeffreys asked: What prior probability over the unknown parame-
ters (μ, σ) leads to the conclusion that $P(H \mid x_1, x_2) = 1/3$, regardless
of the specific values of (x_1, x_2)?

Expressed somewhat differently, Jeffreys's question is: What prior
probability on the parameters preserves the ignorance we have initially
about the relative order statistic for x_3 with respect to x_1 and x_2, regardless
of the observed values of x_1 and x_2? The answer is, of course, the joint
(improper) prior proportional to $1/\sigma$.[6] So, Jeffreys had a new reason for
the two-parameter "ignorance" prior he used in Bayes's rule, based on a
constraint for predictions.

R. A. Fisher was no Bayesian—not in the 1920s when he helped
to create the foundations of significance testing, maximum likelihood,
and the theory of statistical estimation and not in the 1930s when he
set the foundations for randomized experimental design; nor was Fisher
Bayesian in his many presentations (beginning in 1930 and ending only
with his death in 1962) of his "fiducial" solutions to inverse inference. By
1933, Fisher's *Statistical Methods for Research Workers* was in its fourth
edition and Bayes's rule was *not* one of the tools in the toolbox that is
SMfRW! In 1933, Fisher was enjoying his newest invention, the enigma
of fiducial probability. Neyman-Pearson hypothesis testing was a half-

---

5. The problem followed Jeffreys through much of his career. See, e.g., section 3.10 (especially p. 182) in *Theory of Probability* ([1961] 1967) to see the tension between Jeffreys's
Invariance Theory applied to prior ignorance for μ and σ jointly versus separately.

6. In section 3.8 of *Theory of Probability* ([1961] 1967), Jeffreys shows that for a location-
precision model, with parameters (α, h), respectively, the joint prior expressed as $d\alpha dh/h$
yields the desired probability $P(H \mid x_1, x_2) = 1/3$. (Precision is the multiplicative inverse of
the scale parameter.) However, Jeffreys is unable to show the converse—that is, there remain
some open cases whether this prior is unique for all location-scale families.

dozen years old, and confidence interval theory (according to Neyman, that is) was still a year away.[7]

Thus, I speculate it came as no surprise to Jeffreys that Fisher was unwilling to accept the novel derivation of Jeffreys's joint "ignorance" prior for the two normal parameters. For Fisher, as for many non-Bayesians, each probability assertion—whether as prior, likelihood, or posterior probability—had to be grounded on objective (statistical "population") distributions. Thus, statements of likelihood were judged valid because, in taking a statistical parameter as given, they hypothesized the very conditions that made them "objective." But the priors for statistical parameters that Jeffreys adopted were only expressions of ignorance, in the tradition Laplace had created. They were *not* (nor were they intended as) statistical assertions about, for instance, some hyperpopulation of normal distributions from which a particular $N(\mu, \sigma^2)$ was selected at random. Fisher's 1933 paper offered a new fiducial solution to the prediction problem raised by Jeffreys. To appreciate Fisher's contribution, we have to digress for a sketch of fiducial reasoning. How can there be a solution to inverse inference (from sample to population) that does not confront Bayes's theorem? How can there be posterior probability without prior probability?[8]

Consider a simplification of our heuristic example where we know the normal population variance, σ^2, only μ is not known. Fisher reasoned this way: the quantity $v = (\sqrt{n})(\bar{x} - \mu)/\sigma$ is pivotal, having a standard $N(0,1)$ distribution, independent of the unknown mean μ. That is, prior to knowing $(x_1, x_2, \ldots, x_n)$, v is $N(0,1)$. Fisher asserted that ignorance about μ means that after learning $(x_1, x_2, \ldots, x_n)$, still v is $N(0,1)$; that is, Fisher claims that $\bar{x}$ is irrelevant to v in the absence of knowledge of μ. But given $\bar{x}$, "v is $N(0,1)$" is equivalent to "μ is $N(\bar{x}, \sigma^2/n)$."[9] Thus, Fisher derives a statement of inverse probability, apparently, without recourse to a specific prior for the unknown μ. It is no coincidence that the Bayesian reconstruction of this fiducial reasoning yields the same numerical conclusions based on the (improper) uniform prior, $d\mu$.

7. See Levi 1980 for discussion that the noted philosopher, C. S. Peirce, had published the outlines of confidence interval theory fifty years earlier, though it went unnoticed.

8. Modifying Savage's 1963 quip: How could Fisher make a Bayesian omelette without breaking the Bayesian eggs?

9. This reconstruction of fiducial inference as resting on an "irrelevance" step in pivotal reasoning was made clear by Jeffreys in section 7.1 of *Theory of Probability* ([1961] 1967). Hacking 1965 attempts to ground this irrelevance claim on likelihood-based reasoning. I discuss the extent to which Fisher's fiducial methods were Bayesian in Seidenfeld 1992.

In his 1933 reply to Jeffreys, Fisher solves the prediction problem in fiducial fashion, roughly as follows: the quantity $u = (s^2/\sigma^2)$ is pivotal with a χ^2 distribution (on $n - 1$ degrees of freedom). Inverting on this pivotal affords a fiducial distribution for the variance, which we may denote as $P(\sigma^2 \mid s^2)$, an inverse chi-square distribution. Given σ^2, the v pivotal affords a fiducial distribution for the unknown population mean, denoted as $P(\mu \mid \sigma^2, \bar{x})$. These correspond, exactly, to the "posterior" probabilities Jeffreys derived using Bayes's rule and his (improper) joint prior $(d\mu d\sigma/\sigma)$. In other words, Fisher was able to duplicate Jeffreys's predictive probability for a third normal variate, given the first two, without appeal to a "prior" probability, by using fiducial reasoning instead. Fiducially, given (x_1, x_2), the probability is $1/3$ that x_3 lies between the other two.

Foundations and the Appeal to Keynes's Work

Is there better evidence of a statistical dispute being foundational than that the opposing sides agree in the precise mathematical form of their answer while also disparaging the other's reasoning? Thus, by the third of the five papers, Jeffreys's rebuttal (1933) announces the need to explore what the concept "probability" means. Appealing to Bertrand Russell's synopsis of the philosophical problem of induction, Jeffreys quotes that "induction appears to me to be either disguised deduction or a mere method of making plausible guesses" (523), and, with respect to the first alternative, Jeffreys suggests three strategies: (i) induction based on "the law of contradiction"; (ii) induction based on a "law of causality"; and (iii) induction based on the theory of probability.

Of course, Jeffreys opts for the third strategy. That is, he advocates a theory of probability that relates theories and evidence. To carry this off, however, he needs (and knows that he needs) prescriptions for assigning determinate probabilities in specific cases. For that he baldly asserts, "the existence of a numerical theory of probability, however, is not enough for practical application without some rules for deciding what numbers are to be put into it. The fundamental rule is the Principle of Non-sufficient Reason, according to which propositions mutually exclusive on the same data must receive equal probabilities if there is nothing to enable us to choose between them" (1933, 528). And from here it is but a short step to confront Keynes ([1921] 1973, chap. 4) imposing objections to the Principle of Non-sufficient Reason. This he does, in terms of one of

Keynes's well-known examples. I paraphrase Keynes's objection, which Jeffreys quotes in full:

> If we are ignorant of area or populations of different countries of the world, then we should judge a man to be as likely an inhabitant of Great Britain as of France. Also, he should be judged as likely to inhabit Ireland as France, and by the same principle he should be judged equally likely to inhabit the British Isles as France. But, by additivity, the first two judgments make it twice as likely that he resides in the British Isles as in France, contradicting the third judgment.
>
> It will not do to solve this problem, asserts Keynes, by saying that because the British Isles are known to have two subdivisions (which alone tells us nothing about their relative populations), therefore, it is twice as likely for someone to reside in the British Isles as in France. ([1921] 1973, 44)

Jeffreys's reply is simple; he says that in this case Keynes neglects to relativize judgments of equipossibility to the background information of what counts as a "country." Either, argues Jeffreys, the person judges Great Britain and Ireland as separate countries or only as parts of a single country (the British Isles). There is no contradiction, argues Jeffreys, once this background assumption is fixed. That is, Jeffreys adopts Keynes's so-called "logical" interpretation of probability, where probability relates theory and statistical evidence, but he is not moved by Keynes's objections to Non-sufficient Reason.

Of course, Fisher is not satisfied with Jeffreys's reply to Keynes. Fisher agrees with Keynes's objection. There are two senses of the word *country*, and the investigator recognizes this; there is no justification for adopting one sense of country over the other for purposes of using the Principle of Non-sufficient Reason (Fisher 1934, 5).

I suggest the Jeffreys-Fisher exchange about Keynes's example, in criticism of Non-sufficient Reason, sits at the *surface* of their differences about Keynes's views on probability. There are two, more substantial, themes in Keynes's work that divide Jeffreys and Fisher:

1. Keynes argues ([1921] 1973, chap. 3) that, as a quantitative (real-valued) relation between two propositions ϕ and ψ, the "logical" probability $\mathbf{Q}(\phi \mid \psi)$ may not be defined for all pairs.[10]
2. In (the concluding) part 5 of the *Treatise*, Keynes tries to ground

10. See Kyburg's 1955 Ph.D. thesis for an important, early discussion of this theme.

statistical inference on empirical premises only. Particularly for problems of inverse inference, Keynes explores ways of "inverting" the uncontroversial *direct inferences* (such as those Bernoulli's theorem provides), inferences that take us from statistical "population" to "sample" under random sampling.

These two considerations, I suggest, rather than the overt dispute over Non-sufficient Reason, are what separate Jeffreys and Fisher.

Regarding the first question, whether quantitative probability is defined for all pairs of propositions, Jeffreys argues in the affirmative.[11] By contrast, Fisher's theory admits three varieties of inductive support for solving inverse inference in the absence of prior probability for the hypothesis: significance testing, likelihood, and fiducial probability. These take increasingly restrictive background assumptions for their applicability. *Significance testing* requires a well-defined statistical null hypothesis, but (contrary to Neyman-Pearson hypothesis testing) no parametric family of statistical alternatives is supposed. *Likelihood* requires a parametrized family of statistical hypotheses. And *fiducial probability* requires, in addition, a suitable pivotal variable (or pivotal variables, in the case of several parameters). Only in the case of fiducial probability is inverse inference solved by a conclusion expressed as a (conditional) probability for the hypothesis, given the data. Thus Fisher's theory, the non-Bayesian theory, rather than Jeffreys's Bayesian theory, is closer to Keynes's position on the matter of whether (real-valued) probability is defined between all pairs of propositions.

Regarding the second point, whether inverse inference can be grounded on statistical premises alone, Fisher's fiducial probability attempts to do just that. Fiducial inference is the attempt to reduce inverse inference about a parameter to direct inference about a pivotal. By contrast, Jeffreys's Bayesian program offers a refined version of Non-sufficient Reason in which the statistical model fixes the symmetries that are used to determine the equiprobable states of "ignorance." That is, Jeffreys's solution to Keynes's objections about Non-sufficient Reason grounds the representation of ignorance on mathematical symmetries of the "chances."

For example, with a location parameter (e.g., the normal mean μ) the "prior" is uniform, and with a scale parameter (e.g., the normal variance σ^2) Jeffreys's prior is uniform in the log of the parameter. The sym-

---

11. This point is made explicit in Jeffreys's *Theory of Probability* ([1961] 1967), axioms 1 and 5.

metries Jeffreys uses to pick these priors are motivated by mathematical invariances in the statistical model, the empirical part of the model which relates the hypothetical parameter to the observed data through noncontroversial "direct inference." However, Fisher's fiducial solution to the same problem relies on an inversion of the statistically based "direct" probabilities for the pivotal variables. In fiducial inference, there is no appeal to mathematical symmetries in order to apply the principle of Non-sufficient Reason to form an "ignorance" prior probability. The only uses Fisher makes of Bayes's theorem require statistically based probabilities. Thus, on the second point too, I think Fisher's (non-Bayesian) theory comes closer than Jeffreys's Bayesian theory to Keynes's views on solving inverse inference by "inverting" on noncontroversial "direct" probability.

Among contemporary theories of statistical inference, H. E. Kyburg's original program of "Epistemological probability" (1974) captures both Keynesian themes. Regarding the first issue, in many common circumstances the (frequency-based) evidence is inadequate to support a real-valued Epistemological probability for a hypothesis. Then, Epistemological probability is interval-valued, rather than real-valued. With interval-valued probability, not all pairs of propositions are comparable by the simple qualitative relation ". . . is at least as probable as ———." That is, when probability goes interval-valued, it may be that neither of two propositions is at least as probable as the other—they are incomparable under this relation, just as Keynes and Fisher supposed. Second, Kyburg's Epistemological probability theory solves "inverse" inference by inverting on special relations between statistical samples and their populations that behave very much like Fisher's pivotals. Kyburg calls these "rationally representative sample" relations.

Some of the non-Bayesian aspects of Kyburg's theory are discussed (Kyburg 1977) in debates with Levi (1977) and also with me (Seidenfeld 1978). In any case, Kyburg's work on statistical inference shows how one development of the twin Keynesian themes (noted here) leads, naturally, away from the strict Bayesian position illustrated so clearly in Jeffreys's important work.

Nonparametric Inference and Non-sufficient Reason

I want to conclude by discussing how some contemporary work relates to a Keynesian theme in the Jeffreys-Fisher debate. For the specific problem of forecasting x_3, given (x_1, x_2), when the data are i.i.d. normal and both parameters are unknown, Jeffreys's Bayesian method and Fisher's fiducial method lead to the same (numerical) results. Is there an extension beyond the normal model? Are there nonparametric versions, too?

This question is relevant because, in the spirit of the *Treatise on Probability*, if there is an extension to nonparametric fiducial inference that might identify a nonparametric Bayesian "prior," just as Jeffreys's (improper) prior serves as the Bayesian model for Fisher's fiducial inference in the case of normal data. Such a nonparametric ignorance "prior" might stand for a version of Non-sufficient Reason that is applicable *without* any particular knowledge of a statistical model.

Consider, then, the case of 3 i.i.d. real-valued data from an unknown continuous distribution F. The nonparametric version of Jeffreys's prediction problem asks whether there is an "ignorance" prior for the observables such that, given (x_1, x_2), the probability is $1/3$ that x_3 lies between them. Bruce Hill (1988) addresses the general question, for samples of size n. That is, is there a Bayesian model for nonparametric predictions where the following condition $(A_{(n)})$ holds?

$A_{(n)}$:   Given $(x_1, x_2, \ldots, x_n)$, the predictive probability is $1/(n+1)$ that x_{n+1} lies between any two (of $n-1$ many) order statistics, or lies outside either extreme value. That is:

$$P(x_{(i)} < x_{n+1} < x_{(i+1)} \mid x_1, x_2, \ldots, x_n) = 1/(n+1)$$
$$(i = 1, \ldots, n-1), \text{ and}$$
$$P(x_{n+1} < x_{(1)} \mid x_1, x_2, \ldots, x_n) = 1/(n+1), \text{ and}$$
$$P(x_{n+1} > x_{(n)} \mid x_1, x_2, \ldots, x_n) = 1/(n+1).$$

Before reporting Hill's answer, note that there is a simple fiducial argument that satisfies $A_{(n)}$.[12] Let F_i be the c.d.f. for the random variable x_i. F_i is uniformly distributed on the unit interval, $F_i \sim \mathbf{U}[0,1]$, independent of the unknown distribution F. Since the x_i are i.i.d., with common (unknown) distribution F, prior to observing $(x_1, x_2, \ldots, x_n)$, $(F_1, \ldots, F_n)$ is uniformly distributed on the n-dimensional unit-cube. That is, the F_i are independently distributed, and $(F_{(1)}, \ldots, F_{(n)})$ are just the (unobserved) order statistics from n independently distributed

---

12. I find the basis for this argument, ironically, in Fisher's second objection to Jeffreys (1934, 2). Hill (1988, 215) locates it, cryptically, in Fisher's 1939 remarks on "Student."

U[0,1] variates. We use these $F_{(i)}$ as pivotals, in a fiducial argument (sketched below).

Consider $A_{(2)}$, corresponding to the nonparametric version of Jeffreys's problem for predicting the third observation, given the first two. Let $\delta = F_{(2)} - F_{(1)}$, so that $0 \leq \delta \leq 1$. Note that

$$P(x_{(1)} < x_3 < x_{(2)} \mid \delta, x_1, x_2) = \delta = F_{(2)} - F_{(1)},$$

independent of the data, (x_1, x_2). If we take a fiducial step, the observed data are irrelevant to the joint distribution of $\{F_{(1)}, F_{(2)}\}$, that is, fiducially, in densities,

$$p(F_{(1)}, F_{(2)}) = p(F_{(1)}, F_{(2)} \mid x_1, x_2).$$

It is easy to verify that the density function for δ is: $p(\delta) = 2(1 - \delta)$. Then, we can write

$$
\begin{aligned}
P(x_{(1)} &< x_3 < x_{(2)} \mid x_1, x_2) \\
&= \int_\delta P(x_{(1)} < x_3 < x_{(2)} \mid \delta, x_1, x_2) p(\delta \mid x_1, x_2) \, d\delta \\
&= \int_0^1 \delta 2(1 - \delta) \, d\delta \\
&= 1/3.
\end{aligned}
$$

Thus, a simple nonparametric fiducial argument leads to the prediction for the third observation, given the first two, which agrees with Jeffreys's condition for "ignorance" about the underlying (chance) distribution, F, for the observables.

The question for our inquiry is: What "ignorance" prior (over the data) duplicates this nonparametric inference? That is, relying on Fisher's fiducial inference as an acceptable solution to the nonparametric "inverse inference" (about δ), what is the corresponding Bayes model? The answer has interesting consequences for the Principle of Non-sufficient Reason.

Hill 1968 showed that, even for $A_{(1)}$ (and thus for all $A_{(n)}$, since $A_{(n)}$ entails $A_{(n-1)}$), the Bayes model cannot use a countably additive prior probability for the data. This is evidently so in Jeffreys's problem, involving $N(\mu, \sigma^2)$ data, where the improper prior density $d\mu d\sigma / \sigma$ corresponds to a finitely, but not countably additive probability.[13] Thus, Jeffreys's

---

13. This is evident as the "uniform" prior $d\mu$ assigns *equal* prior probability to each unit interval of the form, $k \leq \mu < k + 1$ ($k = 0, k = \pm 1, k = \pm 2, \ldots$). These unit intervals constitute a countable partition of the parameter space. Hence, by finite additivity, each has prior probability 0, though their countable union has prior probability 1.

rule for choosing a prior to depict "ignorance," or (what amounts to the same) the Bayes model for Fisher's fiducial probability, requires non-countably additive probabilities. Hill's analysis reveals this is so also for the nonparametric version.

Apart from the mathematical point, what is urgent about the shift from countably additive to merely finitely additive probability? The following brief discussion illustrates a qualitative aspect of statistical inference that rises or falls with countable additivity. In his discussion of whether or not personal probability needs to be countably additive, de Finetti 1972 formulated the following concept of *conglomerability* of conditional probability: Let $\pi = \{h_1, \ldots, h_n, \ldots\}$ be a denumerable partition and let $E_P[\bullet]$ denote the (finitely additive) expectation with respect to probability P.

Definition: The probability P is *conglomerable* in π if, for each bounded variable X and constants k_1 and k_2, $k_1 \leq E_P[X] \leq k_2$ whenever $k_1 \leq E_P[X \mid h_i] \leq k_2$ $(i = 1, \ldots)$.[14]

About ten years ago Schervish et al. (1984) showed that conglomerability characterizes countable additivity. That is, with respect to denumerable partitions, as is evident, each countably additive probability is conglomerable in each partition; however, each finitely (but not countably) additive probability fails to be conglomerable for some event E, in some partition.[15]

For the particular case Jeffreys uses, predicting the third normal datum given the first two, based on the interesting work of Heath and Sudderth (1978), we learn that there is conglomerability in the margin of the observables (x_1, x_2) and in the margin of the two normal parameters, (μ, σ). However, in light of the Buehler-Feddersen inequality, below, we see that there is *conditional* nonconglomerability. Specifically, let $t = (x_1 + x_2)/(x_1 - x_2)$. Buehler and Feddersen (1963) established the following inequality obtains for all (μ, σ):

$$P(x_{(1)} \leq \mu \leq x_{(2)} \mid \mu, \sigma, |t| \leq 1.5) > .512.$$

Given $|t| \leq 1.5$, and applying conglomerability in (μ, σ), we obtain the

14. Dubins 1975 shows that conglomerability in π is equivalent to disintegrability in π.

15. Note that the failure of conglomerability is for an event—that is, a simple random variable. Also, it depends on details in the mathematical structure of the (merely finitely additive probability P, where the failure of conglomerability occurs can be determined by the unconditional expectations alone. This is discussed, at length, in Schervish et al. 1984.

inequality

$$P(x_{(1)} \leq \mu \leq x_{(2)} \mid |t| \leq 1.5) > .512.$$

However, by Jeffreys's (or Fisher's) analysis, the following obtains for each pair (x_1, x_2):

$$P(x_{(1)} \leq \mu \leq x_{(2)} \mid x_1, x_2) = .5;$$

hence, for pairs (x_1, x_2), which satisfy the inequality $|t| \leq 1.5$, we get:

$$P(x_{(1)} \leq \mu \leq x_{(2)} \mid x_1, x_2, |t| \leq 1.5) = .5.$$

Given $|t| \leq 1.5$, and applying conglomerability in (x_1, x_2), we obtain the contrary equality,

$$P(x_{(1)} \leq \mu \leq x_{(2)} \mid |t| \leq 1.5) = .5.$$

Thus, given $|t| \leq 1.5$, there is *conditional* nonconglomerability.[16]

One upshot of nonconglomerability is that "admissibility" fails—that is, simple dominance is not valid in denumerable partitions. So, of two statistical decisions D_1 and D_2, it may be that $E_P[D_1] < E_P[D_2]$, yet $E_P[D_1 \mid h_i] > E_P[D_2 \mid h_i]$ for each $i = 1, 2, \ldots$ That simple dominance fails raises a somewhat unusual question about the value of cost-free data. In the circumstances above, should the agent make a terminal decision between D_1 and D_2, or is it better to postpone that choice to learn, cost-free, which element of π obtains? The "prior" expectation of waiting for the new evidence and then deciding is negative!

Nonconglomerability of P thus raises a novel issue about the value of new data. Keynes ([1921] 1973, chap. 6) provides a brief but stimulating discussion about the vague notion of *weight of evidence*. For example, on the assumption that the weight of evidence for a hypothesis cannot decrease by learning something new, he shows that the precision (i.e., the inverse of the variance) of a distribution cannot index weight. That is, a conditional distribution may have larger variance. Still, it might be suggested that weight of evidence can be gauged decision theoretically, in terms of the value the new evidence provides in a sequential decision. But we see that, too, cannot serve as a universal index of weight because, for a finitely additive probability it may be that new evidence carries negative expected value; better to decide in advance of the new data!

---

16. See Kadane et al. 1986 for additional discussion.

If we adapt the Jeffreys-Fisher debate to a justification of improper priors in the name "ignorance," if we use that debate to try to restore the Principle of Non-sufficient Reason, then we have the following surprising price to pay: a consequence of "ignorance" is that sometimes it is decision theoretically better to remain ignorant than it is to learn!

I cannot imagine how Keynes would have accepted that. I suspect that on this score, regarding the representation of ignorance, Keynes would have placed himself outside the range of positions bracketed by Jeffreys's and by Fisher's analyses. And surely they would have each responded that that event had probability 2/3 of occurring anyway.

References

Buehler, R. J., and A. P. Feddersen. 1963. Note on a Conditional Property of Student's *t*. *Annals Math. Stat.* 34:1098–1100.

de Finetti, B. 1972. *Probability, Induction, and Statistics*. New York: Wiley.

Dubins, L. 1975. Finitely Additive Conditional Probabilities, Conglomerability and Disintegrations. *Annals of Probability* 3:89–99.

Fisher, R. A. 1933. The Concepts of Inverse Probability and Fiducial Probability Referring to Unknown Parameters. *Proc. Royal Soc. London*, series A 139:343–48.

———. 1934. Probability Likelihood and Quantity of Information in the Logic of Uncertain Inference. *Proc. Royal Soc. London*, series A 146:1–8.

———. 1935. The Logic of Inductive Inference. *J. Roy. Stat. Soc.* 98:39–54 (with discussion, 55–82).

———. 1939. Student. *Annals of Eugenics* 9:1–9.

———. 1973. *Statistical Methods for Research Workers*. 14th ed. New York: Hafner.

Hacking, I. 1965. *Logic of Statistical Inference*. Cambridge: Cambridge University Press.

Heath, D., and W. Sudderth. 1978. On Finitely Additive Priors, Coherence, and Extended Admissibility. *Annals of Statistics* 6:333–45.

Hill, B. 1968. Posterior Distribution of Percentiles: Bayes' Theorem for Sampling from a Population. *J. Am. Stat. Assoc.* 63:677–91.

———. 1988. De Finetti's Theorem, Induction, and $A_{(n)}$ or Bayesian Nonparametric Predictive Inference. In *Bayesian Statistics*. Vol. 3. Edited by J. M. Bernardo, et al. Oxford: Oxford University Press.

Jeffreys, H. 1931. *Scientific Inference*. Cambridge: Cambridge University Press.

———. 1932. On the Theory of Errors and Least Squares. *Proc. Royal Soc. London*, series A 138:48–55.

———. 1933. Probability, Statistics, and the Theory of Errors. *Proc. Royal Soc. London*, series A 140:523–35.

———. 1934. Probability and Scientific Method. *Proc. Royal Soc. London*, series A 146:9–16.

————. [1961] 1967. *Theory of Probability*. 3d ed. Oxford: Oxford University Press.

Kadane, J. B., M. J. Schervish, and T. Seidenfeld. 1986. Statistical Implications of Finitely Additive Probability. In *Bayesian Inference and Decision Techniques*. Edited by P. K. Goel and A. Zellner. Amsterdam: Elsevier.

Keynes, John Maynard. [1921] 1973. *A Treatise on Probability*. Vol. 8 of *The Collected Writings of John Maynard Keynes*. 30 vols. Edited by D. E. Moggridge. London: Macmillan. (CW)

Kyburg, H. E. 1955. *Probability and Induction in the Cambridge School*. Ann Arbor, Mich.: University Microfilms.

————. 1974. *The Logical Foundations of Statistical Inference*. Dordrecht, Holland: Reidel.

————. 1977. Randomness and the Right Reference Class. *Journal of Philosophy* 74:501–20.

Lane, D. 1980. Fisher, Jeffreys, and the Nature of Probability. In *R. A. Fisher: An Appreciation*. Edited by S. E. Fienberg and D. V. Hinkley. New York: Springer-Verlag.

Levi, I. 1977. Direct Inference. *Journal of Philosophy* 74:5–29.

————. 1980. Induction as Self Correcting According to Peirce. In *Science, Belief and Behaviour*. Edited by D. H. Mellor. Cambridge: Cambridge University Press.

Savage, L. J. 1963. Discussion. *Bull. d'Inst. Internat. Statist*. 40:925–27.

Schervish, M. J., T. Seidenfeld, and J. B. Kadane. 1984. The Extent of Nonconglomerability of Finitely Additive Probabilities. *Zeitschrift für Wahrscheinlichkeitstheorie* 66:205–26.

Seidenfeld, T. 1978. Direct Inference and Inverse Inference. *Journal of Philosophy* 75:709–30.

————. 1992. R. A. Fisher's Fiducial Argument and Bayes' Theorem. *Statistical Science* 7:358–68.

Comment

Gregory Lilly

Fisher, Jeffreys, and Keynes

Professor Seidenfeld provides three valuable services to economists intrigued by Keynes and probability theory.

One, Seidenfeld alerts us to the Fisher-Jeffreys debate. It is always instructive (and sometimes amusing) when two giants clash over foundations, especially when, as in this case, the issues are not clouded with overly technical terminology.

Two, Seidenfeld suggests that Fisher and Jeffreys can be reference marks in an explication of Keynes's probability theory. He points out that in two important respects, Keynes is more like Fisher than Jeffreys. I was somewhat surprised at this since the traditional classification puts Jeffreys and Keynes into the Fisher-free category: theorists who tried to develop a "logical" conception of probability. Normally we think about how Jeffreys and Keynes are alike, and how Fisher and Keynes differ; new classifications tend to produce new insights—perhaps this one will, too.[1]

---

1. For example, Cottrell (1993, 43) has advised Keynes scholars who want to explore the connection between *A Treatise on Probability* and *The General Theory* that a focus on the idea that probability is about an objective relation between a hypothesis and an evidence statement is a misplaced focus. Instead of emphasizing the presumed objective logic of a probability-based philosophy of science, an idea that Keynes and Jeffreys share, these scholars should emphasize the idea that the probability relation may not be defined for all pairs of hypotheses and evidence statements, an idea that Keynes and Fisher share.

Three, Seidenfeld introduces some modern results in Bayesian statistics and develops a connection between those results and Jeffreys. Now one can take this connection that Seidenfeld provides and argue that Jeffreys's rationalization of inductive inference is fundamentally flawed. Deriving the proposition that

(1) Sometimes it is better to remain ignorant, even when learning is cost-free. (Seidenfeld, this volume)

within a system that is meant, in Jeffreys's words, to be "a theory of scientific inference that will agree with ordinary beliefs about its validity" (1934, 9) indicates a problem. Something has to go, either the system or the proposition. Given the choice, I will deny Jeffreys's Bayesian system rather than accept proposition (1). But what about the other Bayesian systems? Is the coherence of these systems also threatened by the work that Seidenfeld mentions?

Keynes in 1921, Goodman-Quine, and Grue

Turning to Keynes, what about his rationalization of inductive inference found in the *Treatise on Probability*? Since Keynes and Jeffreys differ, does Keynes escape Jeffreys's fate?

Recall your philosophy 101: induction—the process of jumping to a conclusion about a population when the evidence concerns only a sample of that population—is something we all do in both ordinary life and in science. Philosophers are perplexed, however, by our readiness to regard only some inductions as valid even though *all* are incapable of proof through either logic or observation. On the basis of what he says in the *Treatise*, Keynes believes that he has resolved the philosophical problem of induction, and the key is probability.

An inductive argument affirms, not that a certain matter of fact is so, but that relative to *certain evidence* there is probability in its favour. The validity of the induction, relative to the original evidence, is not upset, therefore, if, as a fact, the truth turns out to be otherwise. . . . The validity of the inductive method does *not* depend on the success of its predictions. Its repeated failure in the past may, of course, supply us with new evidence, the inclusion of which will modify the force of subsequent inductions. But the force of the old induction *relative to the old evidence* is untouched. . . . The validity and reasonable nature of inductive generalization is, therefore, a question of logic and not of experience, of formal and not of material laws. (Keynes [1921] 1973, 245–46)

Goodman and Quine would say that Keynes (in 1921) not only has it backward—the validity of inductive generalization is a matter of experience, not logic—but also he missed the bus: the validity of some inductions (and not others) has little to do with probability. To make sense of the Goodman-Quine position, let us first consider Goodman's ingenious invention, the predicate "grue": "A thing is grue if examined before 2000 A.D. and determined to be green, or is not so examined and is blue; hence at any earlier time, an examined thing is determined to be green if and only if it is determined to be grue" (1972, 359).[2] Since nothing can be both grue and green in that nothing is simultaneously blue and green, we therefore have two logically inconsistent hypotheses,

(2) All emeralds are grue.
(3) All emeralds are green.

which are both highly confirmed by the exact same evidence.

Despite its innocuous appearance, Goodman's grue problem is not easily dismissed. Indeed, Quine (1975) has generalized it, saying that one can have two large and fundamental theories ("systems of the world"), T_1 and T_2, which are logically incompatible yet empirically equivalent.

I fail to see how probability will help here. Goodman and Quine go much further and claim that no logic or calculus, however broadly defined, will be able to distinguish, on the basis of validity, between hypotheses (2) and (3), or between T_1 and T_2. Inductive inference "rests upon chance choices sanctified by habit" (Goodman 1972, 357).

How might chance choices sanctified by habit solve the simpler task of merely differentiating between hypotheses (2) and (3)?

Consider a finite number of agents, and let G stand for the corresponding power set (minus $\emptyset$) comprised of these agents. Suppose that the agents in each element (g) of G consciously follow a method, call it M, applied, at time t_i, to a finite set of hypotheses ($H(t_i, Q)$) which all concern a predicate, Q. Suppose, moreover, that each hypothesis, h, of $H(t_i, Q)$ is susceptible to testing through observation and experiment.

2. Goodman's grue argument first appeared in 1946; an extended discussion can be found in Goodman [1954] 1983.

Hypotheses that fail at least one data test are false; hypotheses that pass all data tests are true.

Method M consists of the following four rules.[3]

> **Rule 1:** Through time $(t_1, t_2, t_3, \ . \ . \ .)$ gather new data and test by experiment, one by one, the elements of $H(t_i, Q)$. So at the end of t_i, G partitions $H(t_i, Q)$ into two subsets: $H^{\text{PASS}}(t_i, Q)$: the hypotheses that passed all the data tests during t_i, and $H^{\text{FAIL}}(t_i, Q)$: the hypotheses that failed at least one data test during t_i.
>
> **Rule 2:** Every $g \in G$ rejects every $h \in H^{\text{FAIL}}(t_i, Q)$; every $h \in H^{\text{PASS}}(t_i, Q)$ is accepted by at least one $g \in G$.
>
> **Rule 3:** If a new hypothesis, h^*, is proposed by some g during t_i, then $h^* \in H(t_{i+1}, Q)$.
>
> **Rule 4:** If h is accepted by g at the end of t_i, then g accepts h at the end of t_{i+1}, provided $h \in H^{\text{PASS}}(t_{i+1}, Q)$.

Note four characteristics of method M. (i) If h is false, then by using M, G will eventually reject h, if h is proposed. If h is true, then by using M, at least one $g \in G$ will eventually accept h, if h is proposed. Hence by using method M, a group can differentiate between hypotheses (2) and (3). (ii) Method M is an example of chance choices sanctified by habit, hence M is a matter of experience, not logic. (iii) Probability has a limited role in method M; it will be used at the level of data testing, enabling a more efficient data analysis. (iv) The structure of M is much like the structure of the old-fashioned scientific method of both Bacon and Galileo (see Rosenberg and Birdzell 1986, 251–56).

Keynes in 1936, the Carnegie School, and Uncertainty Avoiders

What does this have to do with Keynes and economics? Well, consider the following quote from *The General Theory*.

> There is the instability due to the characteristic of human nature that a large proportion of our positive activities depend on spontaneous optimism rather than on a mathematical expectation, whether moral or hedonistic or economic. Most, probably, of our decisions to do something positive, the full consequences of which will be drawn out over many days to come, can only be taken as a result of animal spirits—of a spontaneous urge to action rather than inaction, and not as

3. M is a slight adaptation of a process described in Putnam 1963.

the outcome of a weighted average of quantitative benefits multiplied by quantitative probabilities. (Keynes 1936, 161)

Evidently Keynes in 1936 was thinking a lot like Quine and Goodman; don't the two phrases "a result of animal spirits" and "chance choices sanctified by habit" refer to the same thing?[4] If so, then perhaps we can take the line of thought developed in the preceding section and attain a new perspective on Keynes's economics. In particular, is there a method analogous to M—old-fashioned science—which is applicable to (economic) choices? There does appear to be an informative analogy between valid inductions and rational choices. Choice is the process of jumping to an action on the basis of incomplete evidence; time, after all, waits for no one. And just as, right now, we can only hope that the hypotheses we accept are true, we can, right now, only hope that the choice we make is the best possible given our options and preferences.[5]

Some claim that valid inductions and rational choices are things we can deliberately do, but that depends on controversial definitions of "valid" and "rational." Method M gives us a means to bypass the issue of validity yet still distinguish true hypotheses from false. Is there a method like M that bypasses the issue of rationality yet still differentiates choices in some sort of normative sense?

For help let's turn to the Carnegie school who, like Keynes in 1936, believe that real-world choosers are rarely expected utility maximizers trying to predict the future.[6] The Carnegie school introduces the idea of an uncertainty avoider (Cyert and March [1963] 1992, 166–69) to replace the expected utility maximizer. Uncertainty avoiders do two things. One, they attempt to control their environment, hence increase its predictability. Two, uncertainty avoiders use decision rules, or programs, when choosing.[7] These programs rely on short-run feedback; hence the uncertainty avoider need not make forecasts or depend on expectations. Uncertainty avoiders are content to use a particular program as long as the program produces satisfactory choices: choices that pass the un-

---

4. See Lawlor 1994 for a provocative account of how Keynes in 1921 turned into Keynes in 1936.

5. Were the options considered, the only options truly available? How can we be sure that today's preferences are the same as tomorrow's?

6. The Carnegie school refers to the people associated with Carnegie Tech's Graduate School of Industrial Administration during the 1950s and 1960s—people like Herbert Simon, Richard Cyert, and James March.

7. For an analysis of two important programs, see Lilly 1994.

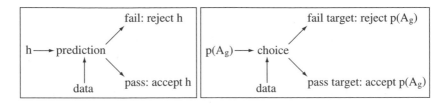

Figure 1

certainty avoider's target or aspiration level. If a program consistently produces unsatisfactory choices, then uncertainty avoiders face an unpleasant task: Do they choose new programs and thus more uncertainty, or do they keep their current programs and thereby risk choosing more choices that will fail their target? Programs are not only for individual uncertainty avoiders; groups use them for organizational and societal choices. In the sphere of social choice, programs provide a means for groups of uncertainty avoiders to achieve coordination and control, hence the desired predictability (March and Simon 1958).

I think Keynes in 1936 would appreciate the idea of an uncertainty avoider. It fits nicely with a Goodman-Quine philosophy; an action that "depends on spontaneous optimism rather than on a mathematical expectation" is quite like a chance choice sanctified by habit, which is quite like an action resulting from a program with a history of producing satisfactory choices.

Now let's take this alternative conception of choice—choice as an example of rule-governed behavior—and find a method, similar to M, that will lead agents to, at the least, accept programs that result in satisfactory choices and, at the least, reject programs that result in unsatisfactory choices.

G and g are used as before. Assume $p(A_g)$ refers to a program that will lead group g (numbering anywhere from one to many) to take an action of type A. The analogy I will push is as shown in figure 1.

The method, call it C, consists of the following three rules.

Rule 1:   Through time $(t_1, t_2, t_3, \ . \ . \ .)$ every $g \in G$ applies a $p(A_g)$.

Rule 2:   If at the end of t_1, g's choice is satisfactory (passes the target), then accept $p(A_g)$ and apply it during t_{i+1}.

Rule 3:   If at the end of t_i, g's choice is not satisfactory (fails the target), then reject $p(A_g)$ and apply, during t_{i+1}, a different program $[p^*(A_g)]$ known to G.

Note three characteristics of method C. (i) If $p(A_g)$ produces satisfactory choices, then by using C, at least one $g \in G$ will eventually apply $p(A_g)$, if it is known to G. If $p(A_g)$ produces unsatisfactory choices, then by using C, G will eventually reject $p(A_g)$, if it is known to G. (ii) Method C is another example of chance choices sanctified by habit. (iii) Method C has an almost trivially simple structure.

Does that mean that method C is almost trivially easy to implement? Not in an economy of uncertainty avoiders!

The difficulty, of course, lies in encouraging uncertainty avoiders to obey C's Rule 3. To reject a familiar program in favor of one totally new is to ask uncertainty avoiders to go against their very nature. This fundamental problem is compounded by further trouble. First, there is a problem of interdependence. For example, g_1 wants to follow Rule 3 and reject their current program in favor of something new: $p_1(A_{g1})$; g_2 wants to keep their current program: $p_2(A_{g2})$. Unfortunately, $p_1(A_{g1})$ and $p_2(A_{g2})$ are incompatible, so g_2 will try to force g_1 to disobey Rule 3. Second, there is a problem of variable rewards. The benefits of applying $p(A_g)$ may be unevenly distributed among the people in g. Those who benefit greatly may be unwilling to do their part in obeying Rule 3 if $p(A_g)$ fails the target.

Does this mean that method C will never be found in an economy of uncertainty avoiders? No, according to Marx, the genius of capitalism lies precisely in its ability to get those uncertainty avoiders with power to obey C's Rule 3. Under capitalism, and at no other time before (or since?), groups with economic power have the incentive to innovate and overturn the status quo: "The bourgeosie cannot exist without constantly revolutionising the instruments of production, and thereby the relations of production, and with them the whole relations of society. Conservation of the old modes of production in unaltered form, was, on the contrary, the first condition of existence for all earlier industrial classes" (Marx [1848] 1978, 476).

So how does capitalism do it—get uncertainty avoiders to obey method C's Rule 3? Rosenberg says it happens in three basic ways: capitalism has managed to (i) reduce the risk of innovation by inventing institutions such as stockmarkets, (ii) offer large financial rewards to the successful innovator, and (iii) give a high degree of autonomy to groups, especially in the arena of investment (1994, 87–108).

Keynes in 1936 seems willing to scrap all three of these features of historical capitalism. Thus my question to Keynes: Would his new version of capitalism be as successful as historical capitalism in implementing method C?

References

Cottrell, Allin. 1993. Keynes's Theory of Probability and Its Relevance to His Economics. *Economics and Philosophy* 9:25–51.

Cyert, Richard, and James March. [1963] 1992. *A Behavioral Theory of the Firm.* 2d ed. Oxford: Basil Blackwell.

Goodman, Nelson. 1946. A Query on Confirmation. *Journal of Philosophy* 43:383–85.

———. [1954] 1983. *Fact, Fiction and Forecast.* 4th ed. Cambridge: Harvard University Press.

———. 1972. *Problems and Projects.* Indianapolis: Hackett.

Jeffreys, Harold. 1934. Probability and Scientific Method. *Proceedings of the Royal Society of London*, series A 146:9–16.

Keynes, John Maynard. [1921] 1973. *A Treatise on Probability.* Vol. 8 of *The Collected Writings of John Maynard Keynes.* 30 vols. Edited by D. E. Moggridge. London: Macmillan. (CW)

———. 1936. *The General Theory of Employment, Interest and Money.* San Diego, New York, London: Harcourt Brace Jovanovich.

Lawlor, Michael Syron. 1994. On the Historical Origin of Keynes's Financial Market Views. In *Higgling: Transactors and Their Markets in the History of Economics.* Edited by Neil De Marchi and Mary S. Morgan. Durham: Duke University Press.

Lilly, Gregory. 1994. Bounded Rationality: A Simon-like Explication. *Journal of Economic Dynamics and Control* 18:205–30.

March, James, and Herbert Simon. 1958. *Organizations.* New York: Wiley.

Marx, Karl. [1848] 1978. Manifesto of the Communist Party. In *The Marx-Engels Reader.* Edited by R. C. Tucker. New York: Norton.

Putnam, Hilary. 1963. "Degree of Confirmation" and Inductive Logic. In *The Philosophy of Rudolf Carnap.* Edited by P. A. Schilpp. La Salle, Ill.: Open Court Publishing.

Quine, W. V. 1975. On Empirically Equivalent Systems of the World. *Erkenntnis* 9:313–28.

Rosenberg, Nathan. 1994. *Exploring the Black Box: Technology, Economics, and History.* Cambridge and New York: Cambridge University Press.

Rosenberg, Nathan, and L. E. Birdzell. 1986. *How the West Grew Rich: The Economic Transformation of the Industrial World.* New York: Basic Books.

An Unfortunate Alliance: Keynesianism and the Conservatives 1945–1964

Jim Tomlinson

> In the past twenty years we have almost ceased to think micro-economically. We have abandoned the micro-economic attempt to balance the economy and to steer its structural changes. We have come to depend wholly on macroeconomic controls.—E. A. G. Robinson, *Economic Planning in Britain*

This article attempts two tasks. First, it offers a broad brush account of the impact of Keynesianism on the performance of the British economy in the twenty years after World War II. Second, it makes a more detailed argument about Keynesianism under the Conservatives, from 1951 to 1964.

Any economic historian dealing with twentieth-century Britain has to come to terms with Keynes. In the sense of continuing intellectual importance with a policy orientation, there is plainly no remotely equivalent figure. This coming to terms is a difficult task, perhaps especially for those who share with Keynes a belief in policy activism and the crucial role of full employment in welfare in its fullest sense. The argument of this article is that, bedazzled by this colossus, much of the existing literature both exaggerates Keynes and Keynesianism's overall impact and plays down the negative impact on policy.[1] This article, it should be emphasized, is centrally concerned with the history of economic policy, along with the impact of Keynesian doctrine and advice on that policy. In

---

1. This exaggeration is apparent in violently hostile work, e.g., Hayek 1978, as much as in sympathetic work. For an earlier attempt at assessment, see Tomlinson 1981.

that sense it has a clearly different approach from those whose concern is the evolution of doctrine.

1. The Impact of Keynesianism

It is abundantly clear that to try and characterize a Keynesian policy regime is to enter a thicket of complex and competing definitions that is almost as dense as that surrounding Keynesian theory. Nevertheless, most authors concur in seeing the policies pursued in early postwar Britain as deserving that name, with however much qualification. Perhaps the best term is *simple or hydraulic Keynesianism* (which could be considered parallel to Joan Robinson's "bastard Keynesianism" in economic theory).

Simple Keynesianism is a term employed by Alan Booth to describe how the very broad agenda of 1930s Keynesianism was narrowed by going through the Whitehall machine in the later years of the war, so that by the late 1940s the Keynesian program focused much more on the simple manipulation of aggregate demand than was likely to have occurred if that program had not had to bend to the demands of administrative acceptance (Booth 1986; 1989, chaps. 8–11). As Booth argues, this program did not have much impact on policy in the early postwar years (1945–47) because of the Labour government's emphasis on controls and planning, but after 1947 it became more important as, to a growing extent, fiscal policy displaced physical controls. After 1951 and the end of the Korean War it came much more into its own as the Conservatives continued the "bonfire of controls" begun by Labour in 1948 and reactivated monetary policy (Rollings 1988).

There was no straightforward transition to simple Keynesianism, however. Howson (1993), for example, has shown how a combination of Keynesian advice and desire to redistribute income led to the policy of cheaper money in 1945 and 1946, and how this was only slowly reversed in the late 1940s. This reemergence of monetary policy was also accompanied by complex arguments about its role, which remained matters of dispute up to the 1959 Radcliffe Report and beyond (Fforde 1992, chaps. 4–10).

The simple Keynesianism that emerged in the 1950s focused attention on aggregate demand and its manipulation via fiscal and monetary policy. In his standard survey of the management of the economy from 1945 to 1960, Dow emphasized that "the chief instruments used by the government have been fiscal policy, which in practice has meant the adjustment of tax rates, and monetary policy. . . . The policies in question are concerned essentially with large-scale effects on the main economic magnitudes: employment, the general price level, and the aggregates which figure in national income accounts" (1965, 1–2). This regime quickly became characterized (and attacked) as one of "stop-go," in which governments generated excessive fluctuations in activity by their Pavlovian responses to either rising unemployment figures or falling foreign exchange reserves. How far policy did act countercyclically as was intended has long been a matter of dispute. Dow, for example, was critical of policy as tending to destabilize rather than stabilize the economy, though this view remains controversial (1965, chap. 15; see also Worswick 1971, 36–60). Another criticism, much heard from the late 1950s, alleged that such short-term fluctuations impeded investment and hence growth (Shanks 1961; Shonfield 1958). In turn, this view has been criticized by those who note that fluctuations in economic activity in Britain were no greater than those in faster-growing western European economies (Whiting 1976; Wilson 1966).

In broader perspective, the impact of this regime in creating the concurrent period of full employment has been much debated. An early postwar generation tended to see a direct line from Keynesian theory to Keynesian policy to full employment. For example, Austin Robinson, writing in 1967, suggested that "if we are looking at the credit side I think we can honestly say that the world today is a different place from what it was in the 1930s–in very large measure as a result of the economic thinking that began in this Faculty in Cambridge in those exciting years of the 1930s" (43).

Few would now accept this strong version of the Keynesian revolution and its impact on policy. In 1968 Matthews showed how postwar fiscal policy at best played only a minor role in the strength of demand in comparison with the 1930s, most of the change coming from private investment and trade. His later more extended work came to a broadly similar conclusion (Matthews et al. 1982, 309–13). The argument was not that government had no favorable effects on demand, but that these effects were mainly indirect:

> Direct injections of demand by fiscal or monetary policy or public sector investment were not responsible for the unusually high average level of activity in the postwar period. It is possible, however, that government policy in a broader sense did contribute to the high average

level of activity, partly on account of the devaluations of 1949 and
1967, partly by the timing of fiscal and monetary measures, partly by
effects on confidence. (Matthews et al. 1982, 313)

A one-sentence summary of the existing literature on the Keynesian
revolution in economic policy with regard to Britain in the 1951–64
period would suggest that "much ado about nothing" would be a considerable exaggeration; nevertheless, the positive benefits to the economy of
this regime have to be set clearly in the context of the international boom
that characterized this period, a boom in which countries with highly
variant policy regimes participated (Maddison 1982, chap. 6; Marglin
and Schor 1991).

The concurrence of the postwar boom has led to the view that the real
importance of Keynes was felt not in domestic policy but in shaping
the international policy regime after 1945. There can obviously be no
dispute that Keynes himself gave the creation of a stable, expansionist
international regime the highest priority in the later years of his life, and
indeed killed himself working to ensure that the regime was superior
to the mess apparent after 1918 (Moggridge 1992, chaps. 16, 28–30).
However, as history too often tells us, heroic efforts don't always yield
a morally commensurate outcome. There would seem to be two queries
which may be entered against the view that, via his role in creating the
"liberal" regime of the International Monetary Fund and GATT, Keynes
played a key role thereby in generating the international conditions for
the "long boom" of 1945–73.

First, much recent work on western Europe has highlighted the rapidity
with which much of the continent recovered in the late 1940s, in a period
when the international regime had not been liberalized to any serious
extent. Milward in particular has emphasized the extent to which even
by 1947 the forces of revival were apparent, and it was precisely the
strength of that revival that exacerbated the "dollar shortage" and balance
of payments problems of western European countries (1984, chap. 1).

Second, this revival of western Europe was sustained via dollar injec-
tions, first by Marshall Aid and then aid under the Mutual Security Act,
rather than by liberalization of the international economy. It was not until
well into the 1950s that the American liberal grand design can be said to
have been realized, by which time the boom had been proceeding for a
decade (Milward 1992). This is not to say liberalization played no role in
the postwar expansion; the concurrence of booms in western Europe is

itself evidence against that view. And while the "grand design" was slow to be achieved, liberalization within western Europe, albeit with tough discrimination against the dollar, was evident from the late 1940s. The point is that liberalization was only one element in the boom.

Another element was that the structural conditions for fast growth and full employment in Europe in this period were particularly favorable, for two reasons in particular. On the one hand, the significant lag between European and American techniques of production (in the broadest sense) provided a scope for the large-scale "catch-up" that was facilitated by the political desire of the United States to export its model of a high-productivity society to its allies. This lag predated the war, of course, but both political conditions and the absence of unemployment meant that efforts to reduce it were greater and more successful than in the interwar period (Abramowitz 1986; Maier 1987). On the other hand, the large agricultural sectors in most western European countries except the United Kingdom meant that rapid growth could be aided by a once-and-for-all transfer of labor from low- to high-productivity tasks. While it of course expanded the labor supply, this productivity-raising shift also meant a surge in demand so that full employment could be sustained (Dumke 1990; Kindleberger 1967).

These points are made to suggest that the basis of the "long boom" did not lie primarily in liberalization of the international economy. This factor undoubtedly played its part, but it came too late to be decisive and it is probably outweighed in importance by the upward shift in investment responding to changes in demand and new technologies (Marglin and Schor 1991).

Another, even more complex issue is raised by the relationship between Keynes and the international economy in the postwar period. This is the counterfactual problem of how far the liberal regime, insofar as it did at least aid the long boom, would have been different if Keynes had died earlier, in, say, 1939. It is certainly plausible that Keynes helped modify features of that regime and make it rather more congenial to countries which, like Britain, wanted to emphasize the centrality of full employment to their policy objectives and at the same time suffered from serious balance of payments problems (Moggridge 1992).[2] The basic thrust of "liberalization" seems to be deeply embedded in U.S. politics

2. On the Keynes approach to the international economy more generally, see Williamson 1983, Wolf and Snook 1988, and Radice 1988.

and economics, however, rather than being dependent on the role of any one person.

By the middle of World War II, the United States was clearly the preeminent economic power in the world, aware of the potential for economic expansion via the liberalization of world markets, but also believing that restrictionism, as in the 1930s, was politically highly dangerous. The United States, like Britain before it in the nineteenth century, believed that only free trade was compatible with peace abroad and prosperity at home. As with Britain and the gold standard, the United States believed that a financial regime of stable exchange rates would underpin the position of the world's most important economic and financial power (Gardner 1955, chap. 1; Maier 1987).[3] It is surely hard to believe that the U.S. government's posture would have been much different even if Keynes had not participated in the debate, and who can doubt that eventually what the United States wanted the United States would get?

2. The Peculiarities of the British

Two broad features differentiated the British economy from those of the other major European industrial powers in the middle decades of the twentieth century: the strength of the commitment to Keynesianism, and the extent of relative decline in its growth performance. The central question addressed by the remaining sections of this article is whether these two features were causally connected. I will use archival sources[4] to assess the hypothesis advanced by, for example, Peter Hall when he argues that "the nation that most avidly embraced Keynesianism also adopted the most arms-length industrial policy in Europe. In that respect, while Keynes's doctrines solved many of the parties' political problems, it by no means solved Britain's economic problems" (1986, 67; see also Bulpitt 1986, 23–28).

The greater impact of Keynesianism at the level of both theory and policy in Britain seems incontrovertible if the comparison is made with other western European economies. Keynesianism was predominantly an Anglo-American phenomenon at the theoretical level, but its policy impact in the United States was significantly delayed over that in Britain.

3. Dispute has focused on *why* the United States was so committed to such a regime and its consequences, not *whether* such a commitment existed.
4. The PRO, HMSO, and CAB are respectively, the Public Record Office, Her Majesty's Stationery Office, and Cabinet Papers.

Table 1   Excess of French, German, and Italian growth rates over that of the United Kingdom, 1873–1973 (percentage of GDP per person per year)

	France	Germany	Italy
1873–1899	0.1	0.3	−0.9
1899–1913	1.1	1.0	2.0
1913–1924	0.5	−1.2	−0.4
1924–1937	0.4	2.0	0.8
1937–1951	0.7	0.0	0.4
1951–1964	2.0	2.8	3.3
1964–1973	2.0	1.8	2.4

Source: Matthews et al. 1982, table 2.5, p. 31.

In the major countries of continental Europe, Keynesianism remained a marginal creed with little or no policy impact, certainly before the late 1960s (Hall 1989; Stein 1969; Tomlinson 1991; Winch 1972, chap. 13). Equally, while the timing and characteristics—let alone the causes— of British relative decline remain matters of keen controversy, the early postwar decades seem a crucial period when, as other European countries started to catch up with U.S. levels of output per head, Britain's growth lagged, yielding a place close to or at the bottom of the "league tables" of growth that made their first appearance in the 1950s (table 1).

In looking at this combination of features, this article focuses on the 1951–64 period of Conservative rule. This choice is partly dictated by the availability of public records: under the thirty-year rule, state papers for the period are now almost all available. Partly because of the workings of this rule, we already have a considerable literature on the economic history and policy of the previous (Labour) government of 1945–51, but there are few archivally based studies that extend into the 1950s (Cairncross 1985; Tiratsoo and Tomlinson 1993; Tomlinson 1993).[5] Beyond the question of sources, however, it seems clear that this period of Conservative rule is sandwiched between Labour governments which, on paper at least, were committed to activist proindustrial growth policies (Blackaby 1978; Tiratsoo and Tomlinson 1993). It is therefore important to establish how governments in this period conducted their economic policy, what

5. Exceptions are Peden 1990, 1992, 1993, and Rollings 1988.

Keynesianism meant to them, and how the policy regime responded to the growing realization of Britain's poor growth performance.

First, all the evidence suggests the contingent nature of support for Keynesianism in the government machine. Attempts to trace the spread of Keynesian ideas among state personnel have previously shown that this spread was extremely slow and that support for Keynesian policy hinged on its assumed capacity to deliver existing, long-standing objectives–in the context of the postwar boom, this meant especially the objectives of low inflation and constraint on public expenditure growth (Peden 1990; Rollings 1988; Tomlinson 1987). Keynesianism had, of course, originally been taken up by the wartime British Treasury because Keynes's approach, embodied in "How to Pay for the War," seemed to provide a congenial program for holding down war-induced inflation. In the postwar period, buoyant levels of activity meant persistent current account budget surpluses, and even when public borrowing in peacetime began again in 1952–53, these borrowings were to finance public investments that yielded a positive money return (Peden 1990, 209–10). Rather than undermine the "fiscal constitution" in this period, Keynesian arguments tended to reinforce the Treasury desire to constrain public expenditure growth by suggesting the need for buoyant surpluses in the boom to offset potential deficits in the event of a slump.

Right through the 1951–64 period, discussion of budgetary policy at the official level is confused by the dual purposes of managing public finances and managing the aggregate level of demand. Most officials continued to regard the first of these as the key task, and this is reflected in, for example, the discussion of the form of government accounts that surfaced periodically in this period. Originally the form of these accounts was organized around parliamentary control of spending and taxation decisions. In the war years, alternative classifications were produced so that budgetary policy could be integrated with economic management. But these different forms of accounts persisted in uneasy cohabitation through the Conservative period (PRO 1960a, 1960b, 1961a, 1962a, 1962b, 1962c). A compromise was reached in 1962 through which the accounts would be presented in two forms designed for both purposes, a result greeted in a characteristic phrase by a senior Bank of England official: "It is a great relief to me that the attempt to combine Dogmatic Theology and Pastoralia in one paper need not be pursued. There are two good new papers on the former for candidates for honours, while the rest of us can concentrate on figures related to the way in which the taxes and expenditure have been authorized by government" (PRO 1962d). This was symptomatic of a failure by most senior officials concerned with budgetary policy (which remained a strictly limited circle) to accept the basic idea that budgetary policy should be determined by the state of aggregate demand. These officials continued to worry about any notion of a budget deficit (however calculated) because of the possible effects on confidence (PRO 1960a). In that context, it is the economic environment in which policy operated rather than the ideas adhered to by officials that had changed significantly since the 1930s.

A well-known feature of this period was, of course, the concern with balance of payments: problems with the payments position, in various guises, usually stimulated the "stop" part of the policy cycle. Reading the policy papers of the period reinforces the impression that, most of the time, it was the payments position that framed the approach to almost every possible issue.

One key part of the debate about the balance of payments in this period was the liberalization of imports. In 1951 the trend toward trade liberalization from the heights of wartime control had already begun. It was reversed under the impact of the Korean War in 1952 but thereafter continued, if unevenly, throughout the Conservative period in office. By 1964, the process was incomplete, but, especially following the "Dillon Round" of tariff negotiations in the early 1960s, it left most of British manufacturing industry with low levels of protection (Dow 1965, 153–58; Morgan 1978).

What is quite apparent from the archives, if not from elsewhere, is that the debate over this liberalization was overwhelmingly concerned with either political issues or with the overall impact on the balance of payments.[6] Liberalization was politically controversial within the Conservative party, especially because of the attachment of an important minority of the party to the idea of Imperial Preference as a way of strengthening the Commonwealth. Only after many a battle did this issue resolve itself in favor of free traders and those who looked to Western Europe as a mainstay of Britain's international economic links (Cairncross 1992, 126–30).

---

6. In this discussion, the view that the balance of payments should govern the pace of liberalization was unopposed. The previous year an alternative prospectus had been proposed by the minister of works: "In the sphere of commercial policy the best approach seems to be a combination of tariffs to protect strategic industries and large plans to expand the productive capacity and to exchange the products of the export industries" (PRO 1953a). Such views seem to have had little impact on the discussion.

More directly pertinent here is the balance of payments/macroeconomic orientation of the discussion of liberalization. The pace of liberalization was largely determined by the perceived strengths of the balance of payments, with the question of the effects on particular industries largely ignored (PRO 1954a). Defenders of liberalization, certainly by the end of the 1950s, framed their position entirely in terms of the argument that the deterioration in the balance of payments was not due to that liberalization (PRO 1960c). The impact of liberalization on individual industries was regarded as a matter of political management, not as raising any issues for the path of economic policy (PRO 1955a, 1961c). The counterpart to this approach was the belief that import competition would increase the efficiency of domestic producers–though this view was more often expressed in the privacy of the committee room than on the public platform. Moreover, this view was seemingly applied indiscriminately in this period: import competition was a panacea, to be supported a priori, without reference to the economic importance of particular sectors. In sum, British policy in this period did not use trade policy in any sense as an instrument of industrial policy (Oulton 1976).

3. The Emergence of Decline

Consciousness of relative industrial decline surfaced early in the postwar period.[7] Even under the Attlee government, while much of the focus on industrial efficiency derived from immediate worries about the balance of payments, the belief existed that the British economy suffered from major long-term defects, which would have serious implications, especially once competitors like Germany and Japan reconstructed their industries (Tiratsoo and Tomlinson 1993). But sensitivity to long-run competitive problems is not, of course, the same as believing that the economy is currently suffering from long-run relative decline. As is well known, Britain has undergone scares about its competitive position going back well into the nineteenth century (Supple 1990; Tomlinson 1994) without this crystallizing into a clear notion of relative decline, as measured, as seems most sensible, by a slower rate of per capita growth than in other comparable countries. The emergence of such a notion of decline became

7. Also of interest here is Colin Clark's discussion in the preface to the 1951 edition of his *Conditions of Economic Progress*, where he predicted that "the main issue in the next decade is not going to be full employment at all . . . but the long-run problems of the production and distribution of real income" (vii).

much more likely once economic growth emerged as a policy concern; consciousness of decline in an income sense assumed that growth was both measured and worried about.

The statistical revolution in National Income Accounting was a by-product of the attempts to manage national economies which, of course, were enormously encouraged by World War II. After that war, all the major industrial countries had such accounts, and these were slowly standardized, making possible the eventual emergence of systematic comparable figures and hence "league tables" of growth. The OEEC (Organisation for European Economic Co-operation) published its first volume of national accounts on a standard basis for member countries in 1954. The first U.N. Economic Survey of Europe to present growth rates of GDP, based on OEEC statistics was that of 1957 (Arndt 1978, 50–51). This firm statistical analysis was the basis for much of the scare about Britain's position at the end of the 1950s (Shanks 1961; Shonfield 1958).

While these statistical productions were important in formalizing the comparative data that were to underpin much of the relative decline debate, concern with growth as an objective in a quite strong sense predates the final products of this statistical revolution. Of course, governments had long been concerned with the material strength of their economies as a major measure of their strategic capacity, but it was really only in the 1950s that the idea of sustained economic growth moved close to the center of the economic policy agenda. The precise dating of this shift is not easy. It is important here to distinguish policies of expanded output to achieve other goals—most obviously in Britain, the desire to rectify balance of payments problems, central to the policy agenda of the 1940s—from the idea of growth as a continuing objective through which the standard of living would show a secular ascent. This contrast was made by Gunnar Myrdal in 1950 when he deplored "a certain tendency in Western Europe to regard present economic programmes as a non-recurrent and exceptional effort, rather than as an initial and integral part of a continued economic growth over a longer period" (Arndt 1978, 37). Once the Korean War was past, and the threat of a major breakdown in the economy because of balance of payments problems receded, this latter notion of growth seems to have spread quite quickly. By the time in 1954 when Chancellor of the Exchequer Rab Butler asked the Conservative party conference, "Why should we not aim to double the standard of living in the next twenty years?" he was harping on a quite well-established theme (Arndt 1978, chap. 4; Dow 1965, 77).

While this prospect was being held out to the electorate, there was growing realization in Whitehall of Britain's failings in comparison with competing countries. Recognition that output was growing faster in countries like Germany and France seems to have come in 1953 (PRO 1954a). Initially, however, the problem of relative economic failure was largely refracted through measures of trade performance. As early as 1952 the president of the Board of Trade circulated a long memorandum on "The Export Situation and Outlook," which offered a gloomy diagnosis and prognosis of Britain's position, reflecting not just the resurgence of German and Japanese competitors but "weaknesses in our competitive position, notably inadequate delivery dates for many capital goods and too high prices for some consumer goods" (PRO 1952a).

Such gloomy prognostications taken alone might be dismissed as part of a syndrome of superficial scares, typical of much of recent British economic history. But they need to be seen alongside more analytical material on the balance of payments position which underscored the perception of a long-term problem of losing ground.

In April 1956 a Board of Trade survey of U.K. export trends showed for the first time that Britain was losing exports not mainly because of an unfavorable commodity or geographical composition, but across the board. Britain's problem, it was argued, was due to a general "weakening in its competitive power, particularly in relation to Germany, the United States and Japan" (PRO 1956a). Subsequent analyses, both official and academic, supported this view (Black 1962, 124–30; PRO 1958a).

Alongside analyses of the trade position that suggested widespread deficiencies in Britain's industrial capacity was evidence of comparative weakness in Britain's investment performance. Even before the publication of full National Income Accounts, the OEEC was drawing attention to this aggregate and suggesting a significant shortfall in the proportion of the National Income devoted to investment in Britain in comparison with other European countries. While skeptical of the precise statistics presented by the OEEC, Whitehall officials seem to have accepted the thrust of this argument (PRO 1953a).

The argument of this section so far has been that the political enthusiasm for growth emerging in the early 1950s was accompanied by a widespread appreciation among officials and ministers that Britain's economy was facing serious, long-term problems of economic performance in relation to competitors. It would be anachronistic before the late 1950s to talk of a clear perception of "relative decline," but nevertheless even before the appearance of growth league tables in the late 1950s Whitehall and Westminster were aware of and responding to strong evidence of serious malfunctioning in the economy. The next section looks at the nature of that response.

4. The Conservatives and Economic Policy

That response has to be seen in the broad context of the Conservative approach to economic policy. Their electoral success of 1951 (albeit with a minority share of the vote) has commonly been seen as reflecting disillusionment with the highly controlled economy which Labour, though to a diminishing degree, saw as necessary to pursue their highly "responsible" strategy of holding down personal consumption to free resources for exports and investment (Cairncross 1992, 7–8). The Conservative counter to this—"set the people free"—involved promises (largely delivered) to raise the level of consumption and to decontrol the economy. While anxious to maintain the "consensus" support of full employment and the welfare state, the Conservative leadership generally saw anticontrols and antibureaucracy rhetoric as a politically successful way of differentiating their approach from that of Labour (Zweiniger-Bargielowska 1994). This antigovernment intervention stance was translated as necessary into a strategy for growth: individual initiative and competition, not government controls and restrictionism, would deliver expansion. While this stance translated readily into policy in some areas, it did so less easily in others. As already noted, it was only after considerable battles that the free traders won the arguments in the party and hence made it possible for import competition to be put forward as a key means of improving the efficiency of British industry (PRO 1953c, 1956b).

The desirability of greater domestic competition was by no means taken for granted in Conservative circles in this period. The Conservatives did pass the 1956 Restrictive Practices Act, but the origin of this was certainly not a straightforward enthusiasm for the rigors of free competition. It has been plausibly argued that a major reason for the 1956 legislation was to try and conciliate industrial hostility to the 1948 Monopolies and Restrictive Practices Act by taking the problem away from government and putting it into the hands of the courts (Hannah 1990; Mercer 1991). Once the act was passed, many firms sought an alternative route to market power via merger, but this development was not met by any strengthening of antimerger policy. On the contrary, the existence of the Restrictive Practices Court seems to have been used as a reason for weakening other aspects of competition policy. In 1959 the Economic Policy committee seriously discussed abolishing the Monopolies Commission, but decided finally against this as too "politically controversial." The Conservatives did eventually pass an act in 1964 abolishing Resale Price Maintenance, but this followed a great deal of controversy (Harris 1972; PRO 1959a).

In other policy areas there was less controversy and more consistency in pursuing the strategy of less government and more competition. Unsurprisingly, tax reductions found much less opposition than competition policy. This focus on tax cuts, together with the concern to raise consumption levels, contributed to the characteristic forms of demand management by the late 1950s: "There has been a retreat from the use of fiscal policy to restrain consumption. To this extent, the main method of ensuring adequate full employment without excessive demand has become one of encouraging or discouraging investment (and to a lesser extent the consumption of durables), together with tax reductions whenever any slack could be envisaged" (Little 1962, 274).

Cuts in direct taxation are seen by Peden (1990, 234–36) as the main sign of policy sensitivity to microeconomic issues in the 1950s. Certainly such cuts were a consistent theme of policy and were often justified in terms of their incentive effects (PRO 1952a, 1960d). On the other hand, in the absence of any compelling evidence that taxation levels are related to output growth, it is surely appropriate to stress the other motives for such tax cuts, not the least of which is their appeal to the traditional Conservative constituency and to the growing number of income taxpayers in the upper working class. If it is appropriate to stress the variety of motives behind Conservative tax cutting in the 1950s, it is also right to note that such a strategy did fit with what many saw as the key to raising Britain's growth performance: raising the level of aggregate investment. As already noted, this was an area in which Britain's deficiencies were recognized very early in the Conservative period of office, and it remained a central issue in most discussions of economic growth (PRO 1953b).

One solution to these deficiencies was to cut the tax on profits, either directly via lower income or surtax (there was no separate corporation tax until 1965) or via investment allowances. Both of these paths were pursued. Initial investment allowances, introduced in 1945, were suspended in 1951 but restored in 1954 and withdrawn but then reinstated over the next decade, though their level remained an object of criticism throughout the period (Dow 1965, 198–200; PRO 1962e).

These policies about exhausted the response to perceived decline. What may be said to characterize them is a general, aggregate focus, involving little direct role for government in industrial affairs rather than any discriminatory and "hands-on" approach. The dominance of such an approach is evident not just in what was done but also in the policies that were rejected. For example, the idea of Swedish-style investment funds, where taxation on profits would be tied to the accumulation of investment funds, to be used only with government agreement, was discussed on a number of occasions but strongly rejected because "industry would feel they were being deprived of the control of their own money" (PRO 1961d, 1962f).

Equally, institutional innovations of the previous Labour government aimed to encourage efficiency were reversed or played down. Development councils were all but abolished. The British Institute of Management was pressured into reducing the scope of its operations. The British Productivity Council survived, but it was never given the role accorded to its predecessor, the Anglo-American Council on Productivity, in the 1948–52 period (PRO 1952b, 1953d, 1956c, 1956d). Parallel to this laissez-faire approach, the Board of Trade with the closest links to industry remained a poor relation of the Treasury in the formulation of economic policy. Typically, when the issue arose of whether the president of the Board of Trade could be told about (not consulted on) the budget, the most senior Treasury official minuted that on this one occasion this might be done because of the personal links between the president and the chancellor of the exchequer but that, "strictly speaking, this is neither necessary nor desirable" (PRO 1961e). The general trend was undoubtedly to reduce any government role in industry. This was not taken for granted, however; at various times the issue of how much government could and should do to encourage greater industrial efficiency was raised.

In 1953 the minister of labor presented a pessimistic assessment of Britain's productivity and output prospects, argued for bypassing the British Productivity Council as too slow to act, and suggested an examination of what role the government might play in such areas as how to spread "production and methods engineering" to less efficient firms and how to encourage the greater use of equipment by double-shift working. But nothing seems to have come of this (PRO 1953d).

The following year the first report by the Productivity and Conditional Aid Committee stimulated a debate at the ministerial level. The president of the Board of Trade proclaimed that "productivity was likely to be less affected by the dissemination of reports and by Ministerial appeals, than by economic and fiscal policies. He wished to avoid provoking a reaction in industry against government interference in this field" (PRO 1954b) and, further spelling out his credo, asserted that "productivity hangs upon demand, upon resources and upon rewards and if we forget these factors we may be sharply reminded of them. Operations outside the main field of economic and fiscal policy can have at the best only a marginal effect upon the problem" (PRO 1954c). The Conditional Aid Committee's advocacy of a more activist role for government was rejected, as it was again the following year (PRO 1955b). The committee was attacked by the president of the Board of Trade as advocating "a degree of interference with industry which industrialists would find intolerable" (PRO 1954d).[8]

5. Continuity and Change in Policy

The previous sections have sought to give an overview of government attitudes to their relationship with industry. But how far can a single picture cover the whole 1951–64 period, when it is commonly believed that attitudes to such issues as growth and the role of government underwent a transformation at the beginning of the 1960s? Brittan, for example, asserted that "a great reappraisal" began in 1960, "the year in which everything really happened but which no-one really remembers" (1964, 204). Undoubtedly, the climate of discussion of economic policy did shift in the early 1960s. On the one hand, attacks on the alleged impact of stop-go on slowing the economy's growth proliferated. On the other hand, and with rather more direct impact on the government, the Federation of British Industry started to advocate a much more explicit policy on growth linked to an enthusiasm for French-style indicative planning. The government did not of course ignore this change in climate and, as is well known, established the National Economic Development Council (NEDC) to demonstrate its new commitment to planning for growth (Harris 1972, 240–42; Leruez 1975, chap. 3).

8. I owe this latter reference to Professor George Peden. The president's views reflected the focus of the Board of Trade's attention on international issues and the neglect of industrial policy (Middlemas 1986, 306–7).

But how far this period saw a basic shift in the government's approach to industrial efficiency and growth remains doubtful. First, it seems clear that creation of the NEDC was largely reactive and its role was intended to be quite limited. This view was summed up by the chancellor of the exchequer in 1961 when, after arguing the limits of "indicative planning," he went on: "On the other hand, there appeared to be a growing weight of public opinion that the economic directions of the country suffered from the lack of suitable machinery for long-term forecasting. He hoped that the machinery he had in mind would be of value in creating a climate of opinion in which the basic economic facts of the country's situation were better understood" (PRO 1961F). It is clear that the contemporary (early 1960s) enthusiasm for growth, in particular the idea that government could do much to affect its level, was viewed with considerable skepticism in the Treasury. But it was seen as a political imperative to respond, while hoping that this new vogue could be put to good use to achieve traditional objectives. The chancellor, after stressing the need to avoid giving the impression that governments could do much to raise the growth level, went on to argue that "the positive idea of 'growth' is a valuable means of presenting many politically difficult decisions, emphasizing that such decisions are a means to enrich people and not to impoverish them." These "politically difficult decisions" related to Treasury concerns to secure an incomes policy and restrictions on government expenditure growth (PRO 1962g). These positions suggest that the turning point of the early 1960s may have been exaggerated, certainly as far as changes in specific policy instruments are concerned, rather than shifts in the rhetoric of policy. Apart from the creation of the NEDC, it is difficult to see other major policy changes that might suggest a turn toward a more interventionist stance on industry. In fact, there was a reinforcement of the focus on competition as a key force for efficiency, with the White Paper on Competition Policy in early 1964 (HMSO 1964).

One area where more intervention did occur was in industrial training. Eventually, in 1962, the government legislated for industrial training boards able to impose a levy on firms to finance the scheme. This was a reversal of previous policy, especially articulated in the Carr report of 1957, which had offered quite searching criticism of current arrangements but still emphasized industry's responsibility for training (HMSO 1958, 1962). This shift was strongly fought in Whitehall, many arguing that it involved too much of an administrative and organizational change, but eventually these objections were overcome (PRO 1962h, 1962i). The significance of this shift should not be overstated: training was an area in which deficiencies had long been recognized and where market failure arguments could most uncontroversially be applied. (Indeed, the 1980s and 1990s have shown how "more training" can be seen as a panacea in many European countries precisely because it does not impinge directly on company autonomy and therefore acts as a kind of lowest common denominator of government intervention.) Rather than the "growth debate" heralding a major new phase in policy toward industry, its main effect seems to have been to reinforce what might be called the growing obsession with the labor market and wage inflation as the key to economic success. Ministers seem to have regarded an incomes policy rather than any intervention in industry as the key to breaking the stop-go cycle (PRO 1961g).

6. Conclusions

The argument of this article is that the Conservative government of 1951–64 failed to rise to the challenge of faltering relative British economic performance, though they were well aware of this faltering from early in their period of office. This failure was partly the result of a combination of long-term features of Conservative ideology and their political priorities in those years. The question this final section attempts to address is how far that failure was also conditioned by "Keynesianism." (It is not, of course, being suggested that Keynesianism caused the underlying weakness of the British economy.)

Economic policy is never the simple translation of economic theory into policy. In this period it is especially clear that major economic decisions—for example, trade liberalization and the decisions to reject, then apply for, EEC membership—were highly political. Nevertheless, economic policy was affected both by the general climate of economic ideas and by the specific advice given to the government by its economic advisers. On the "general climate" it seems right to suggest that Keynesianism did conquer most of academic economics in Britain and did underpin most public debate on economic issues. This did not, of course, mean an absence of controversy on economic issues (Hutchison 1968), but it did mean that most of that controversy took the broad Keynesian approach as given. Above all, there emerged a theoretical synthesis that accepted the case for government regulation of the macroeconomy but linked it to a traditional view that by and large the market was the best allocator of resources. Microeconomic policy, in the sense of government activism, fitted poorly into this, and in that sense at least, as the quote by Austin Robinson given at the beginning of this article suggests, microeconomic thinking was very limited.

The exact state of opinion among the profession at large can only be crudely summarized, but the position among those directly giving advice to the government is much clearer. Even toward the end of the 1951–64 period the number of economists at policy-giving levels in Whitehall numbered no more than twenty. These were overwhelmingly concentrated on just two departments: the Ministry of Agriculture and the Economic Section, which from 1953 was incorporated in the Treasury. Those in the agricultural ministry were obviously highly specialized; almost all the economists working on broad issues were in the Economic Section.

The Economic Section had gained its role in wartime precisely because it carried the "new wave" of Keynesian thought. As one of its senior members put it: "Thanks to Keynesian ideas (and the war) the economist has found his way in [to government]" (Little 1957, 35; see also Henderson 1961). The focus of this section's activities is made quite clear by its historians: "The most important of the Section's duties lay in demand management. Much of their work revolved around issues of macroeconomic policy: the stabilisation of economic activity, investment policy, the maintenance of internal and external balance, and so on" (Cairncross and Watts 1989, 144). For example, when in 1954 the Economic Section discussed "Long Term Economic Policy," the agenda was wholly dominated by macroeconomic issues: the balance of payments, the level of domestic demand, and the control of the aggregate level of investment. There was only brief mention of "problems of particular industries," which suggested some consideration be given to how the government could intervene to speed resource shifts between industry, but the subject seems then to have been ignored (Cairncross and Watts 1989).

The heads of the Economic Section and the chief economic advisers to the government were Robert Hall (during 1947–61) and Alec Cairncross (during 1961–68). Both can reasonably be called Keynesians who strongly believed in the desirability of regulating the macroeconomy, but who were skeptical of the capacity of governments to intervene positively at the microeconomic level or to do much about the rate of economic growth. It is evident from both published and archival sources that their work was very much focused on budgetary policy and related issues.[9]

The Conservatives, it should be emphasized, were not enthusiastic embracers of the Keynesian creed, but that is definitely not the argument here. Cairncross summarizes their attitude as follows: "The Conservatives accepted in principle the use of monetary and fiscal policy in managing the economy but they were reluctant Keynesians and practised demand management only so long as it did not conflict with what they took to be sound principles. Thus they were never prepared to budget for a deficit" (Cairncross 1992, 95). At the macro level, this "reluctance" was of little importance, then, given the generally buoyant economic circumstances of the period.

On the micro side, the Conservatives had a traditional and largely political belief in the undesirability of government intervention and the benefits of free enterprise (Middlemas 1986, 217, 343; Peden 1992). This broadly coincided with the views of their Keynesian advisers (whose predecessors had fought against "planning" in the 1940s) (Tomlinson 1992), who, for example, shared the belief that growth was largely a function of the aggregate level of investment and that the key to expanding investment was to improve incentives via tax cuts.[10]

To put this point in stronger form, we might note that the Economic Section, the chief conduit of economic advice, did nothing to press such issues as industrial finance, the training system, management quality, enterprise organization, and the scale and organization of research and development on the government as possibly relevant to the problem of growth. This is not just a point made with hindsight; many of these issues had been widely discussed in policy-making circles in the 1940s (Tiratsoo and Tomlinson 1993). For the Economic Section, as for the government itself, the proper management of demand, higher investment, and more competition would of themselves secure the best possible performance of the economy. In that sense we can talk of a contingent, and unfortunate,

9. For Robert Hall, see Cairncross 1991; Hall 1959. For Cairncross, see both published comments: Cairncross 1985, 499–500, and his advice to the ministers, PRO 1962j.

10. The issue of investment and growth is, of course, a fraught and complex one, but it seems clear that in the 1950s, most economists (including those in the Economic Section) regarded the volume of investment as crucial to Britain's economic performance. See, for example, Peden 1990, 236; PRO 1954e, 1956e. Note that critics of 1950s policies usually shared this approach, but argued policy had inhibited investment (Shonfield 1958, 267). Criticism of this analysis of Britain's problems was also evident (e.g., Cairncross 1959).

alliance between British Keynesianism and the Conservatives in this period.

I am grateful to a number of people for helpful comments on earlier drafts of this paper; to Allin Cottrell and Neil Rollings; to participants in the New Perspectives on Keynes conference at Wake Forest University, April 1994, especially Donald Moggridge; and to participants at a seminar at Harvard University in April 1994.

References

Abramowitz, M. 1986. Catching Up, Forging Ahead and Falling Behind. *Journal of Economic History* 46.3:385–406.

Arndt, H. W. 1978. *The Rise and Fall of Economic Growth.* Melbourne: Longman Cheshire.

Black, J. 1962. The Volume and Price of British Exports. In *The British Economy in the Nineteen-Fifties.* Edited by G. D. N. Worswick and P. H. Ady. Oxford: Oxford University Press.

Blackaby, F. T., ed. 1978. *De-Industrialization.* London: Heineman.

Booth, A. 1986. Simple Keynesianism and Whitehall. *Economy and Society* 15.1:72–87.

Booth, A. 1989. *British Economic Policy 1931–49: A Keynesian Revolution?* London: Wheatsheaf.

Brittan, S. 1964. *The Treasury under the Tories.* Harmondsworth: Penguin.

Bulpitt, J. 1986. Mrs. Thatcher's Domestic Statecraft. *Political Studies* 34.1:20–34.

Cairncross, A. 1959. Reflections on the Growth of Capital and Income. *Scottish Journal of Political Economy* 6.1:99–115.

———. 1985. *Years of Recovery: British Economic Policy 1945–51.* London: Methuen.

———. 1992. *The British Economy since 1945.* Oxford: Basil Blackwell.

Cairncross, A., ed. 1991. *The Robert Hall Diaries.* Vol. 2: *1954–61.* London: Unwin Hyman.

Cairncross, A., and N. Watts. 1989. *The Economic Section 1959–1961.* London: Routledge.

Clark, C. 1951. *The Conditions of Economic Progress.* 2d ed. London: Macmillan.

Dow, J. C. R. 1965. *The Management of the British Economy 1945–60.* Cambridge: Cambridge University Press.

Dumke, R. 1990. Reassessing the Wirtschaftswunder: Reconstruction and Postwar Growth in an International Context. *Oxford Bulletin of Economics and Statistics* 52.4:451–91.

Fforde, J. 1992. *The Bank of England and Public Policy 1941–1958.* Cambridge: Cambridge University Press.

Gardner, R. 1955. *Sterling-Dollar Diplomacy.* Oxford: Oxford University Press.

Hall, P. 1986. *Governing the Economy.* Cambridge: Polity.

————. 1989. *The Political Power of Economic Ideas: Keynesianism across Nations.* Princeton: Princeton University Press.

Hall, R. 1959. Reflections on the Practical Applications of Economics. *Economic Journal* 69.4:639–52.

Hannah, L. 1990. Economic Ideas and Government Policy on Industrial Organisation in Britain since 1945. In *The State and Economic Knowledge.* Edited by M. O. Furner and B. Supple. Cambridge: Cambridge University Press.

Harris, N. 1972. *Competition and the Corporate Society: British Conservatives, the State and Industry.* London: Methuen.

Hayek, Friedrich von. 1978. *A Tiger by the Tail: The Keynesian Legacy of Inflation.* London: Institute of Economic Affairs.

Henderson, P. D. 1961. The Use of Economists in British Administration. *Oxford Economic Papers* 13.1:5–26.

Howson, S. 1993. *British Monetary Policy 1945–51.* Oxford: Oxford University Press.

HMSO 1958. *Training for Skill.* London: Ministry of Labour.

HMSO 1962. *Industrial Training: Government Proposals.* Cmnd. 1892. Vol. 31. London: Parliamentary Papers.

HMSO 1964. *Monopolies, Mergers and Restrictive Practices.* Cmnd. 2299. Vol. 26. London: Parliamentary Papers.

Hutchison, T. W. 1968. *Economists Economic Policy 1946–66.* London: Allen & Unwin.

Kindleberger, C. P. 1967. *Europe's Postwar Growth.* Cambridge, Mass.: Harvard University Press.

Leruez, J. 1975. *Economic Planning and Politics in Britain.* Oxford: Martin Robertson.

Little, I. M. D. 1957. The Economist in Whitehall. *Lloyds Bank Review* 44:29–40.

————. 1962. Fiscal Policy. In *The British Economy in the Nineteen-Fifties.* Edited by G. D. N. Worswick and P. H. Ady. Oxford: Oxford University Press.

Maddison, A. 1982. *Phases of Capitalist Development.* Oxford: Oxford University Press.

Maier, C. 1987. *In Search of Stability: Explorations in Historical Political Economy.* Cambridge: Cambridge University Press.

Marglin, S., and J. B. Schor, eds. 1991. *The Golden Age of Capitalism.* Oxford: Oxford University Press.

Matthews, R. C. O. 1968. Why Has Britain Had Full Employment since the War? *Economic Journal* 78.4:555–69.

Matthews, R. C. O., C. H. Feinstein, and J. C. Odling-Smee. 1982. *British Economic Growth 1856–1973.* Cambridge: Cambridge University Press.

Meadows, P. 1978. Planning. In *British Economic Policy 1960–74.* Edited by F. T. Blackaby. Cambridge: Cambridge University Press.

Mercer, H. 1991. The Monopolies and Restrictive Practices Commission, 1949–56. In *Competitiveness and the State.* Edited by G. Jones and M. W. Kirby. Manchester:

Manchester University Press.

Middlemas, K. 1986. *Britain in Search of Balance*. Vol. 1 of *Power, Competition and the State*. London: Macmillan.

Milward, A. 1984. *The Reconstruction of Western Europe 1945–51*. London: Methuen.

———. 1992. *The European Rescue of the Nation State*. London: Methuen.

Moggridge, D. E. 1992. *Keynes: An Economist's Biography*. London: Routledge.

Morgan, A. 1978. Commercial Policy. In *British Economic Policy 1960–74*. Edited by F. T. Blackaby. Cambridge: Cambridge University Press.

Oulton, N. 1976. Effective Protection of British Industry. In *Public Assistance to Industry*. Edited by W. M. Corden and G. Fels. London: Macmillan.

Peden, G. 1990. Old Dogs and New Tricks: The British Treasury and Keynesian Economics in the 1940s and 1950s. In *The State and Economic Knowledge*. Edited by M. D. Furner and B. Supple. Cambridge: Cambridge University Press.

———. 1992. Economic Aspects of British Perceptions of Power. In *Power in Europe II*. Edited by E. D. Nolfo. Berlin and New York: de Gruyter.

———. 1993. Modernisation in the 1950s: The British Experience. In *Modernisierung im Wiederaufbau: Die Westdeutsche Gesellschaft in der 50er Jahre*. Edited by A. Schudt and A. Sywottek. Bonn: Dietz Naahf.

PRO 1952a. CAB 134/845 *Economic Policy Committee*. The Export Situation and Outlook. 31 Oct.

PRO 1952b. CAB 134/842 *Economic Policy Committee*. Minutes. 2 July.

PRO 1953a. CAB 134/846 *Economic Policy Committee*. Minutes. 12 Dec.

PRO 1953b. CAB 134/847 *Economic Policy Committee*. Report by Investment Programme Committee on Investment in 1953 and 1954. 2 Feb.

PRO 1953c. CAB 134/846 *Economic Policy Committee*. Minutes. 20 May.

PRO 1953d. CAB 134/848 *Economic Policy Committee*. Efficiency and Output. 3 Dec.

PRO 1953e. T230/267 *Economic Section*. Long Term Economic Policy. 8 April.

PRO 1954a. CAB 134/851 *Economic Policy Committee*. Report by Productivity and Conditional Aid Committee. 6 March.

PRO 1954b. CAB 134/850 *Economic Policy Committee*. Minutes. 18 March.

PRO 1954c. CAB 134/851 *Economic Policy Committee*. Industrial Productivity. 6 March.

PRO 1954d. BT 64/4742 *Report of Productivity and Conditional Aid Committee*. 5 May.

PRO 1954e. T230/284 *Economic Section*. Long Term Surveys of UK Income.

PRO 1955a. CAB 134/855 *Economic Policy Committee*. The Tariff. 14 March.

PRO 1955b. CAB 134/1227 *Economic Policy Committee*. 2d Report of Productivity and Conditional Aid Committee. 12 April.

PRO 1956a. CAB 134/1230 *Economic Policy Committee*. UK Export Trends. 4 April.

PRO 1956b. CAB 134/1229 *Economic Policy Committee*. Minutes. 1 Aug.

PRO 1956c. CAB 134/1231 *Economic Policy Committee British Institute of Management*. 20 April.

PRO 1956d. T228/628 *British Institute of Management* 1954–56.

PRO 1956e. T230/346 *Economic Section.* Long Term Investment Policy 1949–56.

PRO 1958a. CAB 134/1679 *Economic Policy Committee.* UK Export Trends. 4 April.

PRO 1959a. CAB 134/1681 *Economic Policy Committee.* Minutes. 6 March.

PRO 1960a. T171/506 *Budget Committee.* Minutes. 1 Jan.

PRO 1960b. T171/506 *Budget Committee.* Minutes. 11 Feb.

PRO 1960c. CAB 134/1687 *Economic Policy Committee.* The Cost of Liberalising Imports. 2 June.

PRO 1960d. T171/515 *Budget Committee.* Minutes. 12 Oct.

PRO 1961a. T171/515 *Budget Committee.* Minutes. 3 March.

PRO 1961b. T171/593 *Budget Committee.* Summary of Working Party Report on Exchequer Accounts. 12 Dec.

PRO 1961c. CAB 134/1690 *Economic Policy Committee.* GATT Tariff Negotiations. 14 April.

PRO 1961d. T171/592 *Budget Committee.* Minutes. 2 Nov.

PRO 1961e. T171/515 *Budget Committee.* F. Lee to G. Hubback 28 March.

PRO 1961f. CAB 134/1689 *Economic Policy Committee.* Minutes. 3 May.

PRO 1961g. CAB 134/1689 *Economic Policy Committee.* Minutes. 11 Nov.

PRO 1962a. T171/592 *Budget Committee.* Minutes. 15 Dec.

PRO 1962b. T171/593 *Budget Committee.* Minutes. 9 March.

PRO 1962c. T171/593 *Budget Committee.* Reform of Exchequer Accounts. 5 March.

PRO 1962d. T171/593 *Budget Committee.* H. C. B. Myners (Bank of England) to F. Lee (Treasury). 7 March.

PRO 1962e. T171/593 *Budget Committee.* Tax Relief on Industrial Investment. 3 Feb.

PRO 1962f. T171/595 *Budget Committee.* F. Lee to G. Hubback. 12 March.

PRO 1962g. CAB 134/1696 *Economic Policy Committee.* Economic Growth. 28 June.

PRO 1962h. CAB 134/1693 *Economic Policy Committee.* Minutes. 7 March.

PRO 1961i. CAB 134/1695 *Economic Policy Committee.* Industrial Training Arrangements. 28 March.

PRO 1962j. T171/593 *Budget Committee.* A. Cairncross to F. Lee. 30 March.

Radice, H. 1988. Keynes and the Policy of Practical Protectionism. In *John Maynard Keynes in Retrospect.* Edited by J. Hilliard. London: Elgar.

Robinson, E. A. G. 1967. *Economic Planning in Britain.* Cambridge: Cambridge University Press.

Rollings, N. 1988. British Budgetary Policy 1945–54: A Keynesian Revolution? *Economic History Review* 41, 2:283–98.

Shanks, M. 1961. *The Stagnant Society.* Harmondsworth: Penguin.

Shonfield, A. 1958. *British Economic Policy since the War.* Harmondsworth: Penguin.

Stein, H. 1969. *The Fiscal Revolution in America.* Chicago: Chicago University Press.

Supple, B. 1990. Official Economic Inquiry and Britain's Industrial Decline: The First Fifty Years. In *The State and Economic Knowledge.* Edited by M. O. Furner and B. Supple. Cambridge: Cambridge University Press.

Tiratsoo, N. and J. Tomlinson. 1993. *Industrial Efficiency and State Intervention: Labour 1939–51.* London: LSE/Routledge.

Tomlinson, J. 1981. Why Was There Never a Keynesian Revolution in Economic Policy? *Economy and Society* 10.1:72–87.

———. 1987. *Employment Policy: The Crucial Years, 1939–1965.* Oxford: Oxford University Press.

———. 1991. Why Wasn't There a Keynesian Revolution Everywhere? *Economy and Society* 20.1:103–19.

———. 1992. Planning: Debate and Policy in the 1940s. *Twentieth Century British History* 3.2:154–74.

———. 1993. Mr. Attlee's Supply-Side Socialism. *Economic History Review* 46.1:1–22.

———. 1994. *Government and the Enterprise since 1900: The Changing Problem of Efficiency.* Oxford: Oxford University Press.

Whiting, A. 1976. An International Comparison of the Instability of Economic Growth. *Three Banks Review* 66:26–46.

Williamson, J. 1983. Keynes and the International Economic Order. In *Keynes and the International Economy.* Edited by G. D. N. Worswick and J. Trevithick. Cambridge: Cambridge University Press.

Wilson, T. 1966. Instability and the Rate of Growth. *Lloyds Bank Review* 83:16–32.

Winch, D. 1972. *Economics and Policy.* London: Fontana.

Wolf, B., and N. Snook. 1988. Keynes and the Question of the Tariff. In *Keynes and Public Policy after 50 Years.* Edited by O. F. Hamouda and J. N. Smithin. Aldershot: Edward Elgar.

Worswick, G. D. N. 1971. Fiscal Policy and Stabilisation in Britain. In *Britain's Economic Prospects Reconsidered.* Edited by A. Cairncross. London: Allen & Unwin.

Zweiniger-Bargielowska, I. 1994. Rationing, Austerity and the Conservative Party Recovery after 1945. *Historical Journal* 37.1:173–97.

Comment

D. E. Moggridge

I should like to thank Jim Tomlinson for putting a large number of balls into the air. Indeed, there are so many that I could not hope to catch, much less examine, all of them in the space available for this comment, but I trust that I can put a slightly different spin on a few of them.

My first reaction, although this is not perhaps the one that Jim wished me to have, was to say to myself, "How little all of this had to do with Keynes" and "Perhaps this paper needs more of a sense of history." I can illustrate what I mean with a few examples.

The period of Conservative government in Britain coincided with the first decade and a bit of the postwar golden age. Britain's experience in that period was *similar* to that of other western European countries. As elsewhere, the rate of growth of output was twice or more its long-term average, and the rates of growth of output per head, or person-hour, behaved similarly. Acknowledging that Britain's long-term rate of growth was relatively low (which is the central message of Jim's table 1) is, of course, saying nothing new, although a doubling of the underlying rate of growth for all concerned will make that poor performance obvious more quickly. But emphasizing the long-term nature of Britain's relative growth "problem" makes it clear that Keynesianism, however defined, had nothing to do with its origins and little to do with its possible solution.

There are other problems with the article's discussion of the postwar boom. Tomlinson wants to minimize the impact of international Keynesianism—so much so that I think he misreads Maddison (1982, 128–29) and Margalin and Schor (1990, 61–62) to suggest the opposite to the way I read them. He accepts the conventional story that there was a technological lag between European and American best practice that gave scope for European catching up and that, outside Britain, there was a large agricultural sector from which industry could draw labor on favorable terms. However, these conditions were not peculiar to the post-1945 era; they were characteristic of earlier periods. One needs some explanation as to why things differed after 1950. It is here that Tomlinson's article needs to give a bit more thought to two matters.

First, I think he is a bit too quick to reduce the role of the liberalization of the international economy. To regain international economic equilibrium after the war, both Britain and the countries of western Europe needed to increase their exports substantially over those of prewar levels. Some of that rise could, of course, result from higher levels of demand, but I would argue that trade liberalization also played a significant role. True, at least initially, it may not have been the "universalist" liberalization favored by the framers of the initial postwar settlement. True, as well, it may actually have involved a measure of increased discrimination against the United States. But even the reductions in American tariffs and the removal of tariff and nontariff barriers among the members of OEEC stimulated trade. And one must remember that there are too many individual national European stories that seem to hinge on international factors for liberalization to be unimportant.

Second, in relation to the origins of the postwar boom, we are given no explanation as to why the investment so necessary to embody the borrowed techniques in the European capital stock remained at historically high levels after the period of reconstruction.

But enough on the international boom, which, at least as far as Britain is concerned, served to provide a favorable backcloth to its domestic Keynesianism. I now want to turn to a second area where one might regard Keynesianism as being of marginal significance. This is in the article's discussion of microeconomic policy.

I agree with Tomlinson that British Conservative governments have generally been unwilling to get mixed up with discriminating between firms in broadly similar circumstances. But I would ask again, was this something new? Again, I think that the answer would be no. If one wants parallels, all one needs to do is look at the interwar period where there was the same unwillingness to discriminate and, as a result, the same disinclination to do very much (Booth 1988). True, if the private sector did manage to come to an agreement, state power could ratify that fact and preserve the solution. But if the tendencies we are talking about are so deep-rooted, one wonders again whether Keynes and Keynesianism have had that much to do with them.

These were my general reactions. However, I also had a few comments by way of detail.

First, sticking for the moment with competition policy, an acceptable general form of intervention that does not discriminate among firms in broadly similar circumstances, I am surprised that Tomlinson does not make something of the end of Resale Price Maintenance (RPM). As I remember from my misspent youth, worrying about such things as car dealers' margins and the like, the ending of RPM was supposed to have had a significant effect on productivity in the services although, according to the Reddaway reports, the effects of abolition got mixed up with the effects of the Selective Employment Tax, which would have similar effects (Reddaway 1970, 1973).

Second, I am not certain that Jim can get away as easily as he thinks he can without defining Keynesianism a bit more fully. I don't think that just saying it is hydraulic in the sense of Coddington is adequate. Perhaps it became more hydraulic over time, but, for example, the view of monetary policy in 1945–47 was hardly hydraulic in any simple view of the world (Howson 1993). Nor does the text convey the slow groping for a rationale and a role for monetary policy that occurred after the collapse of Dalton's Keynes-inspired exercise in cheaper money (Fforde 1992; Howson 1993). I also think that the view of fiscal policy is very oversimplified, if only because what "Keynesians" thought they could do and the means available to them to do it changed radically in the course of the 1940s and 1950s as more information became available and as techniques evolved.[1] Finally, I think it might be useful to compare the way the world turned out in the 1950s with Keynes's own optimistic 1943 predictions in "The Long-Term Problem of Full Employment" ([1943] 1980, 320–25).

1. Compare Howson and Moggridge 1990 with the discussion of the Treasury's quarterly forecasting model released at the end of the period in August 1964 issue of *Economic Trends* (OECD 1966).

Third, I wonder whether Tomlinson could be more precise in his dating of the renewed concern about long-term growth. He cites Arndt 1978 on the importance of the U.N. Economic Commission for Western Europe's *Survey of Western Europe in 1957*, which was actually published in 1958, as triggering much of the journalistic "scare" about growth in Britain. However, Jim acknowledges that the "concern" "predates the final products of the statistical revolution," but gives no firmer date. Terence Hutchison is not much clearer: in his wide-ranging discussion of opinion on economic policy he takes the relevant date as "about the middle fifties" (1968, 125). However, Hutchison also points out that this dating is not surprising: one needed not only the completion of the statistical revolution but also the completion of the process of recovery and readjustment from the war.[2] True, Hutchison then goes on to take his readers through parts of the *Bulletin of the Oxford Institute of Statistics* 1955 symposium on growth and the balance of payments, but this was well after Hicks's 1953 "An Inaugural Lecture." By the mid-1950s, economic growth was sufficiently in the air that, as Arndt reports (1978, 42), it made the third edition of Samuelson's *Principles*. But when did it really percolate into British policy thinking? And how did it percolate: through the dollar-shortage-inspired literature on trade and growth as in Hicks's inaugural, or through those large PRO files of letters and memoranda from Roy Harrod?

Despite these quibbles, however, I should repeat that we are all in Jim Tomlinson's debt.

References

Arndt, H. W. 1978. *The Rise and Fall of Economic Growth: A Study in Contemporary Economic Thought.* Chicago: University of Chicago Press.

Booth, Alan. 1988. Britain in the 1930s: A Managed Economy? *Economic History Review* 40.4:499–522.

Fforde, John. 1992. *The Bank of England and Public Policy, 1941–1958.* Cambridge: Cambridge University Press.

Hicks, J. R. 1953. An Inaugural Lecture. *Oxford Economic Papers,* n.s., 5.2:117–35.

Howson, Susan. 1993. *British Monetary Policy, 1945–1951.* Oxford: Clarendon.

Howson, Susan, and D. E. Moggridge, eds. 1990. *The Collected Papers of James*

2. If one looks at another Economic Commission for Europe production of the 1950s, Ingvar Svennilson's *Growth and Stagnation in the European Economy* (1954), one can see clearly that taking comparative statistics for 1950 did not seem to show there was much of a problem (see 28–29 and 320 for some comparative material for 1913–50).

Meade. Vol. 4: *The Cabinet Office Diary, 1944–46*. London: Unwin-Hyman.

Hutchison, T. W. 1968. *Economics and Economic Policy in Britain, 1946–1966*. London: Allen & Unwin.

Keynes, John Maynard. [1943] 1980. *Shaping the Post-War World—Commodities and Employment*. Vol. 27 of *The Collected Writings of John Maynard Keynes*. 30 vols. Edited by D. E. Moggridge. London: Macmillan.

Maddison, Angus. 1982. *Phases of Capitalist Development*. Oxford: Oxford University Press.

Margalin, Stephen, and Juliet Schor, eds. 1990. *The Golden Age of Capitalism: Reinterpreting the Postwar Experience*. Oxford: Clarendon.

OECD. 1966. *Techniques of Economic Forecasting*. Paris: OECD.

Reddaway, W. B. 1970. *Effects of the Selective Employment Tax. First Report: The Distributive Trades*. London: Her Majesty's Stationery Office.

Reddaway, W. B., and Associates. 1973. *Effects of the Selective Employment Tax. Final Report*. Cambridge: Cambridge University Press.

Svennilson, Ingvar. 1954. *Growth and Stagnation in the European Economy*. Geneva: United Nations.

Keynes on Aesthetics

Rod O'Donnell

Keynes's philosophy of aesthetics is an area that has received no serious attention. Although his economic views have been intensively explored and various branches of his philosophy have recently come under scrutiny, his reflections on aesthetics as a subject in its own right have been neglected. This is unfortunate because the subject is interesting in itself, is fundamental to several aspects of his thought, and has linkages to his policy stances.

The topic is large, however, and restriction is unavoidable in the limited space provided. I have therefore chosen to concentrate on one topic only—a systematic exposition of Keynes's theory of aesthetics as contained in his unpublished philosophical writings.[1] Other cognate topics will be passed over with varying degrees of silence, including the evaluation of his aesthetic philosophy, a contextual study of his views from a history of philosophy perspective, the issue of continuity in his views over time, the relationship between aesthetics and his short- and long-term practical thinking, and his biography as a devoted supporter of aesthetic endeavors. Each certainly merits discussion, but each would unfortunately require a separate article.[2]

---

1. All Keynes's unpublished philosophical papers will appear in the first volume of a supplementary edition of his writings (see Keynes 1996).

2. There is also insufficient space to comment on issues such as the "art of economics" as practiced by Keynes or the contention that as an economist Keynes was essentially an artist

In focusing on systematic theoretical analysis rather than other issues, my main aim is to help complete an important gap in our knowledge of Keynes's intellectual output. A second objective is to contribute to the cognate topics that depend, directly or indirectly, on such analysis. A third goal is to assist in producing adequate, well-grounded interpretations of Keynes's thought. This requires the thorough and careful investigation of his writings (and of those who influenced him) because his texts, especially his philosophical ones, require multiple readings and a demanding process in which the part under consideration is referred to other parts and to the text as a whole. It is remarkable how easy it is for one to go astray in interpreting his writings, and once one set of writings has been used to clarify another, any weaknesses of interpretation in the former are imported directly into the commentary on the latter. In short, careful theoretical analysis serves important foundational purposes.[3]

Aesthetics and Keynes

Traditionally, aesthetics is that branch of philosophy dealing with the study and evaluation of beauty. Beauty is taken as occurring in two (possibly intersecting) domains—works of *nature*, such as landscapes, flora, fauna, and human forms; and works of *human culture*, such as painting, sculpture, theater, literature, ballet, music, and architecture. In seeking to understand the nature of beauty, aesthetics is concerned with the concepts and arguments used, the states of mind of those undergoing aesthetic experience, and the properties of beautiful objects. In its role of evaluating beauty, it is concerned with the exercise of taste, criticism, and judgment. The common concern with values often results in aesthetics being closely related to ethics.

---

and not a scientist (Buchanan 1987). In relation to Keynes's biography, it may be noted that Shone's view (cited in M. Keynes 1975, 280–81) that the undergraduate Keynes showed no interest in painting (or the arts generally) is clearly erroneous. Keynes's activities, philosophical writings, and correspondence indicate the contrary. For discussion of some aspects of his aesthetic biography, see Harrod 1951, M. Keynes 1975, chaps. 25–27, Moggridge 1992, and Skidelsky 1992.

3. To avoid misunderstanding, I should add that I am contending *neither* that there is only one true interpretation of Keynes on any topic *nor* that all interpretations are of equal value. Briefly put, my view is that the set of interpretations at any given time typically contains a small number of well-grounded, adequate interpretations and a larger number of much weaker interpretations. Our task, by discussion and criticism, is to detect the latter and improve the former.

As a whole, Keynes's writings on aesthetics demonstrate many similarities with, and a few differences from, the traditional conception. Similarities lie in the concern with the beauty of both natural and human creations, the dissection of aesthetic argument, the mental states of recipients, the objects inspiring aesthetic enjoyment, and the nature of taste and evaluation. The connection between aesthetics and ethics is taken to be intimate (as it is in Moore). A notable difference is Keynes's claim that the subject matter of aesthetics is coextensive, not with beauty, but with the wider category of 'fitness.' This new concept, explained below, is central to his theory. While his discussion of the definability of aesthetics and beauty is frustratingly sparse, two general characteristics of his position are that the study of beauty is a department of aesthetics, while aesthetics itself is a department of ethics. Finally, as in many accounts, the visual arts (especially painting) occupy a prominent position in his theorizing.

Keynes and Moore

Keynes's views on aesthetics, like much else in his philosophical writings, were stimulated by G. E. Moore's *Principia Ethica* of October 1903, a work that developed very close links between ethics and aesthetics. These emerged at a theoretical level for three main reasons: because Moore thought beauty definable in terms of goodness; because one of the two greatest goods known to humans was the appreciation of beauty, which is obviously related to aesthetics; and because the other greatest good, personal affection, also has an inseparable (but not so obvious) connection to beauty as a result of Moore's view that love was related to the admiration of beautiful qualities. At a practical or policy level, the links emerged because increases in intrinsic goodness were taken to constitute the rational end of human action and the sole criterion of social progress (Moore 1903, 188–89).

In aesthetics, the relationship of Keynes's thought to Moore's is similar to that obtaining in many other areas. It may be summarized by saying that Keynes was *a critical Moorean*, by which I mean that Keynes was critical of *some of the theories* that Moore developed and sought to improve on them by further analysis and construction, but that he remained within Moore's *general philosophical framework* and did not abandon it for any competing framework. The essential distinction, overlooked by some critics of the position I have advanced, is that between a general framework and theorizing within this framework. Keynes's philosophy of aesthetics serves as a good case study of this *dual* relation to Moore's thought—the criticism and alteration of particular theories, attended by acceptance of the general framework.[4]

Keynes's Writings on Aesthetics

Of Keynes's philosophical writings on aesthetics, six papers written during the period 1904 to 1909 are primary. Other papers, especially those dealing with ethics, also contain relevant remarks but will not be separately discussed here. In general terms, the development of his thought through the six papers may be characterized as an ascent to a theoretical peak in the first three essays, followed by elaborations and extensions in the remaining three (see figure 1, which also provides dates and brief remarks).

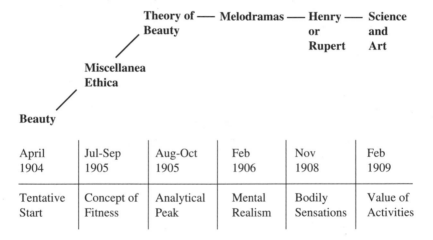

April 1904	Jul-Sep 1905	Aug-Oct 1905	Feb 1906	Nov 1908	Feb 1909
Tentative Start	Concept of Fitness	Analytical Peak	Mental Realism	Bodily Sensations	Value of Activities

Figure 1   Keynes's Main Essays Relating to Aesthetics

In April 1904, not long after the publication of Moore's book, a tentative start was made with "Beauty." "Miscellanea Ethica" then introduced the crucial category of 'fitness.' The analytical highpoint was attained shortly afterward in "A Theory of Beauty," from the somewhat wandering and repetitive discussion of which can be extracted a systematic account of the foundations of his theory. The remaining three essays may be con-

---

4. This viewpoint will be exemplified at various points in the following discussion.

sidered as corollaries or elaborations of this structure. "Shall We Write Melodramas?" emphasized that dramatic realism should be directed toward mental events; the "Prince Henry or Prince Rupert?" dialogue linked the feelings of mental states to bodily sensations; and "Science and Art" gave highest intrinsic goodness to the vocation of the artist.

Before analyzing the six papers in detail, however, it is worth making certain general points. First, aesthetics was not of minor interest to Keynes in the pre-1914 period but was *one of the foremost preoccupations of his early philosophizing.* After reading Moore in October 1903, his second Apostles paper was on probability and conduct, but the third was on beauty, a subject that attracted him theoretically for several years and practically for the rest of his life.[5] Second, Keynes's writings do not amount to a complete outline of the subject; rather, they constitute a fairly systematic set of concepts, suggestions, and proposals, the aim of which was to lay the foundations for a development and improvement of the treatment of aesthetics in his starting point, *Principia Ethica.* Finally, his philosophical papers are not finished pieces of writing intended for public consumption. Most are Apostles papers, the purpose of which was to initiate discussion, as well as to present one's own thoughts. Issues could be left unresolved, terms could be defined incompletely or not at all, and what one wrote might sometimes depend on past discussions between Apostles which are now lost.

Theory

"Beauty," April 1904

This Apostles paper was Keynes's first foray into aesthetics. It is essentially an inquiry into the meaning of beauty and, in keeping with its exploratory nature, consists more of ideas requiring further discussion than a well-articulated argument. As he noted in its first paragraph, "I have vague opinions, indefinite doubts, unfertilised theories on many things that I wish to hear talk of but on which I am incapable of writing an intelligent or coherent paper." Despite this, his primary proposition emerges clearly enough: Moore's definition of beauty is inadequate because beauty (in one central sense at least) is something narrower and more specific than the class embraced by Moore's definition.

---

5. Keynes's first Apostles paper (June 1903) was on obscenity in literature, a subject not unrelated to aesthetics.

Principia Ethica proposed to define beauty as that of which the admiring contemplation is good. Thus, if contemplation of an object is accompanied by admiration, and if this admiring contemplation is also intrinsically good, then the object is beautiful. Keynes's criticism was that there are things of which the admiring contemplation is good but which are not beautiful, not at least in the sense of the word he had in mind. Virtue, for example, was apparently something of which the admiring contemplation was good, but which was not beautiful. Intrinsically good mental admiration was thus not a sufficient criterion for beauty, at least in his sense. But Keynes did not spell out clearly what this sense was, and therein lies the key to much of the imprecision of the essay. The only clue provided is that the beauty of pictures depends on "their colour or their form and outline," but this remark is not developed.

The essay's main question comes down to whether beauty is to be conceived narrowly or broadly. He characteristically offers some ideas, but they seemingly adhere not to one line of thought but to two distinct (although related) lines. Underpinning the main arguments, and apparently representing Keynes's preferred strategy in the essay, is a narrow conception of beauty, but he sometimes moves over to a second line of thought based on a broad conception of beauty. The two mixed lines of argument may be separated as follows:

1. *The beautiful is a subclass of the aesthetic.* This essentially contends that Moore's definition is faulty because it encompasses too much. Many things that are called beautiful in everyday language are not beautiful in the proper, narrow sense, though they are certainly aesthetic. There are thus two categories of the aesthetic— the (truly) beautiful and the nonbeautiful. (A refinement is that certain objects might possess true beauty to varying degrees.)
2. *Beauty possesses different senses.* This contends that Moore's definition is inadequate because the class it admits is too undifferentiated. The existence of different kinds or senses of beauty needs to be recognized within a broad conception because a "picture is not beautiful . . . in the same way as a person or a daffodil."[6]

The two strategies are related in that the narrow conception of beauty in (1) could correspond to one of the senses of beauty in (2).

Matters are not helped by the absence of any definition of aesthetic.

---

6. Moore (1903, 190, 200) did, in fact, recognize the existence of different kinds and forms of beauty, though he declined to engage in their analysis.

"I am not clear as to how I should define 'aesthetic,'" he says, although some ideas are offered as to which things are beautiful in the narrow sense. Natural objects possess this kind of beauty, as do "the real artistic achievements of the world"—some paintings are thus truly beautiful, but most are not.

A second important issue is whether beauty is an attribute of the object itself or our perception of the object. Keynes's answer in this essay is twofold. For beautiful objects of nature, and for a small class of paintings, the quality of beauty *is* possessed by the object itself. Such objects are intrinsically valuable, or good as ends, and correspond to the subset of true beauty within the aesthetic. But for most paintings, beauty lies not in the object but in our *perceptions*. The beauty associated with them belongs to what they suggest to us—the images or mental objects generated in our minds. These paintings are only good as means, and their excellence depends on their powers of suggestion.

> I feel inclined to . . . deny that most pictures have any beauty at all; *we* read beauty into it, we *see* beauty, but we do not see the picture as it really is; it is good as a means, as an instrument for evoking beautiful images in our minds, but it does *not* possess beauty in itself as a daffodil does.

These paintings belong to the nonbeautiful aesthetic. Thus, while the beauty of a beautiful landscape is possessed by the landscape itself, the beauty of a picture of the same landscape lies in our perception of the picture. Things of true beauty have intrinsic value and ought to exist for their own sakes, but nonbeautiful aesthetic things are good only as means for evoking beautiful mental images. A related point is that since images of a picture can vary depending on the standpoint of the observer, the beauty of the image received becomes a function of the 'aspect' from which the picture is viewed.[7]

7. A third issue in the essay concerns the relation between beauty and intrinsic value, especially in the context of originals and imitations. Moore is reported as holding that even if equal beauty be granted, an original possesses higher intrinsic value than its imitation. His reasoning is not given, but it is implied, by a reference to Plato's criticism of tragedy, that the difference lies in the notion of *truth*, imitations being by nature less truthful and therefore less valuable than originals. Using his new ideas, Keynes advanced a different explanation in the context of works of nature. Beautiful natural objects (originals) typically have greater intrinsic value than paintings of these objects (imitations) because beauty is an actual attribute of such objects but not of their representations. (The point is related to the good as end/good as means distinction.)

In his subsequent writings, Keynes developed and clarified his initial probings and pressed them into a more consistent whole. Some ideas were retained, while others were modified or abandoned. In particular, he related the 'aesthetic' to the new notion of 'fitness,' retained the beautiful as an important subset of this wider class, dropped the idea of beauty as an attribute of physical objects, and expanded the idea of different types of beauty to embrace fitness as well.

"Miscellanea Ethica," July–September 1905

As its title suggests, this paper ranges over a number of topics of which aesthetics is one of the more important. It was here, for the first time and at some length, that the novel concept of 'fitness' was introduced.

According to Keynes, most ethical philosophers applied the predicate 'good' both to the object generating a valuable mental state and to the mental state itself. Moore himself was said to make the conflation "though in a less degree." Keynes separated the two constituents, however, applying the term 'fit' to the object generating the mental state or feeling and the term 'good' to the mental state itself. Good thus refers only to states of consciousness, while fit refers to the objects (physical or mental) that inspire them. It is quite possible that Keynes borrowed *the word* 'fit' from Burke's essay on "The Sublime and the Beautiful" while giving it a significantly different meaning.[8]

Keynes defines a fit object as one toward which it is *possible* to have good feelings. In general, objects arouse various feelings, but fitness attaches only to those capable of evoking feelings that are intrinsically good. Fitness is here defined in terms of possibility, not actuality—a fit object need not automatically generate good feelings. However, when a fit object does engender good feelings, the feeling is also called 'appropriate.' Unfit objects also exist, and are those toward which the appropriate feelings are bad.

In his somewhat dispersed discussion, Keynes outlines various of the properties of fitness, some of which are given little or no commentary while others receive more explanation:

1. Like goodness, the notion of fitness is "unique and elementary."

8. See Burke [1757] 1899, 168, 178, 181–87. Burke defined 'fitness' as usefulness or well-adaptedness in serving some end and denied that beauty was in any way dependent on fitness. Keynes read Burke's essay during 1904.

2. The relation between goodness and fitness is asymmetrical. All good feelings are associated with fit objects, but every fit object does not necessarily generate good feelings.

3. There are "different types or classes of fit objects," corresponding roughly to the vulgar use of the words "beautiful," "interesting," "important," "exciting," "amusing," "lovable," and "pitiful."

4. Fitness admits of degrees. An object's fitness is in proportion to the *maximum* goodness it can evoke, not the goodness actually evoked on any occasion. (Thus provided quantities of goodness can be compared, objects could be ranked in order of fitness.)

5. Similarly, appropriateness also admits of degrees. Individuals may have feelings about fit objects which are more or less appropriate, but "*the* appropriate feeling is the most good feeling that any given object can evoke." (It thus corresponds to the maximum goodness used to measure the fitness of objects; the same would apparently apply to unfit objects in reverse.)

6. Good feelings can themselves be fit objects, but their fitness is not in proportion to their goodness (presumably because there is no reason why the goodness of feelings inspired by contemplating good feelings should be commensurate with the goodness of the latter).

7. The quality of fitness is "perfectly objective." Keynes does not explain why, but this would follow from fitness being defined in terms of goodness which is an objective quality in Moorean ethics.

Keynes appears to doubt the objectivity of fitness in a later section of his paper, but careful examination reveals that this is not the case. "I have spoken so far," he says, "as if the quality of fitness were entirely objective and inherent in objects independently of the relation of the objects to us. But I am not clear that this is an assumption which will bear investigation." His questioning, however, is directed *not* toward the objectivity of the concept but toward the *second* part of the assumption: whether fitness is an inherent property of external objects. This is shown by the ensuing discussion, as well as by his very next sentence: "It turns, no doubt, on the question as to whether the sensations set up in us by external objects can, in any sense, be said to be *like* these objects." The result of his inquiry is the following refinement to his analysis, the practical impact of which is not as great as its theoretical importance.

Aesthetic feelings, for Keynes, are not directly evoked by the objects themselves but by the content of our perceptions. If fitness is to refer to that which evokes valuable feelings, then it should refer only to the perceptions and not to the external objects. His previous analysis therefore needs modification. To continue calling the objects themselves fit would require the adoption of some theory of correspondence between mental perceptions and the external world, and this he is reluctant to pursue because it would hobble ethics to possibly inadequate solutions to difficult metaphysical questions.

> Strictly the term fitness ought always to be applied to the mental objects which call up aesthetic feelings, and not to the external objects to which these mental objects correspond. I do not see my way to asserting that to each external object there is only one mental object that really corresponds. . . .
>
> For ethical purposes I do not think it matters. I cannot see that the goodness of our aesthetic feelings depends in the least in any unique correspondence between the mental objects which we alone directly know and the external objects, if any, by which these former are set up. . . .
>
> I would add that I am not endeavouring to answer the question of our relation to the external world, or of our right to attribute qualities and characteristics to external objects. I leave this to the metaphysician. The purport of my argument is to show that the answer is not necessary or relevant to Ethics, nor an essential preliminary to a true theory of aesthetic.

In practice, however, given uniformity in the human constitution, it is permissible to continue to refer to external objects as fit, as a convenient ellipsis: "There is however sufficient uniformity—there may be complete uniformity—in the sense organs of different persons to make it extremely convenient to speak of fitness as belonging to external objects; and it is a practice I propose to continue."

These considerations raise another important question: Is beauty relative or absolute? The fact that feelings are evoked by perceptions, and that perceptions can vary between standpoints and between individuals, might suggest that Keynes is adopting a relativist or subjectivist stance toward aesthetics and ethics. Several of his remarks *seem* to point that way:

Nor can we select one perception and call it and it only the right perception; the beauty of a perceived object is a function not only of the intrinsic characteristics of the object itself, but also of our organs of perception and of our relative spatial position. . . .

If a man sees beauty and feels towards it, the quality of his mental state at the moment is independent of whether others see it also. . . .

The beauty of some pictures depends a good deal upon the particular method in which we fix them. . . .

But again the surrounding discussion indicates that this view is mistaken. The proposition that perceptions are relative does *not* imply that beauty is relative. As Keynes twice emphasized, it "does not in the least affect the question of an absolute standard of beauty." Once a perception has been created, the degree of its beauty is a quite separate matter from its provenance. It is the perceptions themselves that are or are not beautiful, independently of how they have arisen or their relations to the external world. We are dealing with "the beauty of human perceptions, and not with the unknown beauty of their unknown primary causes." After noting the dependence of perceptions on our sense organs, he straight away cut off any movement toward the relativity of beauty:

Nor does this conclusion in the least shake our belief in the absolute standard of beauty. Such perceptions really would be beautiful, just as our perceptions of light may really have that quality. But it is an incorrect deduction to suppose that the external causes of those perceptions also have the quality. They may or may not, for all we know, be like the perceptions that they cause, and independently of this they may or may not possess beauty.

In this way Keynes reconciled the relativity of perceptions with the absoluteness of beauty.

The new notion of fitness was also given a significant role in Keynes's general conception of ethics. The backdrop to "Miscellanea Ethica" was a scheme for "a complete ethical treatise" divided into two main parts, Speculative and Practical Ethics. In both parts fitness was central. One of the tasks of Speculative (or theoretical) Ethics was to develop a "catalogue" of fit objects and good feelings, the "Ethics of Ends" having "the twofold function of analysing and enumerating the different kinds . . . of good feelings and fit objects." (Another task was to discuss the "nature of beauty and tragedy and love.") As regards conduct, Practical Ethics was to concern itself, inter alia, with "the means of producing (a) good feelings (b) fit objects." Keynes also held that the "clear distinction between fitness and goodness had a considerable bearing upon the doctrine of Organic Unities." While denying that this principle (according to which the value of a whole is not the summation of the values of its parts) applied to the goodness of the Universe, he accepted its applicability in relation to its fitness. Since goodness applied only to mental states and not objects, the goodness of the Universe consisted only of the goodness of all the mental states within it—"as an aggregate of conscious being its goodness must be precisely equal to the sum of the goodness of the persons composing it." "But the fitness of the Universe," he declared (using the term loosely as applying to objects), "is an altogether different matter; there I admit the principle of organic unities obtains," although the question had little practical relevance at the level of the Universe as a whole because it was as abstract an issue as "the length of a Chimaera's tail."[9]

Finally, it is worth recalling that Moore's two greatest intrinsic goods (personal affection and aesthetic appreciation) both have a connection with beauty and fitness. The generally neglected link with personal affection is that love and friendship depend to some degree on the admiration of beauty—physical or mental. Both "our love's appearance" and "our love's mind" are capable of evoking good mental states, so each is a fit object. The question of love and the physical and mental characteristics of lovers were much on Keynes's mind in the summer 1905.[10]

John Davis (1991, 64–68) has commented on "Miscellanea Ethica" in some detail, but from the perspective of ethics and epistemology rather than aesthetics. On his account, the paper advances a form of "ethical subjectivism," a "two-fold view of intuition," and the idea that objects "fit" the feelings associated with them. On my reading, Keynes's paper presents goodness and fitness within an objectivist framework, it employs a single view of intuition, and it relates fitness to the evocation of good feelings and not to an unspecified "fit" between objects and feelings.

9. Keynes also accepted in other papers the principle of organic unity at the level of the goodness of individual minds.

10. This is evident from his contemporary correspondence with close friends, as well as a recently discovered manuscript "Miscellaneous papers on love," to be published in Keynes 1996.

Unfortunately, shortage of space precludes closer examination of these differences of interpretation.[11]

"A Theory of Beauty," August–October 1905

This is Keynes's most substantial essay on aesthetics. Written in 1905 and read with omissions in May 1912, it consists of a fusion of new material with more or less unaltered borrowings from "Miscellanea Ethica." His object in the paper is to raise "a bare scaffolding" for a theory of beauty that could later be developed into a more complete system, characteristically aiming at the same time at a general theory applicable to all types of beauty. The underlying structure of the paper is fourfold: it opens with remarks on the present state of aesthetics, then sets out its theoretical or "metaphysical" foundations in two separate parts, and concludes with a preliminary discussion of the types of beauty. A fifth section on "general principles of criticism" was not attempted. But although some of its properties are briefly discussed, beauty itself is again nowhere defined. His somewhat indecisive conclusion is that "the notion 'beautiful' is almost incapable of precise definition."[12]

Keynes is dissatisfied with the theory of art criticism because its principles are vague and inconsistently stated, and because our power of appreciating beautiful objects seems to be greatly superior to our power of saying anything valuable about them. The situation requires a remedy: "surely," he exclaims, "it should be possible usefully to discuss the nature and kinds of beauty, escaping on the one hand the enervating influence of vagueness, and on the other . . . insidious dogmatism." Success here depends on collaboration between philosophy and art. When "the philosopher and artist lose their mutual feeling of suspicion, and the genius of the one check[s] and direct[s] the genius of the other, then the parts and kinds of beauty will be known at last and knowledge and creation may advance together." The gifts of philosophy are analysis, precise and verbal notions, and knowledge centered on parts, whereas those of art are intuitive power, indivisible perceptions of beauty and feelings, and an understanding of what can only be grasped as organic wholes. The two

11. As a digression, it should be noted that Keynes's concept of fitness is totally distinct from the notion, pressed forward during conference discussion, in the context of Nazi propaganda, of political acceptability or ideological propriety.

12. One should not perhaps reproach him for failing to resolve a problem that has long baffled older philosophers.

disciplines actually have a common foundation in *clarity of perception*, for the aim of both is to see "precisely what is there" bereft of all preconception and false association. Although the artist may find translating perceptions into words difficult so that recourse to allusion, allegory, imagery, and suggestion is inevitable, the perception must nevertheless be clear: "he may stammer in his speech, but his vision must never be blurred." But there is also this difference that the artist deals in concrete particulars, the philosopher in abstract forms. The artist must exercise judgment and taste in creation, while the philosopher must examine the nature, foundations, and taxonomy of artistic judgments. But instead of collaborative advance, the subject has been impeded by dogmatism and counterdogmatism.

Three major errors in aesthetics are criticized. The first is "the primitive error of a canon of beauty," pursued, for example, by Dürer, who thought the criterion lay in numerical relations, or by Burke, who proposed a qualitative definition of beauty based on the possession of seven properties (exemplified for Keynes in a "good complexion"). The second error is a version of Moore's naturalistic fallacy, the reduction of beauty to some other thing such as the good (Plato), the useful (Socrates), the pleasurable (Shaftesbury), and the useful for evolution (Spencer). The third mistake is the theory that "beauty is one and indivisible," or that different types or kinds of beauty do not exist, related to which is the error of allowing a "particular kind and type of beauty . . . to usurp the place of the whole of beauty." Keynes's theory avoids these errors—it rejects all canons of beauty, it avoids the naturalistic fallacy, and it accepts a subdivision of beauty into different types.[13]

The "primary metaphysical foundations of the subject" are next laid out, much of which overlaps with "Miscellanea Ethica." However, for the sake of completeness in clarifying Keynes's conception of the foundations and of indicating general continuity with his previous essay, it is helpful to combine the repetitions with the new additions. The points are listed below, roughly in Keynes's order, which is not the most systematic:

1. The (intrinsic) value of beauty lies solely in the feelings generated in conscious beings, and not in the mere existence of beautiful objects. While the mountains of the moon may augment the beauty of the Universe, they do not add to its value so long as they are

13. The same three characteristics are to be found in *Principia Ethica* (Moore 1903, 200–2).

unperceived. Thus "it is not beauty but only the feelings which beauty can create that are good," this following from allowing only mental states to be good in themselves.

2. Aesthetic feelings are evoked by perceptions in the mind, not by objects. This avoids becoming bogged down in the perception-object relation.

3. The perception-dependence of beauty does *not* imply the relativity of beauty. If our eyes, for example, were constructed as a different kind of lens sensitive to different rays, then we would declare a different group of objects to be beautiful. But this only entails relativity if beauty resides in the objects. Locating beauty in perceptions and bypassing the question of the perception-object relation leaves intact "our belief in the absolute standard of beauty."

4. However, general uniformity in human sense organs makes it convenient to omit reference to perceptions and to speak elliptically of beauty as a property of the perceived object. (Such ellipsis would presumably not be necessary if there were a true correspondence between external and mental objects.)

5. Within limits, by adjusting our sense organs and position, we have a certain voluntary control over the perception produced in us. We can see different "aspects" of a painting depending on how we fix it, and from where we view it.

6. Most aesthetic judgments are not based on all the mental facts supplied by the senses, but on a "certain selection" of these, made either consciously or instinctively. Persons with the finest taste and greatest artistic power see "the most beautiful grouping" of these facts.

7. Discrepancies in taste have the following main sources: the image perceived may sometimes vary between individuals; there may be differences of adjustment of organs and position; the term 'beautiful' may be used in different senses; variations may occur in selections from the sense data; and some individuals may suffer pure faultiness of taste (though this last is less common than thought).

8. The theory includes not only physical and natural beauty but also mental beauty. The latter embraces the minds of other people and "the contemplation of abstract images and ideas."

9. In relation to mental beauty, the foregoing arguments require an interesting modification. In cases where the mental objects are

immediately presented by the senses, such as "our friends' appearance," it is (as above) the perception alone that is relevant and not anything related to "objective appearance." But in other cases, such as "our friend's mind," where mental objects are arrived at *indirectly* by mental processes operating on sense data, this proposition no longer holds. We *can* have "true or false views" concerning the object considered. It is possible to be mistaken about the beauty of a person's mind (and presumably of an idea or argument) because our views are inferences from sense data and because inferences are propositions capable of being right or wrong. (Keynes also notes that mental beauty is closely related to issues of human relationships, love, and truth in relationships, but these are subsidiary questions in the present context.)

10. The principle of organic unities holds completely with respect to fitness and beauty—"the beauty of any whole is entirely different from the sum of the beauties of its parts. Any judgment as to the beauty of an entity must be derived from a contemplation of it as a whole and not deduced from judgments concerning its various parts." But as regards "Ethics proper," the principle only applies to the goodness of individual minds and not to the goodness of the Universe which is "precisely equal to the sum of the goodness of the conscious beings in it."

This completes my summary of the "primary . . . foundations" within which Keynes takes the two fundamental propositions to be (1) and (2) above. I now continue with "the second part" of his outline of these foundations, this part being more closely related to ethics.

11. The predicate 'good' (in the sense of intrinsic goodness) applies solely to the mental states of conscious beings and not to objects alone or to wholes combining objects and mental states.

12. Mental states have three constituents—sensations, emotions, and ideas—where the last captures everything not belonging to the first two.

13. For a mental state to be good, "a certain specific relation must exist between the sensation, the idea and the emotion." Less precisely, "the goodness of our states of mind depends upon a certain connection between what we perceive, what we think about the object of our perceptions, and what we feel towards it." Unfortunately, Keynes does not indicate what this specific relation is, beyond

suggesting that it is to do with "a kind of harmony" concerning our surroundings and our senses, thoughts, and emotions.[14]

14. From the dependence of goodness on this (unexplained) harmony, it follows that the idea and emotion appropriate to a given sensation are "partly dependent on the nature and past history of the individual who feels." What a person *can* think and feel will thus be influenced by their circumstances. But putting circumstances aside and assuming "the approximate uniformity of human organs," we can often say what a person *ought* to think and feel.[15]

15. Fitness is distinct from goodness, although defined in terms of it. Strictly speaking, fitness applies only to perceptions, but in looser usage it may be used of the objects inspiring these perceptions. A related but recast definition of fitness is then introduced. A fit perception is one which *ought* to lead to good states of mind, while a fit object is one whose contemplation *ought* to give rise to good mental states. (Combining this definition with that given in "Miscellanea Ethica," we obtain the idea that fitness *can and ought* to evoke good mental states. The recasting now implies something about rationality: faced with fit objects, rational agents ought to experience good mental states.)

16. The class of the fit comprises a great variety of objects and experiences, for anything whatever is fit so long as it is capable of evoking good mental states. Within the fit, the beautiful forms "a large and important" subset. Loosely speaking, the idea of "fit" might be thought of as "a generalised idea" of beauty, but to avoid misunderstanding Keynes preferred not to use "beauty" for the new total class but to employ the different word "fit" in a "not unnatural sense."

17. States of mind themselves may become objects of contemplation and hence may possess fitness as well as goodness. But their fitness need not be in proportion to their goodness. The goodness

14. Keynes's only explanatory sentence is obscure and difficult to relate to the rest of his theory: "Goodness consists in a kind of harmony between our surroundings, as they are presented to us by our senses, our thoughts, and our emotions." Its further discussion would, however, again exceed the permitted length.

15. I don't think Keynes's discussion of this point implies a twofold view of intuition as Davis 1991 suggests. The distinction between "can think" and "ought to think" is similar to that between actual thought and rational thought as deployed in Keynes's fellowship dissertations and the *Treatise on Probability* (Keynes [1921] 1973, 5, 10) and these rely on a single concept of intuition. See also point 15 in the text.

produced by contemplating a state of mind as a fit object is to be distinguished from the intrinsic goodness of the state of mind. All good states of mind have some beauty, but it does not follow that the ethically better state of mind is the more beautiful.[16] In fact, the relation between the beauty (or fitness) of a mind and its intrinsic goodness (or moral excellence) appears to reverse with age.[17] While the minds of the young are highly beautiful and lovable but of lower moral excellence, those of older persons gradually become less beautiful and lovable but acquire greater intrinsic value.

18. In relation to our affections, what we ought to love is the most fit (or most beautiful), for by definition fitness is related to evocable goodness, and the most fit will be that capable of giving rise to the greatest goodness. Thus the most worthy objects of our affection will include the most beautiful physical objects and the most beautiful minds.

19. As outlined in "Miscellanea Ethica," fitness has various properties—it is a unique and elementary notion, it admits of degrees, and its relation to goodness is asymmetrical.

This completes the second part of the foundations in which the key proposition is "the essential distinction between ethical goodness and aesthetic fitness." Keynes acknowledges that "his scheme altogether lacks the precision which a metaphysician would desire," but he trusts that it is consistent with "the testimony of actual intuition and experience."[18]

The final part of the essay seeks to clad parts of the scaffolding with a preliminary account of types of beauty and fitness. Because the total class of the fit embraces an almost endless range of disparate entities, it is evident that further subdivisions are required. The first major division is between physical fitness, which refers to the beauty of art and nature, and mental (or abstract) fitness, which refers to the beauty of minds and ideas. The distinction is the same as that made previously between objects which are directly presented by the senses and those "deduced" or inferred from sense data. "It is with the first perhaps that aesthetics

16. Or, as Keynes wrote shortly beforehand in June 1905 in his manuscript on love (see note 10): "the most beautiful is not always the most good."

17. While Keynes uses moral excellence and intrinsic goodness interchangeably, this seems to me to be a confusing usage needing either clarification or emendation.

18. If one replaces "metaphysician" with "economist," one can imagine him later saying practically the same thing in relation to *The General Theory*.

may be held to deal most properly," Keynes declared, but noted that this was hard to maintain in particular discussions.

Beyond this, however, further significant lines are difficult to draw and can only be suggested. As he remarked early in the essay, beauty is analogous to color for it constitutes a large class within which there is continuous gradation and hazy boundaries: "We may pass from purple to gold, but we do not know at what point we leave the kingdom of the first." Classification into types of beauty remains possible, but controversy over borders is fruitless. In his final paragraphs, Keynes confines himself to four of these types—"pure beauty, the beauty of interest, the beauty of consecutive arrangement and tragic beauty"—at the same time admitting that the description of "what is intended by these names is very baffling."

1. *Pure beauty* has "an eternal mobility and a calm of repose" (even if the subject be tempest and stress), it stands "serene and independent," it has "a certain aloofness," and it is essentially free from "cleverness." There are few objects possessing pure beauty only. It is present in most great works of art, but predominant in a much smaller number. In art, it is present in "a Greek statue or in Keats"; in nature in "a daffodil or in a glacier."

2. The *beauty of interest* is in stark contrast because it is based on "a restlessness and activity of intellect" that pries "into crannies and round corners," has no "modesty or reserve," and refuses no "contortion" or "garbage" for its own purposes. It is a "subtle and penetrating method," arousing feelings by creating interest and fascination.

> As the human race grows older the importance of interest appears to grow; the achievements of the Classical world hinge on pure beauty, but the most original creations of to-day turn on interest. We seem to require the stimulus of its subtlety. Pure beauty we can still worship, but it is interest we need for daily food.

Though some deny its aesthetic legitimacy, Keynes holds that it is as fit as pure beauty. Satisfactory examples are not easy to find, but it is what distinguishes Degas from Botticelli or the Balzac of Rodin from the Venus of Milo.[19]

19. Keynes wrote to Lytton Strachey on 8 July 1905: "I have also read . . . a book about Rodin, with some superb illustrations; do you know the Balzac?—perfectly incredible" (Keynes Papers, King's College, PP/45/316).

3. By the *beauty of consecutive arrangement* is meant "the beauty of perfect logical arrangement," as exemplified by "the 47th proposition of the 1st book"[20] and by "the best work of the greatest philosophers." This type is often evident in music, and possibly in architecture.

4. *Tragic beauty* (in the context of drama) is distinct from other forms but on this "vexed question" Keynes is clearer as to what it is not than to what it is. It is felt by the outside observer and not by its living actors (except in rare cases such as Hecuba), but it does not lie in "the contemplation of the astounding states of mind of the chief actors." His few hints suggest that it arises from viewing the catastrophe from the vantage point of a god, from which perspective the interconnected whole possesses a kind of splendor.

Keynes's most important paper on aesthetics ends with a noteworthy plea for *plurality* in recognizing the fit and the beautiful:

[W]e must refrain from narrowing down too far the fit objects of our senses, and, while it is the delight and the duty of all lovers of beauty to dispute . . . concerning tastes, we must not impose on the almost infinite variety of fit and beautiful objects . . . tests and criteria which we may think we have established in that corner of the field which is dearest to ourselves; nor must we fail to see beauty in strange places because it has little in common with the kind of beauty we would strive to create. . . .

This plea echoes his later championing of *cultural variety* in many spheres, in particular his cry, forty years later, in 1945: "Let every part of Merry England be merry in its own way. Death to Hollywood" (Keynes 1982, 371–72).

"Shall We Write Melodramas?" February 1906

This paper marks a notable switch from painting to the theater. In essence it is a eulogy and defense of melodrama in the course of which Keynes expresses his views on the proper function of plays and the right form of dramatic realism.

20. This is a reference to Euclid's *Elements*, the 47th proposition of the first book being commonly known as Pythagoras's Theorem.

Melodramas, he declares, possess "enthralling dramatic interest," and modern theater affords "no more satisfying product" even if current examples are no longer as superb as past masterpieces. But this is not the prevailing view which, in criticizing melodramas for being excessively unrealistic, uses a canon of realism that stresses both details and essentials:

> [R]ealism in details as well as in essentials is the ideal we set before our playwrights; your play must be real life, we say, only more amusing; you must give us real people in real surroundings; we allow you to compress and to select and even to devise . . . so long as you are not too bizarre; . . . you must represent [the Comedy of Human Life] as it really happens. . . .

Against this canon Keynes protested on two grounds. To begin with, it was rarely, if ever, achieved. But more importantly, it interfered with the essential task of the playwright which was "the development and portrayal of character" and the uncovering of "the workings of the spirit." The proper form of realism is thus *a realism of mental events, feelings, and sentiments.* Realism in other aspects, as insisted upon by the critics of melodrama, is inessential.

> This is the fundamental point to bear in mind in dealing with the problem of realism in the dramatic art; our object is not the optically obvious; we seek by signs and symbols to make known the workings of the spirit. We endeavour to convey through the medium of the eyes and ears not what the eyes and ears immediately perceive, but what of the immaterial and intangible parts of men it is by their means possible to suggest. Mental events compose the essence of the play; *they* must be actual and real to the minutest flicker of feeling, the subtlest suggestions of changing sentiment.

Keynes's objection is thus not to realism in general but to an excessively literal form of realism, in place of which he would substitute a form of mental or spiritual realism.[21] One cannot have both, for the mistaken pursuit of the former sabotages the proper pursuit of the latter—"realism in unessentials seems utterly incompatible with a realistic treatment of

---

21. Interestingly, a similar view was subsequently presented by Lucas (1927, 15–16) while discussing aspects of Aristotle's definition of tragedy. (Lucas was not elected to the Apostles until 1914.)

that which really matters." Understanding feelings, motives, or minds in only one or two hours cannot be achieved by imitating everyday life. The methods required for "laying bare the soul" are those of modern melodrama which, although realistic to some degree, deliberately throws reality aside in three main respects—"violent action, endless conventions, and persons malignantly wicked beyond all known example." It thus relies on a violence of events which "the criminal annals of all countries and ages could not parallel," the employment of abundant conventional devices and tricks of the stage (such as soliloquies, asides, coincidences, slow music, blank verse, rewriting medical knowledge, and altering the legal code), and the presence of "villains" whose existence Keynes interestingly (in view of remarks in later writings) confined to the stage.

> In real life, alas, there are no villains. . . . Villains are . . . an essential accessory of the footlights, which somehow real life succeeds in doing without. We meet stupid men and selfish men and even cruel men sometimes; we meet crass unsympathetic tyrants of their little fields; but men whose souls incessantly keep alive the pallid flame of impersonal unprovoked malignity we never meet.

The paper is also noteworthy in another respect. Rather than implying intellectual elitism, Keynes here defends what he calls "the Drama of People" and argues for the retention and improvement of this "superb artistic whole," which he would endow for the enjoyment of every "errand boy" and "barmaid."

"Prince Henry or Prince Rupert?" November 1908

This paper takes the form of a dialogue between a pair of fictional princes with historical names who are almost certainly Henry Norton (the mathematician and logician) and Rupert Brooke (the poet), the two most recently elected members of the Apostles. The author is hinted to be a certain "King John." On its serious side, the paper is an investigation of the relation between bodily sensations and emotions, the latter embracing both aesthetic and nonaesthetic emotions. As with other dialogues, the author's own views are not always made perfectly explicit, but for the most part they seem to be largely carried by Rupert, with Henry providing useful critical comment.

Rupert advances the central thesis of the essay: that bodily sensations and emotions are intimately related and that the former serves as a criterion or test for the latter. Experiencing a "real emotion," he declares, involves two things: an occurrence in the mind and a sensation in the body.

> [T]he thing which goes on in the mind must be accompanied by a bodily sensation, if we are to have a real emotion. We *think* something or other and at the same time we have a diffused feeling in our body. This we call having a feeling or an emotion. If there were no feeling we should simply have had a thought or a judgment.

Bodily sensations are therefore essential to real emotions or feelings. Mental events on their own are simply thoughts or judgments. If we read poetry or look at a painting and our bodies are not affected in some way, the outcome can only be judgments or opinions, and not true emotions. In short: "The presence of sensation is the test of genuine emotion." The difficult question of causal connection is broached but is not vital to the argument. It seems that bodily sensations do not cause these effects in the mind, so that the process is not analogous to that of "a hot bath" that produces effects on the body which in turn produce effects in the mind. Rather, it appears that "the state of mind is responsible for the state of the body." That is, reading poetry or viewing pictures causes effects in the mind which then cause alterations in the body. But causation and other matters are not the critical issues. The essential point is that bodily sensation is the key to true emotion.

> The important thing is this, that these sensations are a *criterion* of the genuineness of our emotion. If my theory is accepted, we shall be able to know much more clearly than we do at present when we are really feeling. We so easily deceive ourselves about it. An unemotional state of mind towards poetry or pictures may have value, I dare say; but it has not the peculiar value which we attach to genuine feeling unless there is something not merely mental about it.

The theory is regarded as applying to all emotions both aesthetic and nonaesthetic (such as anger and grief). When we truly experience emotion of any kind, there is a necessary bodily accompaniment. But there is this important difference between aesthetic and nonaesthetic emotions that the latter are stronger, more widespread, and thus more confirmatory of the theory than the former.

> They [nonaesthetic emotions] are the best evidence of the truth of my theory; for in most people they are much commoner and much stronger than the aesthetic emotions. . . . In these cases of non-aesthetic emotion the bodily sensation is the best test of what is genuine. Who can feel grief without a certain physical sensation in the head? Do not tears move us because we regard them as a proof of real feeling? They seem to me to be directly caused by the sensation in the head characteristic of certain emotions.

In aesthetic matters, by contrast, the bodily sensations are generally of weaker force and less common. As a result, it is much easier for self-deception to occur and for bad taste to emerge. Some bad taste is the result of being mistaken about the object of one's feelings—people may call a picture beautiful when they experience an emotion, but their emotion actually concerns something other than the beauty of the picture. But most bad taste is the result of passing judgments in the absence of bodily sensations, that is, in the absence of true emotions. If aesthetic judgments were only made when bodily sensations were experienced, differences of opinion would be much reduced and expressions of bad taste more infrequent, for it is "very rare to have a real and bodily emotion which is in bad taste." As always, the occurrence of the bodily sensation is the best test of genuine emotion. In which case, Henry concluded wryly and Apostolically, "disembodied spirits will be cold creatures and we must hope for the resurrection of the body."

"Science and Art," February 1909

This essay is significant for what it reveals about Keynes's evaluation of certain professions which also happen to be of interest in the light of his biography. It opens by posing two questions: Is there a necessary opposition between science and art? And is the present hostility between art and modern science transitory or permanent? But it does not adhere closely to these subjects and becomes preoccupied with a different issue—the comparative valuation of the activities of various occupations.

Restricting himself to the three occupations of art, science, and business, and using a ranking based on the intrinsic value of their activities, Keynes placed the artist first, the scientist second, and the businessperson third, with the scientist closer to the artist than to the businessperson. The artist stands first for two reasons—because more *time* is spent in intrinsically valuable activity and because the *quality* of this activity is greater—although neither reason is particularly well explained. As regards the first, the artist typically spends relatively less time in the process of preparation ("mixing the paints") and thus more time in the process of creative activity. And as regards the second, the notion of "quality" is unclear but seems to refer to the value of the core creative activities of the profession. The process of creating works of art is thus accorded a higher value than the process of creating scientific knowledge, though the reasoning behind this is not made explicit.

The activity of the scientist has intrinsic value on some occasions— such as the excitement of discovery and the appreciation of the beauties of argument—but overall it is not large. In addition, scientists generally have to spend longer periods in preparatory work prior to the creative phase. Mostly science justifies itself by its potential usefulness which far exceeds that of art. The businessperson, by contrast, comes a distant last because his or her activity, comprised partly of "irksome toil" and partly of "bridge," contains little or no intrinsic value, presumably because it produces few intrinsically good mental states. (Bridge in this context appears to imply game-playing based on a combination of skill and chance.)

To avoid misunderstanding, it is essential to note the basis of Keynes's evaluation of these occupations. They are not ranked in terms of their usefulness in any sense or of their value as means, but in terms of the intrinsic value (or value as an end) of the *activity* of the occupation. That is, it is not a question of the value of the outcomes, but of the activities themselves considered from a Moorean ethical viewpoint as ways of spending one's time.[22] Capacity and money aside, asks Keynes, "is there any brother who would not rather be a scientist than a business man, and an artist than a scientist?" He makes his own preferences plain—he would rather be Milton, Wordsworth, or Velasquez than Newton, Leibniz, or Darwin. In real life, of course, he lacked sufficient artistic capacity and expended his energies far more as a (social) scientist than as an artist or businessperson.[23] But it was as a scientist and businessperson who

22. One way of considering this question would be to use Moore's "method of isolation" (1903, 93–94, 187).

23. The extent to which Keynes himself attempted artistic activity is not entirely clear, but it appears to have been very little. One hint that he did venture in this direction is contained in his 1909 paper "Can We Consume our Surplus?": "My poems do not really do my feelings justice. My landscapes even do not truly suggest the influences of nature to which I am most sensitive." On Keynes's considerable business activity, see volume 12 of *The Collected Writings of John*

venerated artistic creation and who would almost certainly have agreed with the message of his essay that "the scientist must admit the artist to be his master."[24]

The Continuity Question

After 1910 Keynes undertook, as far as we currently know, no further *theoretical* work on aesthetics. The question thus arises as to how much continuity there was in his aesthetic philosophy over time. His later writings, which may be considered the primary source of relevant evidence, have two characteristics: they contain few remarks that explicitly hark back to his earlier theorizing, but they are replete with comments reflecting his concern for and involvement with numerous aesthetic matters—the arts in general, different forms of artistic activity, and various manifestations of beauty. Answers to the continuity question must therefore be developed by probabilistic inference from all the available data, a process that might throw up several competing conclusions because of the largely indirect nature of the evidence.

My own conclusion is that the evidence points strongly in the direction of continuity. Briefly put, my reasons are as follows. First, there is no subsequent repudiation of the general theoretical framework established in his early writings on the subject. Second, given that Keynes's aesthetics has such close associations with Moorean ethics, it receives partial and indirect reaffirmation through his 1938 comments in "My Early Beliefs" that much of *Principia Ethica* was "still [his] religion under the surface" and that it is indeed "only states of mind that matter" (Keynes 1972, 442, 444, 449). Finally, and most importantly, his later remarks are all *consistent* with the framework of thought in his early analysis.[25] In the

---

Maynard Keynes, Skidelsky 1992, and Moggridge 1992.

24. The issues raised in this essay are closely related to the questions Keynes subsequently posed in his 1921 presidential address to the Apostles dinner; see Keynes 1996.

25. In general, see Keynes 1982, chap. 3, especially 341–49, 367–72; for a particular instance, see O'Donnell 1994 which analyzes a 1928 letter by Keynes relating to his views on tragedy. The above reasoning does not overlook Keynes's brief statement at the end of "My Early Beliefs" where he fancied that "we . . . illegitimately [expanded] the field of aesthetic appreciation" and misclassified some human experience as aesthetic experience (Keynes 1972, 450). This, however, is a criticism of the perceived scope of the theoretical framework, of a mistake concerning its applicability, rather than of the framework itself. It is possible, from an earlier remark about the quality called 'interesting' (439), that he had in mind one of the types of beauty proposed in his main essay—the beauty of interest. One needs to be generally wary of Keynes's recollections in this memoir, however, as some of them are totally unreliable (see

presence of such strong concordance and no (serious) discordance, it is reasonable to infer that Keynes did not depart from the general framework of his early aesthetic thought and that this continued to serve, directly or indirectly, as a philosophical foundation for later reflections and activities in this area. But however one views the continuity issue, it is distinct from understanding his aesthetic theorizing and from determining whatever significance this theorizing has as a contribution to aesthetic philosophy.

Practice

In principle and in outline, the practical implications of Keynes's ethics and aesthetics are reasonably straightforward. The ultimate goal of human action being greater intrinsic value, we should engage in the pursuit of goodness and its preconditions and the eradication of evil and its preconditions, where what is under consideration is the *comparative value of wholes*. Thus, since fitness is a precondition of goodness, there is a strong presumption in favor of augmenting the number of fit objects and diminishing the number of unfit objects in all realms. Painting, theater, architecture, literature, music, and other artistic activities should be encouraged; the beautiful parts of nature are to be protected and not degraded; and the finer rather than the baser mental qualities of persons ought to be promoted. As he noted in "Miscellenea Ethica" of 1905, one of the preoccupations of practical ethics was with the means of providing fit objects and good feelings.[26] As might be expected, there is much in Keynes's writings, including those of later periods, which exemplifies these ideas. Shortage of space, however, prevents their exploration.[27]

Conclusion

The main aim of this article has been to outline the theoretical foundations of Keynes's philosophy of aesthetics and to open up a new area to discussion and evaluation. Working within a Moorean objectivist frame-

---

O'Donnell 1989, 148–53; 1991a, 92–94).

26. It deserves noting that the concern with wholes allows the possibility of certain cases in which evil in a particular form *might* be a necessary component of wholes possessing positive intrinsic value overall. This does *not*, however, imply acceptance of the "mixed goods problem" presented by Skidelsky 1991, 105–9; 1992, chap. 3; I have argued elsewhere that this problem does not exist in the thought of either Moore or Keynes (see O'Donnell 1994).

27. For a general discussion of the links between Keynes's ethics and his political philosophy and policy making, see O'Donnell 1989, chaps. 8, 13, 14; 1991b.

work, Keynes sought to extend his modified version of Moore's ethics to the cognate realm of aesthetics, a realm touched on but not investigated by *Principia Ethica*. His main contribution was the invention and articulation of the concept of 'fitness,' this property of things denoting their capacity to evoke good mental states. The article has also indicated at various points that Keynes's views on aesthetics are an important constituent of his philosophy of practical reason. They are therefore related to his theory of ethically rational conduct, his political philosophy, and, broadly conceived, his economic policy making.

I would like to thank Mike Lawlor and Allin Cottrell for organizing the conference; the conference participants for their helpful discussion; King's College, Cambridge, for permission to quote from the Keynes Papers; and the Australian Research Council for funding assistance. This article is a shortened version of the conference paper.

References

Buchanan, J. M. 1987. Keynesian Follies. In *The Legacy of Keynes*. Edited by D. A. Reese. Nobel Conference 22. San Francisco: Harper & Row.

Burke, E. [1757] 1899. A Philosophical Inquiry into the Origin of Our Ideas of the Sublime and the Beautiful. In vol. 1 of *The Works of the Right Honourable Edmund Burke*. London: John C. Nimmo.

Davis, J. 1991. Keynes's Critiques of Moore: Philosophical Foundations of Keynes's Economics. *Cambridge Journal of Economics* 15:61–77.

Harrod, R. F. 1951. *The Life of John Maynard Keynes*. London: Macmillan.

Keynes, John Maynard. 1972. *Essays in Biography*. Vol. 10 of *The Collected Writings of John Maynard Keynes*. Edited by D. E. Moggridge. London: Macmillan.

———. [1921] 1973. *A Treatise on Probability*. Vol. 8 of *The Collected Writings of John Maynard Keynes*. Edited by D. E. Moggridge. London: Macmillan.

———. 1982. *Social, Political and Literary Writings*. Vol. 28 of *The Collected Writings of John Maynard Keynes*. Edited by D. E. Moggridge. London: Macmillan.

———. 1983. *Economic Articles and Correspondence, Investment and Editorial*. Vol. 12 of *The Collected Writings of John Maynard Keynes*. Edited by D. E. Moggridge. London: Macmillan.

———. 1996. *Eton Essays and Cambridge Philosophical Papers*. Vol. 1 of *The Further Collected Writings of J. M. Keynes*. Edited by R. M. O'Donnell. London: Routledge.

Keynes, M., ed. 1975. *Essays on John Maynard Keynes*. Cambridge: Cambridge University Press.

Lucas, F. L. 1927. *Tragedy, in Relation to Aristotle's Poetics*. London: Hogarth Press.

Moggridge, D. E. 1992. *Maynard Keynes, An Economist's Biography.* London: Routledge.

Moore, G. E. 1903. *Principia Ethica.* Cambridge: Cambridge University Press.

O'Donnell, R. M. 1989. *Keynes: Philosophy, Economics and Politics.* London: Macmillan.

———, ed. 1991a. *Keynes as Philosopher-Economist.* London: Macmillan.

———. 1991b. *Keynes's Political Philosophy.* Vol. 6 of *Perspectives on the History of Economic Thought.* Edited by William J. Barber. Aldershot: Edward Elgar.

———. 1994. *Keynes on Aesthetics.* Research Paper No. 380. Sydney: School of Economic and Financial Studies, Macquarie University.

Skidelsky, R. 1991. Keynes's Philosophy of Practice and Economic Policy. In O'Donnell 1991a.

Skidelsky, R. 1992. *The Economist as Saviour, 1920–1937.* Vol. 2 of *John Maynard Keynes.* London: Macmillan.

Comment

John B. Davis

O'Donnell intentionally passes over "a contextual study" of Keynes's views on aesthetics from "a history of philosophy perspective" en route to "presenting a systematic account of Keynes's theory of the subject as contained in his philosophical writings." I don't think, however, that one can in fact produce an adequate accounting of Keynes's views on aesthetics without attending to the historical philosophical context in which they developed. It's as if someone were to attempt to explain Keynes's economics without ever mentioning anything about the history and development of modern macroeconomics! One just doesn't quite get at the issues that concern an author unless one is aware of the context in which he or she operated. Thus here I give a brief account of two principal issues involved in the philosophical analysis of aesthetic experience in the early decades of the twentieth century, describe a spectrum of reactions to these issues by three of Keynes's leading contemporaries in philosophical aesthetics, and then note difficulties in explaining Keynes's thinking apart from attention to a framework such as this.

Of the two principal issues, the first concerns objectivity. Having an aesthetic experience involves more than merely *thinking* that one is having an aesthetic experience, since it is clear that people can be wrong about whether they have had aesthetic experiences. While there may be considerable ambiguity involved in saying just what it is that makes an experience a genuinely aesthetic one, nonetheless we know that, for example, the remark, "I felt a sense of injustice," wrongly reports an aesthetic experience. (Indeed, probably the most common cause of mistaken aesthetic response involves judging a work of art on religious or moral grounds.) Thus, explaining an aesthetic experience involves explaining what is objectively an aesthetic response to the world. Typically the answer involves saying that one must exercise a certain special sort of perceptiveness, or be able to notice something characteristically aesthetic in one's range of experience. This raises a second issue—the key issue, it seems, for early twentieth-century aesthetics.

When we attempt to account for an experience we believe genuinely or objectively aesthetic, we are inclined to begin by arguing that more is involved than our registering mere likes and dislikes, and say that somehow the object of experience itself exhibits, say, an inherent delicacy, warmth, dynamism, unity, and so forth. The business of noticing something characteristically aesthetic is thus fundamentally a matter of *perception*, and not just a way of thinking about things or interpreting them. We cannot divorce aesthetic experience from perception, and perception involves recognizing something actually in the world. However, we may also perceive things as delicate, warm, dynamic, unified, and so on *non*aesthetically. What is it, we must thus ask, that makes a perception of one of these qualities aesthetic? The principal problem of aesthetic experience, then, is to distinguish experience of things in an aesthetic mode of perception from experience of things in the perceptual modes that ground our nonaesthetic characterizations of the world (Aldrich 1963, 7). Putting it somewhat differently: How does one *detach* oneself from the ordinary concerns of life and ordinary modes of perception in perceiving the world in an aesthetic manner?

A number of Keynes's contemporaries attempted answers to this question. I. A. Richards (1926) said that when we detach ourselves from a scientific worldview, we bracket questions of truth and falsity. Art creates an inner, psychological harmony in the individual, and aesthetic experience is thus essentially subjective. A more mixed sort of view was developed by George Santayana (1896), who explained aesthetic experience in terms of objectification, or the mind's objectifying something subjective as features perceived present in objects in the world. Beauty is the feeling of pleasure objectified, and objectification makes this feeling appear to be a quality of the thing experienced as beautiful. For José Ortega y Gasset (1956), one gains detachment or psychic distance from ordinary interests in the world by distancing oneself from things taken as physical objects, and then regrasping them as "ultra-objects" that possess only aesthetic qualities. These qualities are abstract properties of aesthetic objects and are thus detectable only by a special aesthetic perception.

This of course is not the place to investigate whether these views begin to explain what is distinctive about the aesthetic mode of perception; rather, the purpose of this sketch is to lay out a spectrum of contemporary views—from Richards's subjectivism, to Santayana's subjective objectification, to Ortega's ultraobjectivism—against which we can compare Keynes's opinions on aesthetics and assess his grasp of the two issues set out here. Keynes's own early views are encapsulated in his "A Theory of Beauty" Apostles paper of August–October 1905 (a close companion of his "Miscellanea Ethica" paper of July–September 1905). Most distinctive about both papers is Keynes's introduction of the concept of fitness, where mental states are alone said to be good and the objects generating such states are then said to be "fit." "Fit" objects, that is, are those toward which one indeed can have good feelings, and among "fit" objects are things generally associated with aesthetic experience. Keynes comments that though "I have spoken so far as if the quality of fitness were entirely objective and inherent in objects independently of the relation of the objects to us . . . I am not clear that this is an assumption that will bear investigation." In fact, "strictly the term fitness ought always to be applied to the mental objects which call up aesthetic feelings, and not to the external objects to which these mental objects correspond," though were there "sufficient uniformity" in human sense organs, it would be "convenient to speak of fitness as belonging to external objects." Nonetheless, though fitness only properly applies to mental objects, that the perception of beauty can vary across individuals "does not in the least affect the question of an absolute standard of beauty."

Why should this be so? If we emphasize the idea that only mental states are good, and that the concept of fitness ought only be applied to them, we seem to recall Richards's subjectivism, and thus undermine Keynes's desired conclusion regarding an absolute standard of beauty. If, alternatively, we emphasize the notion that external objects are "fit," Santayana's subjective objectification is suggested, and a "sufficient uniformity" in human constitution then might justify ascribing fitness to external objects. Finally, should rather Keynes's emphasis on there being "an absolute standard of beauty" be primary, then Ortega's Platonic-like "ultra-objects" seem to be involved. Of course, Keynes's early unpublished papers were hardly polished efforts—at times bordering on being collections of notes—and consequently it would be unwise to attempt to match them too closely with full-blown theories of aesthetics. One can, however, look to Keynes's later philosophical commitments and read them back into his early papers for indications of how his views may have developed.

One key later commitment was to G. E. Moore's 1903 theory of analytic definition and indefinability thesis, where such notions as good and probable were for Keynes simple Platonic qualities incapable of definition. In the *Treatise on Probability* Keynes states, "a *definition* of probability is not possible. . . . We cannot analyse the probability-relation in terms of simpler ideas" (CW 8:8). In "A Theory of Beauty" Keynes asserts that "beautiful" is essentially indefinable, and then uses Moore's naturalistic fallacy argument to justify that conclusion. I cannot here enter into an analysis of the Platonic metaphysics this involved (but see Davis, 1994), but it should be noted that this apparatus relies on a theory of intuition as a form of unmediated, pure insight into the underlying real nature of things. Intuition thus understood would function as an *intellectual* mode of perception that grasps the simple, essential qualities of things, where as for Plato, phenomenal things would be "fit" to the extent that they conformed, in the world of appearance, to our specially defined mental states. Fitness, on such a view, thus applies to mental states, and, while perception of phenomenal objects varies across individuals, this does not affect our ability to speak of "an absolute standard of beauty."

All this would consequently seem to imply that Keynes ought to be aligned with the most objectivist of philosophers of aesthetics, to account for psychic distance or detachment in aesthetic perception in the strongest of terms. The second (and principal) problem with which we began—distinguishing aesthetic and nonaesthetic perception—would then require an analysis of the logic of intuition as a special human faculty. Yet, there is a difficulty with this interpretation of Keynes's early views. The first of the two issues noted at the outset concerned identifying objectively aesthetic experience, where the term *objective* was used in a quite different sense than is involved in speaking of Platonic intuition. There the issue was whether an experience is genuinely aesthetic, where this presupposed that one could be mistaken about whether one was having an aesthetic experience. In Keynes's early thinking, however, it is not clear how—or even that—one can be wrong in having an intuition, so that, in effect, Keynes is unable to distinguish between when people merely *think* they are having aesthetic experiences and their objectively having them. Put in terms of the example above, it is not clear how Keynes could demonstrate that the remark, "I felt a sense of injustice," wrongly reports an aesthetic experience, especially, it might be added, when his discussions of intuition in ethics and aesthetics are cast in such similar terms. His view, it thus appears, though purportedly an objectivist one, seems to lack the conceptual resources to clearly avoid being subjectivist or subjective objectificationist. That Keynes later criticized himself on the topic of intuition, first in response to Frank Ramsey's criticism of the notion in the *Treatise*, and then later (in quite sarcastic terms) in his "My Early Beliefs" memoir of his undergraduate years, suggests he also had doubts about his early positions (CW 10:338–39, 437–38).

What all this implies is that since Keynes's early views on aesthetics were arguably not quite stable, we must be cautious about claiming either that they constituted a systematic whole, or even that they remained Keynes's views after his early years. It should also be noted that the questionable metaphysics on which Keynes's early aesthetics rested, and from which he later distanced himself, also underlay his other philosophical positions in ethics and logic. Thus, difficulties in his early metaphysical substructure presumably had wide-ranging effects, which it would not be unreasonable to think Keynes later addressed. This suggests Keynes's philosophy generally is best approached from a perspective of a development in thinking—the approach, of course, long used to explain the transition from his early to later economics.

References

Aldrich, V. C. 1963. *Philosophy of Art*. Englewood Cliffs, N.J.: Prentice-Hall.

Davis, John B. 1994. *Keynes's Philosophical Development*. Cambridge: Cambridge University Press.

Keynes, John Maynard. 1905a. Miscellanea Ethica. Unpublished. King's College Library, Cambridge.

———. 1905b. A Theory of Beauty. Unpublished. King's College Library, Cambridge.

———. 1971–89. *The Collected Writings of John Maynard Keynes*. 30 vols. Edited by D. E. Moggridge. London: Macmillan. (CW)

Moore, G. E. 1903. *Principia Ethica*. Cambridge: Cambridge University Press.

Ortega y Gasset, J. 1956. *The Dehumanization of Art, and Other Writings on Art and Culture*. Translated by W. R. Trask. Garden City, N.J.: Doubleday.

Richards, I. A. 1926. *Science and Poetry*. New York: Norton.

Santayana, G. 1896. *The Sense of Beauty*. New York: Scribner's.

Keynes and Marshall: Methodology, Society, and Politics

Peter Groenewegen

The importance of Keynes's Marshall heritage is increasingly being acknowledged in the discussion and interpretation of his economics. This is not surprising. After all, Keynes was a product of, and early participator in, the Cambridge school that Marshall had created. Moreover, he had the distinction of being one of the few personal students of Marshall among the many teachers who made that school so important in the period between the two world wars. As editor of the *Economic Journal* (Moggridge 1990) Keynes initially operated when many of the problems raised in the journal were thrown up by direct, and indirect, discussions of the Marshallian research program. This had been spelled out in the oral tradition of his teaching (for a brief definition, see Groenewegen 1988, esp. p. 650) to be interpreted by his anointed successor to the Cambridge chair, by his indirect pupils (that is, the pupils taught by pupils) in the pre–World War I period, and by the later, post-1918 generation which taught economics at Cambridge until the end of the 1920s (cf. A. Robinson 1990). The major economic links between Marshall and Keynes have been long understood, despite the introduction of occasional biases (J. Robinson

This article draws on research financed by the Australian Research Council in connection with my Marshall biography, here gratefully acknowledged. I am indebted to the Faculty of Economics and Politics, University of Cambridge, for permission to quote from the Marshall Papers; the Master and Scholars of Trinity College, Cambridge, for permission to draw on the Layton Papers; for assistance from King's College archivists in giving me access to the Keynes Papers relating to Marshall and to allow me to quote from this material. Comments from participants at the Keynes Conference are gratefully acknowledged, as are those from Mark Blaug which rescued me from some embarrassing errors.

1962, 79), even though the details will continue to be elaborated (for example, Clower 1989; Leijonhufvud 1994).

It may be helpful at the outset to clarify the subject matter of this article. For a start, it does not deal with Marshall's possible influence on aspects of Keynes's economics in a technical sense. Instead, it explores aspects of the implications of a closeness in the relationship between these two major Cambridge economists based on my biography of Alfred Marshall (Groenewegen 1995). This was sparked by a reading in draft of O'Donnell's discussion of Keynes's projected works which were never written (O'Donnell 1992), providing fruit for interesting speculation.

A previous article (Groenewegen 1993) contrasted the perspective of the Marshall biographer with that of two recent Keynes biographers—Moggridge 1992 and Skidelsky 1983, 1992. This found both wanting in fathoming what I presume to have been the depth of the Keynes-Marshall relationship. The first section of this chapter gives a brief account of the essentials of its findings slanted toward matters of special relevance to the potential connection between the two on methodology—society and politics; these then form the subject for subsequent parts of the chapter. A final paragraph attempts some conclusions.

In short, my stance is that of one who has poured over the writings of Marshall but who is rather innocent of the far more voluminous Keynes papers. Insights from that comparative advantage of familiarity with the Marshall papers are useful for shedding light on aspects of Keynes's thinking, thereby modifying and perhaps even adding to the rich interpretations already available. In this way, a Marshallian intruder in a gathering of Keynes scholars may serve a useful purpose or, at worst, may learn from his audacity in trespassing on the field of study devoted to Marshall's greatest and most influential pupil.

Marshall and Keynes: The Biographical Record

When Keynes first met Alfred Marshall can only be guessed at.[1] Joan Robinson's comment that "Keynes . . . drank Marshall with his mother's milk" (1953, 6) is metaphorical (he was one and a half years old when his mother, Florence, attended Marshall's lectures in early 1885), but it points to the fact that Keynes would have met Marshall as a visitor to Harvey Road at an early age. Keynes ([1924] 1972, 213–14) himself mentioned

---

1. This section draws heavily on Groenewegen 1993.

dinner parties he attended at Balliol Croft, in particular remembering meeting Pierson (probably in 1904) and Wagner (probably in 1913) on such occasions. Individual social meetings between the two therefore commenced not long after Keynes had turned twenty-one in June 1904.

From the time Maynard Keynes graduated as twelfth wrangler in 1905 until Marshall's death in July 1924, there seem to have been three phases of especially close contact between the two men. The first covers the period of twelve months from June 1905 to mid-1906 when Marshall in the end unsuccessfully lured Keynes to attempt the second part of the Economics Tripos. This brought Keynes under Marshall's spell for virtually the whole of Michaelmas term 1905. The second period of close contact covers the period after Marshall's retirement in June 1908 to the outbreak of war in 1914, when Keynes was lecturing in economics at Cambridge. This period coincides with Keynes's substantial book writing program, covered in what O'Donnell (1992, 771–78, 805–6) calls the first document of such plans. The third period covers the years of World War I, when contact seems to have been largely by Marshall-initiated correspondence and during which he proferred advice to his pupil, now ensconsed in the Treasury on aspects of the war and its finance. Much of this occurred during the early years of the war when Marshall can be said to have still been reasonably mentally alert.[2] The contact appears therefore one-sided, though this picture is perhaps exaggerated from the fact that Keynes's responses, if any, have not been preserved among Marshall's papers.

There is also a fourth period, largely of posthumous "contact," during which Keynes once again immersed himself in Marshall as "pupil" of the "master." This started in May 1924 when Keynes visited Marshall at the start of his "final illness," a visit he tenderly described in a letter to Lydia (Hill and Keynes 1989, 195) and when Keynes may also have pumped the old man for reminiscences about his early years (Keynes [1924] 1972, 172 n. 2). It can be said to have lasted for two years thereafter. These cover the period when Keynes first wrote his *Memoir* of Marshall (Keynes 1972)[3], then when he assisted Pigou in editing the *Memorials*

2. On Mary Paley's account, Marshall's mental strength and memory began to deteriorate very sharply from 1921, making him virtually incapable of constructive work. This implies that much of *Money, Credit and Commerce* was based on his former work, edited by her, rather than on original rewriting.

3. That is, from 13 July when Marshall died until early (probably 4) September, or in less than two months. I intend to write more fully on the Keynes *Memoir* as Marshall biography for a book of Marshall essays to be edited by Marco Dardi, in a chapter provisionally titled,

(Pigou 1925, v), and finally when he himself edited Marshall's *Official Papers* for the Royal Economic Society, a task completed by June 1926, the date given in its preface (Marshall 1926, v). This posthumous contact between Keynes and Marshall's work is important because it largely coincides with documents 2–4 of Keynes's writing program, as described by O'Donnell (1992, 778–93, 306–12) and with some of the *Essays in Persuasion* on social and political matters (Keynes [1931] 1951), which these writing plans may have helped to assist. Marshall's death gave Keynes privileged access to the Marshall papers, including their thoughts on economic progress and ideals for that final volume, of which only draft outlines and scraps of notes are extant. As pure speculation, it may be suggested that some of Keynes's writing projects for the early 1920s may well have been produced as a conscious, or subconscious, desire to explicitly complete some of the "master's" unfinished work that had been placed before him during the months after his death.

The first phase in the chronology of the Marshall-Keynes relationship as summarized here was quite intense, an intensity in my view that is perhaps best captured by Harrod's account (1951, 105–21). This provided a brief period of very concentrated economics training by Marshall. In an as yet rather barren Economics Tripos, it is not surprising that Marshall used this contact with Keynes to put enormous pressure on what he saw as his potentially most gifted pupil, to win him for professional economics. Keynes's solid economics reading over the summer of 1905 is reflected in the list of books he claimed to have read on enrolling for Marshall's classes in 1905 (reproduced facsimile in Groenewegen 1988, 667). He attended Marshall's 1905 Michaelmas lectures on advanced political economy, including the special difficulties class held on Saturdays, and he wrote a substantial number of essays for Marshall, which Marshall vigorously corrected, and praised, in red ink (Keynes [1924] 1972, 215–16 and n.). Layton's lecture notes[4] for these classes indicate that the lectures were ostensibly devoted to international trade and government action and that they commenced with a brief discussion of the history of the subject and introduced encouraging autobiographical fragments of how the lecturer himself had come to economics.[5] The lectures

---

"Marshall Biography after Keynes."

4. Preserved at Trinity College, Cambridge, Layton Papers, Layton 15[6].

5. The autobiographical remarks were noted by Layton as follows: "Marshall intended to work at Maths and Physics under Stokes. Got on to metaphysics which he thought was the key to human life. Up at 5 in the morning to read Kant's Critique. Got on to ethics—as solving

also discussed the following: methodological issues, including the view that flexible definitions were the most useful and that definitions in any case should be treated as a "matter of convenience"; issues in capital theory; economic progress, with special reference to Britain; aspects of coal and steel production and their importance for that progress; taxation and rent; the association between religious ideas and the durability of primitive socialist societies (probably illustrated from Marshall's 1875 experience with the Shakers in the United States); and the effect of permanent peace on the level of the rate of interest. Marshall's second-term (Lent) lectures for 1906 elaborated the quantity theory of money, the heading used by Layton in his notes. This is presumably the reason why Keynes ([1924] 1972, 190 n.1, 191 n.2, 216) later recalled having attended them, even though by then he had already dropped any plan of taking Tripos examinations, instead of recalling the 1905 Michaelmas term lectures, of which some of his brief notes are extant. Both sets of lectures stressed the association of economics with ethics—the practical nature of economics and its relevance to human improvement—a lesson, which Austin Robinson (1947, 25) suggested, Keynes never really forgot.[6] For our purpose here, the point to be made from Keynes's attendance at these lectures is on the broad moral and social context and problem solving to which Marshall introduced his pupils in advanced economics. The practice sharply contrasted with Pigou, whose lectures emphasized the analytic rather than the practical.[7]

The second period of contact between the two is of greater interest. Before retiring from the chair, Marshall had arranged the appointment of Keynes to the economics teaching staff as a lecturer. In the years immediately afterward, he assisted his young protégé in various ways. Marshall gave Keynes easy access to his personal library by offering him material on virtually permanent loan. When Keynes was appointed as official custodian of the economics books for students in the Tripos (most of them at this stage effectively donated by Marshall), Keynes was

---

practical problems got to Economics. Returned to ethics to find out what were not Ethics or Economics. Found one set: How far is a man bound to express opinion that what others hold to [as] good for them to believe but [which are] untrue" (Layton Papers, Layton 15[6], p. 25). The essentials of this brief paragraph match Keynes's longer account in the *Memoir* ([1924] 1972, 167–71).

6. Austin Robinson then recalled that beneath Keynes's "Georgian skin there peeped out from time to time an almost Victorian sense of moral purpose and obligation." Cf. Pollard 1994, 147.

7. As indicated in Layton's notes, for example, Layton 15[5] (May 1905 term lectures on taxation).

necessarily placed in some contact over their treatment with their previous owner.[8] Given Keynes's interest in writing papers on topics such as "the 'long run' in economics" with reference to "the element of doubt in the determination of value," "commercial fluctuations," "English gold reserves," "official index numbers of prices," "proposals for an international currency,"[9] "the riskless rate of interest," and "mathematical notes on the median," as well as texts on money and the "mathematical organon of economics" (O'Donnell 1992, 805–6), these forays into the Balliol Croft bookstacks would have been quite helpful. Preserved correspondence shows the nature of some of that assistance. On 20 November 1906 (therefore outside the period under consideration) Marshall wrote Keynes to persuade him to enter the Cobden Prize, inviting him to call on either 24 or 26 December to glance at a meager bibliography on the history of interest he had prepared and of which, nevertheless, he had several items to show Keynes. Whether his list included Wicksell's *Interest and Prices* can only be speculated on. In December 1910, Marshall informed Keynes that he had found his copy of Rau, with its curves of supply and demand in the fifth edition, and that he was in no hurry for its return.[10] The letter also gave Keynes some gossip about Marshall's acquaintance with Fleeming Jenkin's work in the 1870s and the demonstration of Henry Cunynghame's "very original" machine for drawing rectangular hyperbolas at an 1873 meeting of the Cambridge Philosophical Society.

The degree of closeness the Marshall-Keynes relationship could reach at this time is neatly illustrated in the well-documented Pearson controversy, an event probably closely associated with Keynes's intention to write on "the logical basis for correlation" (O'Donnell 1992, 805).[11] The episode itself is described in some detail in Skidelsky 1983, 223–

8. Marshall offered to give Keynes some of these books if he had "the space" so that they "could come to you without waiting for my demise" (Marshall to Keynes, 30 May 1909).

9. The last were two hobby-horses of Marshall, particularly the first. See his "Remedies for Fluctuations of General Prices" (1887) in Pigou 1925, 188–211, the *Official Papers* (for example, Marshall 1926, 11–12), and his correspondence with Irving Fisher (Pigou 1925, 474–78).

10. For a discussion of these curves, see Humphrey 1992 and an earlier working paper by Hennings (1979). The curves appeared in an appendix to editions of Rau from the fourth edition of 1841 onward, hence also in the fifth edition of 1845 which Marshall lent Keynes.

11. O'Donnell 1989, 186–88 indicates that Keynes's critical attitude to Pearson's statistical methods had been sparked off initially in the context of Keynes's work on probability and that, more specifically, it addressed the logical validity of the entailed "induction" in these statistical exercises.

27 and Moggridge 1992, 205–7 in a way that fails to do full justice to Marshall's role in the affair. Marshall had entered the fray by writing to the *Times* on 7 July 1910, since the matter of parental alcoholism and its effects on their offspring was an issue that greatly interested him. This was before he realized that Keynes had replied to Pearson on the subject at article length for the *Journal of the Royal Statistical Society*, as Keynes indicated in a letter to Marshall dated 11 July. This letter mentioned that Keynes himself had been unsuccessful in reaching the *Times'* readership and included for Marshall a copy of the proofs of his article attacking Pearson, intended for the July issue of the *Statistical Journal*. From then on, the two economists acted as comrades-in-arms intent on verbally thrashing the "insolent" Pearson, until the controversy concluded in early 1911. During the battle, Marshall fed Keynes recollections of his talks with Todhunter, possibly going back to 1866, about what Marshall took to be his opinion on the inapplicability of the method of least squares to *all* types of statistical data (Marshall to Keynes, 14 September 1910). He also referred Keynes to new material coming from the enemy, sending him his copy of Pearson's specific reply in pamphlet form to the two Cambridge economists,[12] asking him whether he wished to reply to a letter from Galton to the *Times* in support of Pearson, and urging Keynes to finish the controversy on his behalf since he had foolishly told the *Times* in his third letter that this would be his last word on the subject.[13] However, as late as 31 January 1911, a letter from Marshall alerted Keynes to Pearson's abusive letter in the December issue of the *Journal of the Statistical Society*, offering Keynes, if he wished to reply, his own copy of the letter with critical notes thereon. As Skidelsky 1983, 226n* briefly notes, the debate shows the close affinity between Keynes's and Marshall's medical views on the potential for heredity from alcoholic parents to their offspring, an affinity that can be widened to embrace support for the eugenics movement but not, as Skidelsky (225) wrongly

12. That is Pearson 1910, an annotated copy of which is preserved in the Marshall Library. The fact that Marshall alerted Keynes to its existence is indicated in Keynes to Marshall, 13 September 1910, in which Keynes thanked Marshall for lending him his copy of Pearson's pamphlet.

13. Marshall to Keynes, 2 November 1910; Marshall's third letter to the *Times*, published 19 August 1910, invited the public to adjudicate between him and Pearson from their published correspondence, but suggested also that in this context they should study Keynes's detailed reply in the *Statistical Journal*. It indicated that he "had finished" his public participation. Mary Paley wrote Keynes (21 September 1910) not to interrupt Marshall's holiday by involving him further in the Pearson controversy.

surmises, encouragement of a "selfish" abstention from children to enable intellectual married couples to lead the good life.[14] It also suggests a methodological kinship in skepticism about the worthiness of certain statistical techniques in the social sciences. Reading this and their other correspondence of the prewar period made me realize how strong was their rapport at this stage, making it all the easier to understand Keynes's critical perspective on Marshall in his obituary assessment and his criticism of the sentimental and maudlin approach of Pigou to the subject.[15]

Although the First World War phase of the Marshall-Keynes relationship is largely irrelevant to the purpose of this discussion, this is not true of the fourth, mainly posthumous phase, starting with Keynes's final visit to Marshall on 16 May 1924.[16] On 20 July, Keynes spent three and a half hours with Mary Paley gathering material from her for his *Memoir*. On 12 October, well after the *Memoir* had been completed, Keynes spent "two or three hours with her working through papers and things" (Hill and Keynes 1989, 227–28, 233–34). In between, Mary Paley Marshall had bombarded Keynes with letters about her husband, both before and after completion of the *Memoir* by early September.[17] The *Memoir* itself expressly thanked Mary Paley Marshall for her assistance (Keynes [1924] 1972, 161 n. 1), which included a set of detailed notes she had prepared for Keynes and from which Keynes quoted freely in the *Memoir*.[18]

14. There are favorable references to eugenics in the *Principles* (for example, Marshall 1920, 248, while pp. 201–3 comment harshly on the selfishness of some middle-class parents in not having children). Marshall wrote Keynes (18 May 1911) congratulating him on the local Eugenics Society and promising to pay him a life composition membership fee as soon as possible. The fact that the Marshalls had no children is discussed at some length in my biography (Groenewegen 1995, chap. 8) without definite conclusions as to the reasons for this.

15. Keynes's reactions to Pigou's Marshall Memorial Lecture in October 1924 is given in a letter to Lydia (Hill and Keynes 1989, 241), which indicates Keynes's strong dislike of its sentimental stress on "the feeblest side of Marshall" before saying "that it was what we ought to admire." Keynes's measured admiration for Marshall in the *Memoir* is discussed in the next paragraph.

16. Maynard Keynes was present at Marshall's funeral on 17 July, unlike his parents.

17. On 4 and 5 September 1924, Florence and John Neville Keynes congratulated their son on the *Memoir*, the latter praising son Maynard for his magnificent coordination of "appreciation and criticism" and a completeness which, in his view, made a formal "life" redundant because there was nothing "really important" on the subject left to say. However, by 30 August, Edgeworth had seen proofs and by 6 September, Edgeworth, who had probably invited Keynes to write the obituary in the first place, complimented him on the result as "a great success, . . . not a mere eulogium but a portraiture" (letters preserved in Keynes's Marshall File, King's College, Cambridge).

18. Sometimes too freely, by trying to improve the story with his own literary embellishments, as for example, in Keynes [1924] 1972, 161–62, 164–65, 169 dealing with Alfred Marshall's

The *Memoir* also obviously owed much to his parents (including especially his father's extensive diaries) and to Edgeworth (Keynes [1924] 1972, 205, 207 n.2), while the version printed in the *Memorials* (Pigou 1925, 1–65) corrected errors that had been pointed out to him by former Marshall acquaintances who had read the *Memoir* (Keynes [1924] 1972, 161). Last, but not least, Marshall's own papers were used on a number of occasions (Keynes [1924] 1972, 192 n.1, 201–3, and 231 for some of the more important references to them), but the evidence is ambiguous on what Keynes gleaned for himself from this source or what, as evidently was rather frequently the case, Mary Paley had selected for him. This makes an important aspect of the potential Marshall heritage rather difficult to ascertain.

Apart from writing the *Memoir*, this posthumous phase in the relationship involved compilation of Marshall's bibliography for publication in the December 1924 issue of the *Economic Journal*,[19] assisting Pigou in his editorial task on Marshall's literary remains for the *Memorials* and editing Marshall's *Official Papers* for publication. Work on Marshall's bibliography would have reinforced the impression Keynes so clearly gave in his *Memoir* that Marshall was a person of wide and diverse interests and that the *Principles of Economics* to which he had devoted so much of his life only presented a very incomplete picture of the range of his thought. No details have survived about the nature of Keynes's task in assisting Pigou's editorial work on the *Memorials*. His October visit to Mary Paley may have been partly undertaken to assist in this matter, though other objectives for the visit are equally plausible.[20] To what extent this editing involved a thorough search of Marshall's manuscripts housed in "the nests of drawers" of his study (Keynes [1924] 1972, 213) is also not known. Editing Marshall's *Official Papers* likewise provided an opportunity to revisit a wide array of Marshall's economics. This was

---

father, William, his Uncle Charles and Marshall's alleged missionary pretensions. Details are in my Marshall biography (1995), but see also Coase 1984 and 1990, esp. pp. 20–24.

19. *Economic Journal* 34 (136) December 1924, pp. 627–37. Keynes's list benefited greatly from a list of Marshall's published writings made by Mary Paley Marshall (and preserved in the Marshall Library) and from the Marshall's scrapbook of newspaper cuttings, which included copies of most of Marshall's many letters to the press.

20. One such objective could have been looking through Marshall's books to select ones unwanted by Mary Paley for library purposes. These visits also indicate the close rapport between Mary Paley Marshall and Maynard Keynes, which lasted for the whole of her life and which was undoubtedly far closer than her relationship with Pigou, the official literary executor of Marshall's will.

a useful reminder that Marshall's government evidence went beyond the famous testimony on trade depressions, monetary theory, and the fiscal policy of international trade to reflect on the aged poor and pension schemes and on government finance in general (cf. Groenewegen 1990).

For the more than fully occupied Keynes of the mid-1920s, this pious devotion to the "master" is a striking tribute of the admiration Keynes felt for him. This admiration shines through some of the phrases in the *Memoir* on Marshall the economist: "within his own field, the greatest in the world for a hundred years"; "Much, but not all, of this ideal many-sidedness Marshall possessed. . . . His mixed training and divided nature furnished him with the most essential and fundamental of the economist's necessary gifts—he was conspicuously historian and mathematician, a dealer in the particular and the general, the temporal and the eternal, at the same time"; Jevons's work "lives merely in the tenuous world of bright ideas when we compare it with the great working machine evolved by the patient, persistent toil and scientific genius of Marshall . . . [in sitting] down silently to build an engine" (Keynes [1924] 1972, 173, 174, 184–85). Is it a wonder that this "absurd little man" who had brought Keynes to economics, left his mark on so many parts of Keynes's own work?

Methodological Parallels

Keynes's *Memoir* contains references to two important methodological aspects where Marshall's opinions can be described as rather similar to his own. Hence they may quite possibly have influenced Keynes's perspectives on the subject. One dealt with some essential features of the nature of economics; the other raised the well-known issue about the dangers of mathematical reasoning in economics, including that of employing sophisticated mathematical and statistical techniques to draw inferences from the data. This section emphasizes methodological aspects of the first of these issues, though for the purpose of this article, the second issue cannot be totally ignored.

The general characteristics of Marshall's economics highlighted by Keynes are its practical nature: "the whole point lies in applying the bare bones of economic theory to the interpretation of current economic life" (Keynes [1924] 1972, 196). This quality also gave economics its transitory nature, because the "profound knowledge of actual facts of industry and trade" are constantly and rapidly changing (196), as was so strikingly illustrated in Marshall's own *Industry and Trade* (228). Economics was therefore "far from a settled affair—like grammar or algebra—which had to be learnt, not criticised," to use Sanger's words which Keynes approvingly quoted (223). This implied the importance of developing an engine of analysis rather than a body of settled principles. Such an analysis had to be capable of organizing and selecting relevant facts and assisting in finding solutions to actual problems. It should be emphasized in the quite different world of economics in 1994 that this meant that determinate solutions to theoretical problems had relatively little importance in Marshall's foundations of economics. He was interested in comprehending an actual economic situation and on that basis to try to grasp the economic and social mechanisms by which certain desirable social and economic consequences over the longer period could be achieved. Facts went hand in hand with theory, justifying Marshall's factory inspections and his preference for reading factual books which he confessed to J. B. Clark (in Pigou 1925, 417). Application was as essential as explanation, whether to temporal problems like structural and periodic unemployment, depressed industry, or an overstimulated war economy, and shortage of the major monetary metal or deficiencies in government revenue-raising capacity or to the more eternal and higher themes of economic and social progress through human improvement in its widest sense. The final chapter of book 1 of the *Principles* illustrates Marshall's philosophy of economics to perfection.

The engine that Marshall built in those *Principles* enabled him to deal with the particular in terms of the general; to explain a wide range of economic issues by the sophisticated analytical armory that he brought into action under the rubric of the theory of value or, more broadly, the theory of supply and demand. Marshall's theory of supply and demand in this context should not be narrowly conceived in terms of stable functions of price. These were only a minor part of the analytical apparatus, despite the attention lavished on their detail by some of his early pupils (cf. J. Robinson 1953, 22). Marshall used the terminology of supply and demand as shorthand for the major forces in economic and social life: wants and activities, production and consumption, to use his terminology for variously titling books 3 and 4. These categories were capable of assisting in explanations of the theory of relative prices and the theory of factor prices, the theory of output and the theory of employment, the theory of money and the theory of crises, the theory of taxes and the theory of trade. They were to be seen as drawer labels in the filing cabinet for storing and classifying relevant detail, to paraphrase Friedman's metaphor. They had to be handled with the greatest of care because they needed *caeteris paribus* clauses with respect to time, with respect to interdependence, with respect to space, with respect to institutions, for a person is a poor economist, Marshall once remarked (1920, 368) who claims to find the theory of value easy. In building his apparatus for the mind, Marshall was searching for the holy grail of the ability to discover temporary, relevant truths, not looking for timeless, universal, equilibrium positions, useful though these could be in devising preliminary and exploratory strategies for analysis. Economics was a way of thinking, not a fund of ready-made conclusions and propositions.

Keynes's sympathy with this program is clear from the introduction he wrote for the *Cambridge Economic Handbooks*, whose publication commenced in the early 1920s (Keynes 1922, v–vi). Although this paid homage to both Marshall and Pigou as the persons who have "chiefly influenced Cambridge thought for the past fifty years," it was Marshall's influence that stayed dominant in this context as far as Keynes was concerned. Keynes's emphasis on the virtue of the relative imprecision in economics contrasts sharply with the formal mathematization in which Pigou liked to indulge when writing theory and the manner in which he tried to present those parts of his system which Marshall had left purposefully untidy and allusive in a way that made them unambiguous, precise, clear, and often enough, banal (Vaizey 1976). This difference in style was already noted in connection with Marshall's and Pigou's lectures when Layton and Keynes attended them; moreover, Pigou's attempts at tidying Marshall's theory by simplification annoyed Marshall personally on several recorded occasions (Marshall to Pigou, 12 April 1916, in Pigou 1925, 43–44; see also Bharadwaj 1972). It makes for a substantial wedge between Marshall and the Marshallians, particularly those Marshallians who developed Pigou's neat theorems, whose actual foundations in the volumes of Marshall's principles and applied economics were invariably qualified in the way Marshall himself had left them to his students. Pigou never absorbed Marshall's message on method, conceptualization, the nature of abstraction, style, and vision— parts of Marshall's economic legacy that Keynes found attractive and emphasized, not only in his tribute to Marshall but also in the practice of his own work. Keynes tentatively acknowledged this in his preface to the Japanese edition of *The General Theory* which sharply differentiated Marshall from his immediate followers on the subject of the need for a theory of output and consumption as a whole (Keynes [1936] 1973a, xxix).

This Marshallian methodological legacy is visible in *The General Theory*, which uses important parts of Marshall's analytical engine. One of these is Marshall's limited emphasis on the virtues of market clearing as compared with Pigou, and his hesitancy in applying the supply and demand apparatus to the labor market. Another is the sure awareness of the monetary nature of economic life in his analysis, despite the explicit intention to omit such monetary considerations from his *Principles*. However, Marshall drew attention to the dangers from this omission in matters like the rate of interest (Marshall 1920, 593–95), while his concluding paragraph in the book alerted readers to the provisional nature of its contents. The first volume was unable to reach "practical conclusions" because "nearly every economic issue depends, more or less directly, on some complex actions and reactions of credit, of foreign trade, and of modern developments of combination and monopoly" (722).

It can also be argued that Marshall's main engine of analysis, here broadly presented as the theory of supply and demand, played a major part in the conceptual apparatus of *The General Theory*. After all, its key elements were aggregate supply and demand, with the supply analysis very Marshallian in its conception. Supply and demand as broadly conceived are also embodied in many of the key variables of the analysis, even though sometimes in startling new dress (for example, the theory of interest). Moreover, given Marshall's feelings about the transitory nature of economic principles and his acceptance of the fact that texts like his *Principles* had the inevitable fate of becoming "waste paper" (Marshall to Fay, 23 February 1915, Pigou 1925, 489–90), I doubt whether he would have been as upset about Keynes's treatment of part of his theory of saving-investment as some of his indirect pupils were. Marshall may in fact even have welcomed Keynes's treatment as a solution to the conundrum of his implicit supply and demand analysis of the capital market with its ambiguities in labeling the horizontal axis and his doubts about portraying saving as a simple increasing function of the rate of interest. Interesting though such speculations may be, they are far removed from the topic of methodological empathy between Keynes and Marshall. Enough has been said on the last to show that this empathy had clear antecedents in the Marshall-Keynes interrelationship as here outlined.

Marshall's critical perspective on mathematical economics was fully captured in Keynes's own ([1924] 1972, 185–88), which likewise recognized Marshall's claim to being "the founder of modern diagrammatic economics." This drew on the preface to the first edition of the *Principles* (Marshall 1920, x–xi) where Marshall suggested such criticisms and expressed a qualified preference for diagrams, which could only be used for illustrative purposes or for self-clarification. Ten years before, Marshall had made this point to Edgeworth, arguing that "curves" were to be preferred to algebra because "they bear more obviously on the science of statistics." However, in the specific case of the labor market where Edgeworth wanted to use them, Marshall argued that supply considerations of labor were so complex, that his use of curves in this context "had been disappointing."[21] Keynes's reluctance to use diagrams in *The General Theory* is also well known; the one diagram in that book, and in fact the only one used in his published economic writings, was "suggested to" him by Harrod after prolonged debate (Keynes [1936] 1973a, 180 n.1; 1973b, 558, where Keynes told Harrod as a loyal Marshall pupil that such a diagram could never constitute a theory of interest). Diagrams could only accommodate the elementary, and they tended to freeze specific assumptions about elasticity from the specific shape of the curve given in the illustration, thereby implicitly constraining the generality of the analysis.

Keynes's criticism of econometrics in correspondence with Harrod and Tinbergen has been too frequently elaborated to require much comment here. However, its association with Marshall's critical comments on the subject deserves more discussion. Their joint assault on Pearson was highly critical of the regression techniques which Pearson was employing on social data, and it induced Marshall to inform Keynes about earlier methodological criticisms of this nature which he had heard Todhunter make. Marshall expanded on such criticisms in correspondence with H. L. Moore. This concerned Moore's *Laws of Wages*, of which he had been sent a complimentary copy and whose method Marshall criticized from the casual dips he had made into its contents on the basis of longstanding beliefs. These told him that

> no important economic chain of events seems likely to be associated with any one cause so predominantly that a study of the concomitant variations of the two can be made as well by mathematics, as

21. Marshall to Edgeworth, 28 March 1880 (British Library of Economics and Political Science, Collection Misc. 470, M469).

by a comparison of a curve representing these two elements with a large number of other curves representing their operative causes: the "*caeteris paribus*" clause—though formally adequate seems to me impracticable. [Secondly,] nearly a half of the whole operative economic causes have refused as yet to be tabulated statistically.

Over long periods of time, results from this method were particularly dangerous. Marshall enclosed a letter he had written to Edgeworth making similar points on Moore's book in a different way. Much later, Marshall wrote Moore (15 December 1921) that he had tried to solve issues of interrelating many variables during the 1870s by means of statistical data recorded in his Red Book. This contained, on an annual basis for both the nineteenth and earlier centuries, consecutive statistics of basic economic variables along with political and other events, and by this means he had tried to obtain "*a posteriori* results by the method of concomitant variations. . . . The result was that I found the depth of my ignorance as to the relations between the development of different economic phenomena to be even greater than I had supposed, and that is saying much."[22]

The methodological empathy between Marshall and Keynes, far greater than that existing between Keynes and Pigou, undoubtedly owed much to their close relationship over the last two decades of Marshall's life. As Keynes had written in the context of Pigou's Marshall memorial lecture, Pigou had failed to grasp this strong side of Marshall's work, the aspect which Keynes had specifically highlighted in his own appreciation of Marshall. Keynes of course went much beyond Marshall's position, but he shared Marshall's strong distrust of theory for theory's sake, his love for facts, and his aim of the practical nature of economic science.

Social Progress and the Good Society:
Two Cambridge Views of the 1920s

The penultimate paragraph of Keynes's *Memoir* ([1924] 1972, 231) draws attention to the fact that Marshall's last two years were devoted to an attempt at constructing a final volume dealing "with the possibility of social advance." At one time, Marshall described his intentions to his wife as writing a twentieth-century Plato's *Republic*, a sketch of a Utopia

22. Marshall to Moore, 5 June 1912, 15 December 1921 (Columbia University Libraries, Ms Coll. H. L. Moore, Rare Book and Manuscript Library).

in which the ideal was to be blended with the realities that made achievement difficult. Marshall's sharply declining powers of concentration and memory from 1922 onward meant that the task effectively got no further than a bundle of notes. These contained various outlines, sketches for some of the chapters, and reflections on 'utopias' either to be admired or to be condemned and forgotten. Whether Keynes gleaned the information about this project from Mary Paley Marshall and the preface of *Money, Credit and Commerce* (Marshall 1923, vi) or from a perusal of these notes in the Marshall papers during the months after Marshall's death is not clear. What is clear is that some time during the early 1920s Keynes himself was sketching an outline of essays on the "Economic Future of the World," a project to which his mind was probably turned by the pessimistic outlook for humanity during the aftermath of World War I (O'Donnell 1992, 778–81, 806).

Marshall's association with this topic had been long-standing. As Keynes also wrote in his *Memoir* from autobiographical snippets of the later years of Marshall's life (Keynes [1924] 1972, 170–71), Marshall's need to understand the economic constraints on the possibilities for social progress had driven him initially to study political economy in the second half of the 1860s. Marshall's enduring support for this basic aim in economic study is also clear from at least part of the opening chapter of the *Principles*, concerned as it is with progress as a means of alleviating, and ultimately removing, the human degradation involved in poverty. Moreover, the high theme of progress, an almost inevitable consequence of human evolution, permeates substantial sections of the book. Alas, these fall precisely in the parts now least studied or read in that volume.

"Aims for the Future" had been a separate book for the second volume of the *Principles* as projected in 1887 to Macmillan (Whitaker 1990, 195); and, though dropped from the 1903 outline of that volume (201), it resurfaced when the final volumes actually started to take shape. In his eightieth year, Marshall partly transformed the separate volume on the future, into the more realistic project of a volume of previously published essays dealing with functions of government and possibilities for social advances,[23] but the separate volume was not forgotten. Preserved outlines

23. This was partly achieved in Pigou's *Memorials*, some of whose contents reprinted major Marshall essays on social progress he had published over his lifetime. Examples are Pigou 1925, reading 2 on the future of the working classes; item 5 on housing the London poor, which resembled the later garden city proposals; item 10 on cooperation; and item 17 on the social possibilities of economic chivalry, Marshall's most outspoken platform for social policy and reform.

gives a good indication of the form it was intended to take (see Whitaker 1990, 217, for an example).

The flavor of Marshall's thinking on this subject can be given from fragments preserved in the Marshall Library:

> Attainable ideals
>> rus in urbe, urb in rure.
>> Variety in life, even when hands are monotonously at work.
>> A right economic government by the people of their governors.
>> Equal early opportunities: graduated take of opportunities, stimuli, fruition?
>> Steadiness of employment, provision against unsteadiness groups unselfishness.
>> Struggle without ferocity.

Thus our ideals are: work for all intelligent but not carried to the length to exhaust the nervous[?] energies (unless of course under the pressure of exceptional emergency). This is not a rule for the student or the artist, when a divine frenzy is on him, he must let it have its head.

True human progress is in the main an advance in capacity for feeling and for thought, yet it cannot be sustained without vigorous enterprise and energy. A certain minimum of means is necessary for mankind's well being, something more than that minimum is necessary for a high class life.

Difficulties of the businessman in risk-taking. . . . This is apt to be overlooked by ardent social reformers. They recognise the necessity for capital—that can be annexed by the State and handed over as the basis of self-governed businesses: and they assume, with some measure of justice, that the workers themselves will be able to supply a good deal of faculty for routine management. But they do not seem to recognise that industrial progress is dependent on the right selection of ventures: they do not make provision for the control by the State of the action of the workers in regard to these risks. If no considerable risks are taken, there will be no progress: if considerable risks are taken at the expense of the State by men who have no special genius for handling them, the State will lose much of its capital. Meanwhile those who have the faculties needed for the higher work of business are likely to have escaped to seek any capital over which they may have control in other lands.

Collective enterprise now has several advantages

(i) joint stock management—like the difficulties government enterprise is open to

(ii) government corruptability reduced by publicity.

Conclusion: Government business must extend and ought to extend: but its extension brings great evils: and ought to be opposed save when it can make a strong *prima facie* case for efficiency and economy.[24]

Other notes raised issues to be specifically addressed when writing on the future of industry. These included the international distribution of progressive industries among nations; the international spread of improvements; and the benefits from trade, including access to the products of mines and agriculture of new countries. Marshall stressed the problem of western European countries without natural resources in maintaining their comparative economic strength. This was to be achieved by fostering essential business qualities, especially innovative skills and ability of informed decision making, both chief factors in the production of material wealth. Marshall discussed the incentives required for economic progress in terms of wealth and the stimulus of success: "Wealth, distinguished from a competency—is valued more for the power and distinction which it gives. Honours and prestige can give the same. This is the logical basis for heavy taxation of private wealth, proving the proceeds is [*sic*] well spent."[25]

How does this Marshallian conception of the future, economic progress, and ideals compare with Keynes's contemporaneous sketch for the study of the economic future of the world? Reproduction of its dozen lines facilitates comparison.

Essays on the Economic future of the world

1. Transitional character of the 19th century

2. Relative prices of agricultural and industrial products

3. Population

---

24. Marshall Library, Red Box 1 (5), "Progress and Ideals," fragments dated early 1920s apart from the first, which is dated 7 April 1903.

25. Marshall Library, Red Box 1 (5), "Progress and Ideals," fragments titled "Book III—The Future of Industry," dated 23 July 1920. Several of the sentiments expressed in these fragments parallel those given in "Social Possibilities of Economic Chivalry" (Pigou 1925, 323–46) which had first appeared in the *Economic Journal* in March 1907.

4. Climate v Race Patriotism

5. Present average wealth, and value of output

6. Importance of inequality to civilisation
   Value of wealth to the individual

7. Prevention of great fortunes

8. Theoretical socialistic framework

9. Psychology of reward and incentive

10. Education, Eugenics and Quoei Soudri
    (O'Donnell 1992, 806)

Although, as O'Donnell (779–80) convincingly points out, Keynes's outline for these essays drew on work on which he had been sporadically engaged both immediately before and after World War I, the similarity between part of the outline and some of Marshall's ideas is nevertheless striking. Examples of the former are Keynes's proposed introduction in terms of the transitional character of the nineteenth century, reminiscent of the opening pages of his *Economic Consequences of the Peace.* Population, the Malthusian specter, and eugenics were likewise recurring themes in Keynes's writing of the early 1920s, though with prewar origins. Particularly interesting are their apparent roots in 1912 lecture notes dealing with factors influencing labor supply, which in itself carries a strong Marshallian flavor, given the attention Marshall had lavished on the topic in both books 4 and 6 of the *Principles.* The same can be especially said about topics six–nine of Keynes's list, dealing with equality and inequality in progress broadly conceived,[26] the need to curtail great fortunes, the psychology of reward and incentives, and the need to examine a theoretical socialist framework in order to preserve its good, humanistic values while at the same time not eliminating some of the values of capitalism so essential to economic progress. Those values are abundantly present in Marshall's extant notes on economic progress and ideals, just as earlier, but in a more restrained way, they had been pub-

26. Thus Marshall pleaded specifically for inequality in work practices and distribution for artists and intellectual workers in order to enable them to use their scarce talents to the full, and thereby to make an essential contribution to civilized life to the maximum extent possible, a position already hinted at in the *Principles* (Marshall 1920, 70 and n. 2, 194–96 and n. 1), the second of which also raises issues of race and climate in this context.

lished in his last journal article on the "Social Consequence of Economic Chivalry."

Various inferences are possible on the basis of such broad similarities. To a large extent, they reflect the zeitgeist of those years, in which all thinking persons dwelled on the possibilities for progress in a future which the horrendous experience of the great war could only portray in the darkest colors, particularly when, with the peace terms imposed on Germany at Versailles, a recurrence of this catastrophe within a generation was highly feasible.[27] In addition, the specter of socialism as a reality which the successful 1917 Bolshevik revolution imparted colored all serious speculation on an economic future for the world at that time, both with respect to the survival of capitalism and the future of socialism. However, a Marshallian influence cannot be ruled out with reference to some of the specific ways Keynes posed the questions. Several aspects of the economic research agenda for the post-1919 future featured strongly in Marshall's oral tradition and were reflected in fragments among Marshall's papers and even occasionally in published material.

Political Perspectives on a Neoliberal Tendency to Socialism

Both Marshall's and Keynes's political positions can be, and have been, described as neoliberal with tendencies toward socialism (Clarke 1988; McWilliams Tullberg 1975; O'Donnell 1989). Although Keynes at least for part of his life (the 1920s) was actively politically committed to the liberal party, Marshall stayed clear of such formal commitments except on the fringes. Examples are his brief association with the Cambridge Reform Club in the early 1870s and, more enduringly, with the Cooperative Movement especially during the 1880s. The liberal creeds they adopted were those befitting their age and their class. However, their respective flirtations with notions of socialism and critiques of capitalism are the topics of interest here.

Marshall's tendency to socialism was unashamedly Millian and reformist. However, given the range of political opinion to which the name, socialism, was then applied (the Christian socialism of Maurice, Hughes, and Ludlow; the social critiques of William Morris; the Georgist movement of land taxation and land reform; Fabianism; and the Marxism of

---

27. Alfred Marshall had himself speculated on this possibility in letters to Taussig (37 [*sic*] March 1915) and Maynard Keynes (21 February 1915), both in Pigou 1925, 290 and 482, respectively.

Hyndman's Social-Democratic Federation), a person with Marshall's political and social opinions could easily describe himself as a socialist.[28] The characteristics of that socialism are not difficult to document for Marshall. He expressed a measure of support for state enterprises and for what was called "municipal socialism" at the turn of the century; for progressive tax and social welfare policies to redress social inequality and poverty; and for schemes of profit-sharing and cooperative enterprise as more satisfactory forms of working-class industrial organization than that suggested by the "new" and more militant trade unions of unskilled labor which had begun to flex their muscles from the late 1880s. Much of this platform was enunciated in Marshall's "Social Possibilities of Economic Chivalry." It was to have been reiterated and developed for the final volume on economic progress.

However, the degree of support Marshall believed he could offer to these socialistic policies was constrained by their adverse effects on incentives and efficiency, particularly the incentives to work, save, accumulate, and, above all, take risk. Public enterprise he saw in general as adverse to risk taking, while the overall incentive to enterprise in such organizations tended to be very limited because this depended largely on the motivations that only ownership could provide. As shown in the previous section, the growing importance of joint stock companies mitigated this conclusion. Such large conglomerates also divorced management and enterprise from ownership, while their increasingly bureaucratic form reduced proclivities to risk taking. Moreover, Marshall reacted strongly against the ambition of strong job expansion schemes in municipal enterprises, especially in public transport, because this entailed the same detrimental productivity effects from overmanning that he ascribed to what he called the "make-work schemes" of new unionists in the engineering and other sectors of British manufacture.[29] The type of public endeavor

28. "We are told sometimes that everyone who strenuously endeavours to promote the social amelioration of the people is a Socialist—at all events, if he believes that much of this work can be better performed by the State than by individual effort. In this sense nearly every economist of the present generation is a Socialist. In this sense I was a Socialist before I knew anything of economics; and, indeed, it was my desire to know what was practicable in social reform by State and other agencies which led me to read Adam Smith and Mill, Marx and Lassalle forty years ago. I have since then been steadily growing a more convinced socialist in this sense of the word" ("Social Possibilities of Economic Chivalry," in Pigou 1925, 334).

29. Marshall to Edward Caird, 22 October 1897, 5 December 1897 in Pigou 1925, 398–401, for example: "Leisure is good, if it is well used. But the laborious laziness, which has come into many English government workshops, and some private ones, engenders a character to which leisure is useless" (401).

Marshall most strongly supported was in town planning, education, the arts, and those activities not likely to be undertaken by private enterprise, either because of the collective benefits they bestowed or because they entailed health, sanitary, and humanitarian costs which private owners were not likely to meet. No broad appeals for nationalizing the commanding heights of the British economy came from this Cambridge economist.

Marshall also supported fiscal measures at distribution. Although originally opposed to redistributive taxation with progressive rates because of adverse incentive effects on work and thrift, during the last decades of his life he admitted that such disincentive effects had been grossly overstated.[30] Such taxes were a useful social policy instrument, especially if their proceeds were satisfactorily spent. From an early age, Marshall also had progressive views on the policy of giving outdoor relief—the policy is so heavily criticized by the 1834 Poor Law because of its disincentive effects on self-help, thrift, and work—to assist unemployed workers and, more importantly, those destitute in sickness and old age, where he gave cautious support to the payment of age pensions ("Social Possibilities of Economic Chivalry," in Pigou 1925, 345–46). Universal assistance was decried for such reason, and because of its costs, including the excess burdens if such schemes were financed from general taxation.

Marshall's adherence to the principle of self-help as crucial to labor organizations—so visible in his support for "old" trade unionism with its emphasis on voluntary, mutual assistance schemes, for profit sharing and for organizing cooperative ventures in retailing and other activities—needs little attention in this context. However, his critical perspective on laissez-faire and on unrestrained competition (for example, Marshall 1920, 6–10; Pigou 1925, 274–77) bear some reiteration. They can be summed up in his definition of laissez-faire as "let the State be up and doing" (Pigou 1925, 336), implying that an active State is essential to regulate and control the mixed consequences of vigorous competition under free enterprise, thereby enabling it to sift out the detrimental from the desirable. Marshall's attitude to capitalism and free enterprise is comparable to that of a late twentieth-century social democrat: the state is required as regulator and as redistributor to remove the undesirable consequences from an economic and social system (competitive free enterprise) otherwise superior to any of the others that are known.[31]

---

30. Marshall to Lord Reay, 12 November 1909, in Pigou 1925, 461–65, esp. p. 463.

31. Vaizey's 1976 perceptive comments that Marshall set far less store on the market-clearing properties of a competitive system than Pigou did is of relevance here. It should not be forgotten

Such sentiments are replicated in the projects Keynes was developing in the mid-1920s in his outlines for a "Prolegomena to a New Socialism" and the associated project of a "Critical Examination of Capitalism" (O'Donnell 1992, 781–93, 806–12). The thrust of the new socialism lay in the end of laissez-faire, the theme on which Keynes later published an essay (Keynes [1931] 1951, 312–22) which in fact was one of the few major published outcomes of these projects. It associated the individualism of laissez-faire with the "technical superiority of small units in certain cases," possessive "instincts of risk-taking . . . [and] of avarice and hoarding" and a "criterion of profit" for which any new system should "preserve opportunities." These qualities gave it superiority over the State, but such "alleged disadvantages of the State [became] equally disadvantages of the large scale entrepreneur using other people's money" under the joint stock system that separated ownership from control and developed general bureaucratic tendencies (cf. Keynes [1931] 1951, 314–15). The "large" this brought with it for business organization appeared therefore to the two Cambridge economists as not necessarily beautiful and efficient, an idea which Marshall had in fact partly adopted to deal with his so-called "Cournot problem" of the possibility of increasing returns destroying effective business competition.

Keynes's prolegomena in its subsequent two parts intended to develop the philosophical foundations in order to explore the role of "benevolence," the public good, and, more particularly, the means thereto in "economic well-being." It then planned to address the chief preoccupations of the State under six different heads: population, including eugenics; money;[32] enterprise issues lumped together as "adequacy of saving, investment of fixed capital, public utilities"; labor matters lumped together, including "wage levels, [employment and social] insurance, industrial disputes"; "natural resources"; and last, and an almost total

---

that Marshall's *Principles* (book 5, chap. 13) had explicitly criticized those who were drawing naive welfare implications from competitive equilibrium while Marshall was also very skeptical, particularly as compared with Pigou, about the ease with which government action could address the situation. Marshall's scattered comments on the subject of unemployment suggest also that he never entertained flexible wage solutions to this problem, except as a form of fantasy when exercising the mind in the realms of pure theory.

32. Obviously placed second because of Keynes's conclusions in *The Tract on Monetary Reform*, which he had completed the year before and which stressed the positive and important role of the state in securing price stability. As indicated earlier, Marshall had stressed the importance of price stability for facilitating good business decisions and urged a government role therein in providing official price indices.

inversion of the priorities in the classic treatment of the subject by Adam Smith, "defence, peace" (O'Donnell 1992, 807).

Many of these indications of proposed content were directly inspired by Keynes's own interests at the time. Monetary reform and the need for "a drastic remedy for unemployment" with its explicit rejection of "the old principle of laissez faire" as passé for both the labor and capital markets (see Harrod 1951, 345–49) are clear examples. Much of the thrust of these arguments fit equally with some of Marshall's published and unpublished pronouncements on the matter. Of special relevance are his thoughts on the impact of developments in joint stock companies on the case against public enterprise and, more generally, the "master's" recognized emphasis on the transitory nature of economic phenomena. The particular developments in joint stock companies mentioned were a striking example of this transitional quality, as was the general demise of laissez-faire in its traditional, late-Victorian meaning. Moreover, there was little in this list of proposed government responsibilities that Marshall could not have endorsed with the exception perhaps of its perspectives on saving and fixed capital investment.

The first outline for a critical examination of capitalism, which O'Donnell (1992, 785–86) provisionally ascribes to November 1924, followed closely therefore on Marshall's death and in particular, Keynes's October visit to Mary Paley when he went through "papers and things." This, in my view, may explain the structure of "ideal, actual and practicable" as a model for organizing Keynes's views on the subject equally well as the appeal to Moore's ethical foundations made by O'Donnell 1992, 788. Justice in distribution with critical remarks on inheritance and, more pertinently, observations on the structure and purpose of an ideal society (utopias) were important aspects of Marshall's outlines for his projected final volume which Keynes, when looking through Marshall's papers, could hardly have missed. Many of the themes to be raised by Keynes under "the possible" had likewise gained the attention of Marshall in his prognostications on potential postwar developments in his *Industry and Trade*. These included reflections on state saving; alternative social organizations based on state socialism, guild socialism, and copartnership; and the necessity of devising regulatory mechanisms for controlling public utilities and trusts. These seem good reasons to think that Keynes's project to critically examine the contemporary operations of capitalism had a strong Marshall pedigree since this was part and parcel of the research program which Marshall had laid out for himself in his study of economics, and which in fact had partially achieved in his *Industry and Trade*. (Cf. Keynes [1924] 1972, 228, whose reading of *Industry and Trade* is not inconsistent with this view.)

Drawing such parallels is much easier than documenting the influences in question. The last need not be done. The point to be made is that in developing his own brand of liberal socialism, Keynes more than likely drew on the similar ideas of this subject the "master" had left to his "pupils" and of which Keynes himself was clearly aware (Keynes [1924] 1972, 214). The two perspectives on politics by the two Cambridge economists resemble each other in some of their approaches to specific questions, and insofar as those of one is concerned, formed a substantial part of the roots of the other.

Conclusion

A wider look at Marshall's influences on the system of thought developed by his most outstanding pupil may pay considerable dividends in the interpretation of Keynes's thought. In settling interpretative debates on the meaning of parts of *The General Theory*, as well as aspects of the economics of Keynes before that book, this is an increasingly recognized procedure. A closer look at the nature of the relationship between the two men aids this process, particularly if it includes the posthumous contact with Marshall's views which Keynes imposed on himself in the two years after Marshall's death. Misunderstanding of the extent of Marshall's influence on Keynes owes much to an inadequate grasp of this biographical aspect; it also arises from inadequate perception of the thrust and objectives of Marshall's own enormous, albeit incomplete, opus. *Principles*, and *Money Credit and Commerce*, and especially the monetary evidence, have received the focus of attention in the Marshall-Keynes relationship; if this article has convinced Keynes scholars that this may not be enough, it will have served its purpose in assisting our understanding of the thought of the greatest twentieth-century economist.

References

Bharadwaj, Krishna. 1972. Marshall on Pigou's Wealth and Welfare. *Economica* 39.153:32–46.

Clarke, Peter. 1988. *The Keynesian Revolution in the Making 1924–1936*. Oxford: Clarendon.

Coase, R. H. 1984. Alfred Marshall's Mother and Father. *HOPE* 16.4:519–27.

————. 1990. Alfred Marshall's Family and Ancestry. In *Alfred Marshall in Retrospect*. Edited by Rita McWilliams Tullberg. Aldershot: Edward Elgar.

Clower, Robert W. 1989. Keynes General Theory: the Marshall Connection. In *Perspectives in the History of Economic Thought*. Edited by Donald A. Walker. Aldershot: Edward Elgar.

Groenewegen, Peter. 1988. Alfred Marshall and the Establishment of the Cambridge Economics Tripos. *HOPE* 20.4:627–67.

————. 1990. Marshall on Taxation. In *Alfred Marshall in Retrospect*. Edited by Rita McWilliams Tullberg. Aldershot: Edward Elgar.

————. 1993. Marshall and Keynes: Observations on the Treatment of the Relationship in two Recent Biographies. *Marshall Studies Bulletin* 3:21–35.

————. 1995. *A Soaring Eagle: Alfred Marshall 1842–1924*. Aldershot: Edward Elgar.

Harrod, R. F. 1951. *The Life of John Maynard Keynes*. London: Macmillan.

Hennings, Klaus. 1979. Karl Heinrich Rau and the Graphic Representation of Supply and Demand. *Volkswirtschaftslehre* 35 Fachbereift Wirtschaftswissenschaften, Universität Hanover.

Hill, Polly, and Richard Keynes, eds. 1989. *Lydia and Maynard*. London: André Deutsch.

Humphrey, Thomas M. 1992. Marshallian Cross Diagrams and Their Uses Before Alfred Marshall: The Origins of Supply and Demand Geometry. *Federal Reserve Bank of Richmond Economic Review* 78.2:3–23.

Keynes, John Maynard. 1922. Introduction to *Money* by D. H. Robertson. Cambridge Economic Handbook. London: Nesbitt and Cambridge University Press.

————. [1924] 1972. Alfred Marshall 1842–1924. In *Essays in Biography*. Vol. 10 of *The Collected Writings of John Maynard Keynes*. 30 vols. Edited by D. E. Moggridge. London: Macmillan. (CW)

————. [1931] 1951. *Essays in Persuasion*. London: Rupert-Hart Davis.

————. [1936] 1973a. *The General Theory of Employment, Interest and Money*. Vol. 12 of *The Collected Writings of John Maynard Keynes*. 30 vols. Edited by D. E. Moggridge. London: Macmillan. (CW)

Layton Papers, Trinity College, Cambridge.

————. [1936] 1973b. The General Theory and After. Part I: Preparation. Vol. 13 of *The Collected Writings of John Maynard Keynes*. 30 vols. Edited by D. E. Moggridge. London: Macmillan. (CW)

Leijonhufvud, Axel. 1994. Hicks, Keynes and Marshall. In *The Legacy of Hicks*. Edited by H. Hagemann and O. F. Hamouda. London: Routledge.

McWilliams Tullberg, Rita. 1975. Marshall's Tendency to Socialism. *HOPE* 7.1:75–111.

Marshall, Alfred. 1920. *Principles of Economics* 8th ed. London: Macmillan.

————. 1923. *Money, Credit and Commerce*. London: Macmillan.

————. 1926. *Official Papers*. London: Macmillan.

Moggridge, D. E. 1990. Keynes as Editor. In *A Century of Economics: 100 Years of* the *Royal Economic Society and the Economic Journal.* Edited by John D. Hey and Donald Winch. Cambridge: Cambridge University Press.

————. 1992. *Maynard Keynes. An Economist's Biography.* London: Routledge.

O'Donnell, R. M. 1989. *Keynes: Philosophy, Economics and Politics.* London: Routledge.

————. 1992. The Unwritten Books and Papers by Keynes. *HOPE* 24.4:767–817.

Pearson, Karl. 1910. Questions of the Day and of the Fray No. 1. Supplement to the memoir entitled *The Influence of Parental Alcoholism on the Physique and Ability of the Offspring. A Reply to the Cambridge Economists.* London: Dulan.

Pigou, A. C., ed. 1925. *Memorials of Alfred Marshall.* London: Macmillan.

Pollard, S. 1994. New Light on an Old Master. *Economic Journal* 104.422:138–53.

Robinson, Austin. 1947. John Maynard Keynes 1883–1946. *Economic Journal* 57.225:1–7.

————. 1990. Cambridge Economics in the Post-Marshallian Period. In *Alfred Marshall in Retrospect.* Edited by Rita McWilliams Tullberg. Aldershot: Edward Elgar.

Robinson, Joan. 1953. *On Re-Reading Marx.* Cambridge: Students' Bookshop.

————. 1962. *Economic Philosophy.* London: Watts.

Skidelsky, Robert. 1983. *Hopes Betrayed, 1883–1920.* Vol. 1 of *John Maynard Keynes.* London: Macmillan.

————. 1992. *The Economist as Saviour, 1920–1937.* Vol. 2 of *John Maynard Keynes.* London: Macmillan.

Vaizey, John. 1976. Keynes and the Cambridge Tradition. *Spectator,* 19 May:20–21.

Whitaker, John. 1990. What Happened to the Second Volume of the Principles? The Thorny Path to Marshall's Last Books. In *Centenary Essays on Alfred Marshall.* Edited by J. Whitaker. Cambridge: Cambridge University Press.

Comment

A. W. Coats

Peter Groenewegen's paper covers a trio of complex and controversial topics extending well beyond the conventional boundaries of economics. I have no quarrel with the general thrust of his argument, and in comments of this kind it is obviously impossible to examine the details at length. I shall therefore treat his contribution as a starting point for some selective observations on the relationship between Marshall and Keynes, those twin peaks of Cambridge economics.

Keynes is a fascinating figure who has, understandably, received the attention (if not always the benefit) of several major biographers and numerous lesser ones. By contrast, and remarkably so, Groenewegen stands alone as a comprehensive biographer of Marshall, and I have been privileged to read the entire early draft of his manuscript (Groenewegen 1995). The book is a substantial, revealing, and invaluable rectification of a glaring omission. Quite apart from the question of his intellectual stature and importance, on which there are still conflicting interpretations, Marshall was in many ways a difficult and elusive—at times even evasive—character, and the sources available to a scholarly biographer are on the whole far less abundant and illuminating than in the case of Keynes.

Groenewegen emphasizes certain broad similarities between the two economists by focusing on three aspects of their work that are rarely

considered together. This procedure is legitimate, for it is generally recognized that Keynes bore a considerable weight of Marshallian and late
Victorian intellectual and cultural baggage throughout his early and middle years—and, indeed, in his economic theory right up to the time he
began serious work on *The General Theory*. Wisely, Groenewegen makes
no attempt either to unpack that baggage and attach precise labels to its
contents or to assess Marshall's overall influence on Keynes. But his
forthcoming biography provides abundant new resources for scholars
who do wish to undertake these tasks.

Nevertheless, despite the undeniable similarities, it is the differences
between Marshall and Keynes that are so striking, particularly with respect to personality, tone, style, and objectives. Groenewegen's treatment
of the final, partly posthumous phase of the relationship is particularly interesting, and I shall concentrate on this period in part because it affords
an opportunity to test Robert Skidelsky's hypothesis that biographers
commonly assume their subjects are more frequently the product of their
background than of their times. In so saying, however, he adds the caveat
that "this method works perfectly well in most cases. It breaks down when
the times become turbulent, when the mentality or sensibility of society
starts to shift" (Skidelsky 1992, 194). The early 1920s were just such a
time; and it raises the question of how far the postwar disintegration of the
prewar culture disrupted the basic continuities in the Marshall-Keynes
nexus.

In the most intriguing section of his paper, Groenewegen compares
Marshall's projected volume of previously published essays on the future, economic progress, and ideals, with Keynes's plan for a study of
the economic future of the world. He suggests that the broad parallels
between their respective visions, both of which have utopian touches,
may "reflect the zeitgeist of those years [i.e., the early 1920s] in which
all thinking persons dwelled on the possibilities for progress which the
horrendous experience of the great war could only portray in the darkest
colors" (Groenewegen, this volume).

However, these visions do not represent a direct response to the postwar
crisis, as Groenewegen implies, for he notes that Marshall's essays had
been written much earlier, while Keynes's outline "drew on work on
which he had been sporadically engaged both immediately before and
after World War I" (Groenewegen, this volume), the latter elements partly
before Marshall's death. Beyond this, the narrowing lists of topics are
so cryptic and abstract that it is difficult to assess their meaning and

significance. Indeed, in parts they resemble the brief note headings that examinees offer when they are unable to complete their exam paper, in the hope that a sympathetic examiner will interpret them generously as evidence of the candidate's knowledge. In this case, the evidence seems to reflect Marshall's and Keynes's backgrounds rather than the postwar "times."

During the 1920s, at a time when he might have chosen to dedicate himself to the development, refinement, and extension of Marshall's ideas, Keynes was fully engrossed in current affairs, functioning as a high-level journalist, publicist, and expert pundit rather than as an economic theorist. In fact, his interest in the development of theory was limited throughout the 1920s, and he was anything but a cloistered academic, the role Marshall preferred. Keynes's practice directly conflicted with Marshall's belief that the economist, qua economist, should avoid active involvement in debates over current controversial public issues. Whereas Marshall eschewed controversy wherever possible, believing it inimical to the progress of science, Keynes embraced it enthusiastically, frequently engaging in polemical campaigns, and at times deliberately overstating his case in order to shock his audience. He was unusually frank on one occasion, when he declared, "we have to invent a new wisdom for a new age. And in the meantime we must, if we are to do good, appear unorthodox, troublesome, dangerous, and disobedient to them that begat us" (quoted in Skidelsky 1992, 230).

It is inconceivable that Marshall, with his exaggerated respect for the accumulated wisdom of the past would have used such language, or even thought such thoughts! Keynes, by contrast, knew perfectly well when he was breaking with tradition, usually undertaking the task with relish. In discussing the gold standard problem, for example, he protested that the Bank of England and the Treasury were tackling postwar problems with prewar ideas and emphasized the need to replace old men and outmoded habits of thought (quoted in Skidelsky 1992, 154, 194). In theoretical matters he was less innovative, at least up to the later 1920s when his faith in the orthodox Cambridge framework of monetary analysis began to be undermined, as he worked on the *Treatise on Money*. But a more dramatic example is his admission that the completion of *The General Theory* involved a long and difficult process of emancipation, a "struggle of escape from habitual modes of thought and expression." The Marshallian legacy could not easily be repudiated, for "the difficulty lies, not in the new ideas, but in escaping from the old ones, which ramify, for those brought up as most of us have been, into every corner of our minds" (CW 7:xxiii).

The sheer volume of Keynes's activities, and his intense preoccupation with immediate pressing problems, help to explain his well-known inconsistencies, periodic self-contradictions, and shifts of emphasis to accommodate changing circumstances—a direct consequence of his multiple roles and his penchant for "firing on all cylinders," to cite Peter Clarke's expressive phrase (1994, 127). What a contrast with Marshall's "elaborately unsensational and underemphatic style" in which "the minimum of controversy was provoked," to cite Keynes's famous memorial essay (CW 10:210–11). Both Marshall and Keynes were engaged in persuasion, but their audiences and their methods were dramatically different. Marshall never attempted to write polemical works comparable to Keynes's *Economic Consequences of the Peace* or *The Tract on Monetary Reform*, both of which were masterpieces of prose designed to shock, as well as to persuade. Undoubtedly, at times Keynes overdid it, as in some early drafts (and some would add, also the final version) of *The General Theory*, ignoring the pleas of some of his admirers that in so doing he would reduce its effectiveness. As he himself remarked: "In economics you cannot *convict* your opponent of error; you can only *convince* him of it. . . . Even if you are right, you cannot convince him, if there is a defect in your own powers of persuasion and exposition" (CW 12:470).[1]

Keynes criticized Marshall's style in the *Principles* because of

> The lack of emphasis and of strong light and shade, the sedulous rubbing away of rough edges and salients and projections, until what is most novel can appear as trite, allows the reader to pass too easily through. Like a duck leaving water, he can escape from this douche of ideas with scarce a wetting. The difficulties are concealed; the most ticklish problems are solved in footnotes, a pregnant and original judgment is dressed up as a platitude. The author furnishes his ideas with no labels of salesmanship and few hooks for them to hang on in the wardrobe of the mind. (CW, 10:212)

Recently Warren Samuels has pointed out that Marshall's style was designed to reinforce his scientific authority by presenting himself as autonomous or convenient, and in policy matters giving the impression that

---

1. There is a fascinating examination of Keynes's style of argument and the structure of *The General Theory* in Maurizio Gotti 1994. The essays by Alessandra Marzola and Riccardo Bellofiore in the same volume are also of interest.

he was personally independent of or above the controversy (Samuels and Patchack-Schuster 1993, 160). What a contrast with Keynes, who was—at least apart from the *Treatise on Probability* and *The General Theory*—often only too eager to get his ideas in print before they had been fully worked out.

References

Clarke, Peter. 1994. Keynes in History. *HOPE* 26.1:117–35.

Gotti, Maurizio. 1994. The General Theory as an Open-Ended Work. In *John Maynard Keynes: Language and Method.* Edited by Alessandra Marzola and Francesco Silva. Aldershot: Edward Elgar.

Groenewegen, Peter. 1995. *A Soaring Eagle: Alfred Marshall, 1842–1924.* Aldershot: Edward Elgar.

Keynes, John Maynard. 1971–89. *The Collected Writings of John Maynard Keynes.* 30 vols. Edited by D. E. Moggridge. London: Macmillan. (CW)

Samuels, Warren, and Thomas W. Patschack-Schuster. 1993. Aspects of the Structure of Marshall's Principles. In *Economic Thought and Discourse in the Twentieth Century.* Edited by Warren J. Samuels, Jeff Biddle, and Thomas W. Patchack-Schuster. Aldershot: Edward Elgar.

Skidelsky, Robert. 1992. *The Economist as Saviour, 1920–1937.* Vol. 2 of *John Maynard Keynes.* London: Macmillan.

Keynes: An Archivist's View

Jacqueline Cox

This is a paper about papers, boxes and boxes of them; the accumulated evidence of sixty-two years' energy and ideas. It sets out to describe how the paper mountain was built and how it has been mapped and scaled since its maker's death. The Keynes Collection at King's College is certainly the largest in the library's Modern Archive Centre, as well as the most heavily used. It is also significant in that it attracts the widest variety of scholars. In recent years, economists have had increasingly to share the reading room with philosophers, with historians of social policy or elite culture, with art critics, even with librarians. They have had to acknowledge that to concentrate on the drafts of his economic theories alone is to grasp at only part of his contribution and that inadequately. They have begun to widen their focus and adopt something of the approaches of, say, the philosopher or the historian. The abiding richness of the Keynes Papers can only encourage this interdisciplinary contact. Continued archival research will allow for the drawing of more and more considered pictures of Keynes.

By way of introduction, a note on the current setting. King's College possesses a collection of "modern" (that is nineteenth- and twentieth-century) manuscripts that is unrivaled in importance by any other college library in the United Kingdom. Since 1930 and the transfer of the papers of Rupert Brooke, King's College Library has acquired the records of many eminent "Kingsmen" and of individuals associated with them, among them C. R. Ashbee, architect; Clive and Vanessa Bell, art critic and painter, respectively; T. S. Eliot, poet; E. M. Forster, novelist; Roger Fry, art critic; Richard Kahn, Nicholas Kaldor, J. M. Keynes, Joan Robinson, and Richard Stone, economists; and Alan Turing, computer scientist. The Modern Archives include the papers of many other former members of the college, such as former fellows Oscar Browning, G. Lowes Dickinson, J. T. Sheppard, and Nathaniel Wedd. Activities of junior members are also documented in the records of King's College clubs and societies.

The Centre continues to acquire records as gifts from former members and their families and, to a lesser degree, as purchases from individuals and at auction. In the past decade, accessions have been dominated by the papers of former fellows and honorary fellows in economics. The records of Keynes, Kahn, Kaldor, Robinson, and Stone now constitute more than 65 percent of the 2,000 feet of total records held.

The Modern Archive Centre is housed in part of the newly refurbished extension to the library. Its splendid reading room seats twelve and is open to scholars throughout the year. Reader numbers have risen steadily since the archives were given accommodation separate from the main library in 1982 (they topped 900 in 1991). The majority are established academics pursuing postdoctoral research for books and articles. Among an international readership, North Americans and the Japanese are particularly well represented. Document consultation is free. The records are stored in two adjacent strong rooms, secured against fire and theft and, for long-term conservation reasons, maintained at a constant temperature and relative humidity.

The needs of collections and readers are met by a single, full-time archivist. A graduate professional, the modern archivist liaises with record donors, arranges and catalogues the papers once received, and assesses their confidentiality and conservation needs. She gives advice on the contents of collections and on issues of copyright and reprography to visiting scholars, correspondents, and junior and senior members of the college.

In his will, drawn up in 1941, Keynes instructed his executors, Geoffrey Keynes (his brother) and Richard Kahn, to divide his papers into the "personal" and the "economic"—Keynes to take responsibility for the former and Kahn the latter. The will further requested that both men destroy the greater part of their portions and transfer to King's College and the Marshall Library (at the University's Faculty of Economics and Politics), respectively, only that material, personal and economic, which they deemed worthy of permanent preservation. The will seemed to suggest that at the end of such a survey Keynes's archive would amount to no more than a couple of boxes.

But it was probably false modesty on his part to pretend that his executors would tear up anything. After all, he came from a family of hoarders and recorders. His father had sustained a lifelong pursuit of butterflies and stamps. His mother had garnered his childish scribbles, school essays, and Eton bills. She had doggedly compiled scrapbook after scrapbook of cuttings of his press appearances, that is, articles by and about him charting his public reputation from 1905 onward. And he knew that he was a "great man." An unwillingness to do some spring-cleaning in his own lifetime was the result of more than simple inertia, or the "out of sight is out of mind" convenience of large houses with rambling attics in London, Cambridge, and Sussex. It must also be explained by a self-conscious sense of his own place in history. As we shall see, his executors were at least as sensitive to his international reputation and the interests of posterity as was Keynes himself.

Keynes's prodigious talents and industry combined with the self-confidence of his class are a commonplace. The man was a prolific writer, snatching up his pen to tackle university, college, government, editorial, or investment business at turns; "words," he said, "are the assault of thought upon the unthinking" (1933 in CW 21:244). From 1919 on he employed part-time secretarial assistance, at least for the typing of business correspondence and the dictation of some newspaper articles. Carbons of his daily out-letters survive to swell his archive from that date. He would either have someone come in from Miss Pates's agency or poach on the college office staff when in Cambridge, or he would arrange for a "Missy," as he called her, to arrive at 46 Gordon Square just half an hour or so after he did on his return to London every Tuesday or Wednesday evening during term.

For the last twelve years of his life, as work pressures steadily rose and his health declined, he employed full-time help in the person of Mrs. M. S. Stephens. King's College also paid Mrs. Stephens a retainer of thirty shillings a week from 1939 to secure her services in the college office when she was not required by Keynes (Council minutes, vol. 13, King's College Muniments). Mrs. Stephens followed Keynes to Ruthin when he was in the hospital and then convalescing after his heart attack in May 1937. She joined him at the Treasury in 1940 and accompanied him to Washington in 1941. Such loyal, hard work was rewarded on his death by an annuity of £150, a not inconsiderable sum at the time.

Keynes's working habits were orderly. He composed his essays and books in long-hand, often in pencil, on a writing board as he sat in an armchair by the fire, then sent off drafts to be typed. For *The General Theory of Employment, Interest and Money*, these drafts survived in sufficient quantity for the editors of *The Collected Writings of John Maynard Keynes* to devote half of one volume (Vol. 14) and a third of another (Vol. 29) to an analysis of their evolution. He lectured from the book's successive proofs and circulated galleys for comment in the meantime to Harrod, Hawtrey, Kahn, and Joan Robinson.

His powers of concentration, economy, and facility as a journalist were equally enviable. Here, his response was speedy; *one* draft of each article was usually the first and final version with a minimum of crossing out. A typical article of, say, 1,200 words (there survive 300 or so of varying lengths for the quality and popular press among his papers) might take him no more than a couple of hours to be ready for the typist and dispatch to the printer. Or less. "The *New York Evening Post* telephoned me for a short message about how it [the Wall Street Crash] looked to an Englishman," he wrote to his wife, Lydia Lopokova, on 25 October 1929. "'$250,' I replied, 'not a penny less.' After lunch came another message accepting these terms, so I spent *half an hour writing it* and then another 25 minutes, which gave me a headache, dictating it down the trunk telephone" (Keynes Papers PP/45/190; emphasis added).

But I am doubtful how much of a complete success secretarial help was in maintaining an orderly office during his lifetime. The man was too peripatetic—too used to working alone and at speed to wait on the bureaucracy of others. Richard Kahn told my predecessor as modern archivist that Keynes had no filing system, except perhaps as editor of the *Economic Journal*.

He allowed papers to accumulate in "files" [of which he enclosed a dog-eared example]. These files were to be found all over the place—in the College Office, in his College room, at Gordon Square or at Tilton. And of course during the War in his room at the Treasury. Then he would, when he had finished with them, place them in the drawer of a splendid piece of furniture. It was a frightful business assembling his papers after his death. How the bursarial office functioned so efficiently

I can't explain, though I was second Bursar. (letter to M. Halls, 6 December 1986, Keynes Papers accessions files)

"I have found my long lost article on Malthus!" [first written in 1924], Keynes wrote to Lydia on 10 October 1930. "The bed maker turned it up dusting" (Keynes Papers PP/45/190). And on 3 December 1933, at the end of a particularly hectic day at King's, he groaned, "after that I did my final piece of hard work in my office and even did the enormous act of strength of clearing out my baskets and the old stale smelly matters which lie on my desk" (Keynes Papers PP/45/190). In 1937, visiting Stanley Woolston's antique saleroom in Cambridge he discovered, in one of the drawers of a piece of furniture recently discarded by Lydia and there on display, "a lot of my papers, including all my patents of nobility signed by King George and other monarchs, CBs, Chevaliers of Leopold etc.; also a lot of photographs of you" (24 January 1937, Keynes Papers PP/45/190).

It fell to Mrs. Stephens to begin to sort out Keynes's paperwork in the year after his death in preparation for his biographer, a "heroic task," according to Roy Harrod (1951, xiv). Harrod had unrestricted access to the archive, now all seemingly assembled at Gordon Square. By 1951, this project complete, Geoffrey Keynes was again giving his attention to the terms of his brother's will. "You will have to come to London to envisage the problem of Maynard's papers," he wrote to the King's Librarian, A. N. L. ("Tim") Munby. "The next move must be organised by us jointly. Everything is getting very dirty and has been left too long already" (13 March 1951, Keynes Papers accessions files). Imagine, then, in April 1951, Tim Munby and Piero Sraffa, then librarian of the Marshall Library, driving up to London to join Geoffrey Keynes and begin the division of the spoils into the personal and economic, or, more properly, the private and public lives of Keynes.[1]

Back at King's College, the personal papers, comprising his juvenilia, his voluminous correspondence with Bloomsbury friends or on the subject of his books, manuscripts, pictures, or the Cambridge Arts Theatre, amounting to some ten boxes, were packed into Keynes's large Empire bookcase, one of his "splendid pieces of furniture," now standing in the librarian's room. Here they joined the collection of rare books

---

1. The division of archive collections by executors is not a practice advised by archivists, keen to stress the interrelatedness of the parts and integrity of the whole, and to avoid the subjectivity inherent in the selection of material for one "half" or the other.

Keynes had assembled during his life: early editions, that is, of authors prominent in the history of thought, such as Bacon, Hobbes, Hume, Descartes, Rousseau, and Voltaire; sixteenth- and seventeenth-century English poetry and prose; seventeenth-century drama; books from the library of Edward Gibbon; nineteenth- and twentieth-century literature; and an outstanding group of Sir Isaac Newton's manuscripts, together with the papers of his executor, John Conduitt.

By the mid-1950s, Munby had provided the personal papers with a summary listing, box by box. All applications to read them were referred for approval to Sir Geoffrey. In deference to the sensitivity of persons still living, certain personal letters exchanged with Keynes were reserved from view during their lifetimes. In the case of the correspondence between Keynes and Lytton Strachey, where the deaths of both men did not, to the mind of the executors, reduce the sensitivity of the contents, the entire collection, amounting to 1,000 letters over the period 1905–31, was sealed up and ordered embargoed until 1986. This represented a hard-won compromise exacted from Geoffrey Keynes by Roy Harrod on learning of his intention to burn this evidence of Keynes's homosexuality (letter from Roy Harrod to R. F. Kahn, 8 July 1969, Kahn Papers RFK 12/2/6). Rather than that mere indifference to the quality of the archive hinted at in Keynes's will, fear of its potential to undermine his reputation and the reception of his ideas, particularly in the United States, was the greatest threat to its survival.[2] But survive intact it did.

In subsequent years, further additions to the personal papers were made by members of the Keynes family and others, including Roy Harrod. The most recent large-scale transfer to King's from Milo Keynes, Geoffrey Keynes's son, has been the papers of Lady Keynes, the former Lydia Lopokova, ballerina.

Meanwhile, at the Marshall Library, the situation of the papers was altogether different. Elizabeth Johnson has described elsewhere the sight that greeted her arrival as the first editor of the projected *Collected Writings of John Maynard Keynes* in the mid-1950s (Johnson 1978, 1–16). The papers, in bundles, files, and boxes, were literally jammed one stack on top of the other into a big, a very big, cupboard without any shelves and into locked filing cabinets. Many were dirty, crumbling, and stained with rusty paper clips. The ten boxes at King's were dwarfed beside the

---

2. Little did they know that Keynes's letters to Strachey, which had been in the possession of James Strachey, had already been copied and that their contents would be made public in Michael Holroyd's biography of Lytton Strachey in 1967–68.

acres of papers and volumes dubbed "economic." A skeleton catalogue of the material had been produced by a Mrs. MacDonald at about the same time as Munby was working at King's.

According to Elizabeth Johnson, the structure of this list followed an order by subject and date already divined by Mrs. Stephens in her work for Harrod. So there were batches of files for the drafts and related correspondence of each of Keynes's published works, subject files in other words, together with a chronological sequence of letter files on wholly miscellaneous issues; there were files bringing all his speeches together, qua speeches, or all his memoranda together, qua memoranda, alongside envelopes of notes and papers, including speeches or memoranda, on particular subjects, Malthus for instance. The papers included sections for material illustrating his official work for the India Office, the Treasury or one or other government committee, his editorial and society activities, and his business interests. It was on the basis of this arrangement that the editors of *The Collected Writings* produced their volumes in the next twenty-five years. What was originally envisaged as a series of twenty-one, mushroomed to twenty-five and then twenty-nine volumes, with the uncovering of more and more of the collection's potential and the unearthing of Keynes material in other archives. Finally, for all its seeming completeness, the mountain grew again in 1976 with the discovery at Tilton of a laundry hamper of further drafts and correspondence, much of it dating from the mid-1930s. That necessitated a further volume. Manuscripts and xeroxes of manuscripts identified subsequently to Mrs. MacDonald's list were merely tacked on to its end for administrative convenience, regardless of provenance, and dubbed "Miscellaneous."

Throughout the project, scholarly use of the papers was limited, in view of the editors' need for untrammeled access and the slender means available to the Marshall Library for supervised consultation, detailed cataloguing, or document conservation. As the project neared completion in the mid-1980s and the Faculty of Economics and Politics found itself unable to house the collection permanently, the editors, together with the Marshall Librarian, Lord Kahn, and the librarian and archivist at King's College, considered the transfer of the economics portion to join the rest of the papers at King's. Reunion was finally effected in June 1986.

Since the amalgamation of the papers at King's and my arrival in 1990, the opportunity has been taken to produce an integrated, more detailed catalogue—one that would take account of the accumulation of material since the initial transfers to Cambridge and further recognize that Munby and Sraffa's division into the personal and the economic had resulted in some anomalies. Philosophy papers, for instance, appeared in both parts.[3] Already, in 1984, Keynes's engagement diaries had been transferred from the Marshall Library to King's in an attempt to iron out one discrepancy. But it was ever thus with the arranging of personal papers. Archivists are trained to expect and recognize the types of record produced, say, in the administration of a business or a town council. The internal structure of such organizations into departments or committees is retrievable from their documentary output and can be readily reflected in the arrangement of an archival catalogue. But the leavings of an individual may be as multifarious as her life and equally as chaotic. There are few hard and fast rules for cataloguing here, beyond the application of common sense and the preparation of detailed indexes to compensate for the seeming opacity of the author's "system."

In this specific case, identifying the original order or disorder was hindered by the checkered administrative history of the papers since 1946 and the number of hands that had combed through them for personal, biographical, or editorial purposes. Freedom of movement was further constrained by the number of scholars who were familiar with the collection on the basis of the existing if inadequate catalogues. Imagine the footnote implications if I changed anything!

Completed in 1993, the new catalogue has, for the material formerly housed at the Marshall Library, largely retained the arrangement of the former list, where papers were filed by subject. Within subject sections, however, certain files have been reorganized, their contents amalgamated with papers on the same subjects from later transfers, especially from among that material previously called "Miscellaneous," and their descriptions enlarged. By contrast, the original box list of the personal papers has been completely reworked. In certain cases, to improve coherence, material has been moved from one subject section to another or from the personal to the economics "halves" of the collection; the rounding up of Keynes's philosophical papers to the "Apostles" would be a good example here. A concordance of former and current document references has also been drawn up to aid in tracing these alterations in position,

3. In 1946, disposing of Keynes's "working library of economics books" (so described in his will), Kahn told John Saltmarsh, then librarian at King's College, "I have difficulty in accepting the view that the Theory of Probability is part of the Theory of Economics" (2 August, Kahn Papers RFK 3/44). One can assume the same outlook affected the division of his papers five years later.

together with a subject, name, and place index. In the cause of a logical, consistent, and full description of the papers for future scholars, I trust I have not overly confused readers used to the Ancien Regime.

I want to comment now on the way the collection has been used by scholars. I will confine my remarks to the period of my tenure at King's, that is from September 1990, after the reunion of the entire collection and completion of *The Collected Writings*. The published volumes of Keynes's papers, the first point of contact for intending scholars, have undoubtedly influenced the use of the originals. I cannot comment on the work produced from the published source material alone, but the editors themselves acknowledged that, while they had aimed at completeness in the publication of, for instance, his works of theory, his drafts and related discursive correspondence, his journalism and committee evidence, they had been selective and less conscientious in the treatment of other areas. Philosophical papers in particular were described as "outside our brief" (1989 in CW 30:xiv). So increasingly over time readers have returned to the papers to pursue themes only lightly touched on in *The Collected Writings* and to begin research into subjects formerly considered irrelevant to the man's development as an economist. After all, the thirty volumes represent only a third of the bulk classified as economic. And the personal papers were barely touched. Rod O'Donnell's projected five- to six-volume series to publish Keynes's philosophical writings, together with other previously overlooked material on economics, politics, and the arts, may redress the balance in part (O'Donnell 1994). It may also reduce demand for the originals. Perhaps the publication in 1993 of the entire collection on microfilm will, for those institutions sufficiently well endowed to afford the £9,700 necessary for 170 reels, remove much of the need for their academics to visit King's.

In the three and one-half years since I have been modern archivist, more than 120 researchers, chiefly North American, British, Italian, Japanese, and Australian, have consulted the Keynes Papers. Roughly two-thirds are economists interested in the development of Keynes's thought. Of the remainder, students of Bloomsbury aesthetics and modernist literature make up a significant proportion, followed by historians of interwar politics and economics in England, Continental Europe, and the United States; historians of thought and social policy; and critics of the fine and dramatic arts. Others come to scour the archive for the evidence it throws on the contributions of other major figures of the era—for example, the Cambridge economists in Keynes's circle, or the liberal and conservative politicians and social policy theorists with whom he corresponded. Here are a few research titles to illustrate the range of interests: the demise of Pigovian economics; Keynes, Kahn, and imperfect competition; Keynes's ethics; the interventionist mind, 1930–45; the reception of Keynes in Germany, 1929–35; progressivism and the British Labour Movement, 1935–45; the economics of rearmament, 1936–39; Anglo-American relations during World War II; the Arts Council; the Provincial Insurance Company; Walter Sickert; Ludwig Wittgenstein; Herbert Hoover.

What is particularly noteworthy about the body of researchers, however, is the fact that the economists, so long content simply to read the scribbles, notes, and drafts of dry theory, to participate exclusively in the internalist debate about Keynes's thought, are now broadening their archival trawl. Granted, for many this open-mindedness extends only to the inclusion of the early philosophical writings, in the analysis of which the methodology of the economist is perhaps little challenged. But for the more historically aware, I wonder whether this does not indicate the beginning of an acceptance that all theorizing or modeling takes place in contexts wider than those of the theory or model itself. Robert Skidelsky reminds us that "the rise or fall of ideas in economics is as much connected with attendant circumstances, including ideological and political circumstances, as with their logical properties or their power of passing any test of prediction" (Skidelsky 1986, xviii).

History *does* matter in Keynes scholarship. Neoclassicals can do without it seemingly, but how can we understand the debunking of standard equilibrium theory without appreciating the practical imperative of persistent, long-term unemployment in Britain throughout the 1930s? "Keynes's interests in economic theory were almost completely practical" (Moggridge 1975, 74). His long and short runs were modeled in real time, in the changed conditions of the twentieth century in which the traditional tenets of capitalism were patently not working. In Bradley Bateman's recent work, wide reading in the records of the Economic Advisory Council and the Macmillan Committee has located the elaboration of a theory of uncertainty squarely in the political and economic circumstances of the summer of 1933; it was not fixed immutable in Keynes's undergraduate musings on probability (Bateman 1994). In part, the preface to Don Moggridge's biography of Keynes reads as an apologia to his fellow economists for bringing the man's life and times into a consideration of his economics (Moggridge 1992, xvi–xxvi). Robert Skidelsky, out of a completely different stable, feels no such need. Perhaps part of the explanation for this growing interest in the contextualizing of Keynes's thought can be found in the desire to stand up to the monetarists, to explain Keynesian analysis anew in the wake of the discrediting 1970s. It may also stem from a broader desire to demonstrate the value of a time when economic theory was influenced by what was happening in the world.

So, installed in the archives, how do these new converts to the delights of documentary research conduct themselves? They make their notes by hand or laptop, which are, depending on the strength or otherwise of their English, succinct précis or laborious transcripts. Their document selection is either methodical or serendipitous; sidetracking diversions may uncover gems. They are reverential, excited (one academic who shall be nameless always speaks of "fondling the files"), or indifferent to the mystique of the original document that bears Keynes's own autograph. Many of the foreign visitors fight a battle of conscience between cramming in all they have to achieve in a week or two's study leave and making the most of Cambridge's seductive charms. Then there are those who, through fear or disdain, ignore the archivist and those, wise readers, who quickly appreciate that the way to archival nirvana is via her good offices! The more historically aware will ask questions about the administrative history of the collection and how the catalogue is arranged. The more pressed will immediately ask about xeroxing; the more hedonistic about the city's best pubs.

Despite the variety of interest shown in the Keynes Papers, I think there remain several areas of research comparatively unexplored. The first of these is a detailed study of Keynes as a journalist. It would consider the journalistic impulse as part of the armory of the "persuader," the rhetorician, intuiting the world and its problems for others. In this incarnation, Keynes described himself as both "propagandist" and "prostitute," yet he urged his fellow economists to "leave to Adam Smith alone the glory of the quarto . . . pluck the day, fling pamphlets into the wind, write always *sub specie temporis*, and achieve immortality by accident, if at all" (1933 in CW 10:199). This project would consider the political agenda to his writing on economics, particularly as proprietor of *The Nation* after 1923 when he was preoccupied with the relaunch of the Liberal party. Scholars might compare the man's style and content on the same issue, theoretical or practical, in both the quality and popular press. They would assess Keynes as an "outsider," a lobbyist, and weigh his influence on public opinion and the government. The archive material necessary to such a project survives in the manuscript and typescript drafts of the hundreds of articles he wrote in the 1920s and 1930s; in the scrapbooks of the published product compiled by his mother; and in the voluminous correspondence with editors and syndication agencies, politicians and civil servants, and contributors to his *Manchester Guardian Commercial Supplements* or *The Nation*.

Another project, one which I am sure I can predict as forthcoming, is that which examines more closely "group process" in the development of Keynesian economics, reading the Keynes Papers together with the records of other members of the Cambridge Circus. The records of Joan Robinson are already in the public domain at King's. But they are scanty. Analysis will benefit from the addition of the papers of Austin Robinson now at the Marshall Library, the opening of the Sraffa Collection at Trinity College, and the cataloguing of the records of Richard Kahn, on which I am currently engaged.

Keynes described himself as controversialist and a prima donna, unable to resist putting people right where he perceived stupidity, be it in managing the economy, running the university, or promoting the arts. There is sufficient archival evidence to bear out both titles and proof that his achievements lay in the combination of his talents, exactly that combination—mathematician, historian, statesman, philosopher—he so prized in Marshall (1933 in CW 10:173), rather than preeminence in any one area. For all that he frequently bemoaned his lack of leisure time, it is apparent that he understood his own nature. "When I sit as today," he wrote to Lydia on 1 February 1925, "at the matters of my book all day long, I feel it would be better if I had nothing else to think about. But I daresay it is not truly so. The mind becomes quickly stale and infertile (at least mine does) if it thinks only about one matter, so the distractions do not lose so much time as it seems" (Keynes Papers PP/45/190). Both archivist and academic can be grateful for his lack of repose.

References

Bateman, B. W. 1994. In the Realm of Concept and Circumstance. *HOPE* 26.1:99–116.

Harrod, R. F. 1951. *The Life of John Maynard Keynes*. London: Macmillan.

Holroyd, M. 1967–68. *Lytton Strachey: A Critical Biography.* 2 vols. London: Heinemann.

Johnson, E. S. 1978. Keynes from his Papers. In *The Shadow of Keynes: Understanding Keynes, Cambridge and Keynesian Economics.* Edited by E. S. and H. G. Johnson. Oxford: Basil Blackwell.

Kahn, R. F. Papers. King's College, Cambridge.

Keynes, John Maynard Papers. King's College, Cambridge.

Keynes, John Maynard. 1971–89. *The Collected Writings of John Maynard Keynes.* 30 vols. Edited by D. E. Moggridge. Cambridge: Cambridge University Press. (CW)

Moggridge, D. E. 1975. The Influence of Keynes on the Economics of His Time. In *Essays on John Maynard Keynes.* Edited by M. Keynes. Cambridge: Cambridge University Press.

———. 1992. *Maynard Keynes: An Economist's Biography.* London: Routledge.

O'Donnell, R. M. 1994. Editing Large Unpublished Writings: The Case of J. M. Keynes. Research Paper 388, School of Economic and Financial Studies, Macquarie University.

Skidelsky, R. 1986. *Hopes Betrayed, 1883–1920.* Vol. 1 of *John Maynard Keynes.* New York: Viking Penguin.

Comment

Michael S. Lawlor

I complement Jacky Cox on a job well done and welcome her careful and well-crafted presentation of the history, structure, and current use of the raw material of which Keynes scholarship is made.

As Jacky says, "this is a paper about papers, boxes and boxes of them." From the standpoint of the historian of ideas, and, after reading this article, also from the standpoint of the archivist, it is clear that the papers of a figure as intellectually important and as interesting as Keynes are a far cry from a collection of "wrong ideas of a dead man." Rather, they are a living record from which modern scholars can both draw insight about the life, work, and times of this great man, and they often form a basis by which to project his concerns onto current issues.

As I have next to nothing to criticize in Jacky's account, I wish instead to use my space here to suggest some ways in which her account raises issues of importance for the history of economics, remembering that this volume is an attempt to showcase the diverse nature Keynes scholarship is now assuming. Thus my reflection on the Keynes papers will consist of a number of questions and speculations suggested by her fascinating paper.

First, as a service to the community of scholars of economic thought, it would be interesting to know more about the character of the Keynes papers in comparison with other collections of similar import. I wonder what is distinctive in this regard about Keynes, compared to other scientific or intellectual figures of his stature. For example, is the treatment of personal versus professional papers and the attendant difficulties of classification that Jacky details at all peculiar to Keynes, his time, or his place? Just as a suggestive comparison, it strikes me that there is often little distinction between these spheres in the case of many literary figures. Think of James Joyce or D. H. Lawrence and their work, in which the personal is the raw material of the art and the personal papers, chiefly correspondence, have been a major factor in literary scholarship. On the other hand, might it be the case that modern scientists leave no personal papers whatsoever? Or that, if they do, there is very little interest expressed in them by chroniclers of their achievements?

Second, and related, are some questions about the organization, possible destruction, and public access of the Keynes papers—an issue about which, it seems to me, Jacky has much insight and some new evidence. She details the particulars of Keynes's will, the subsequent division of the papers by executors and archivists into the personal and the economic, and the controversy over the release of certain parts of the papers concerning Keynes's sexuality. This last topic would seem to merit further work, particularly given that Jacky's footnotes indicate the still-closed Kahn papers shed new light on the subject. It is exactly this type of issue that illuminates the living nature of a historical archive, for it is obvious that the treatment and use of at least these personal aspects of the Keynes papers tell as much about the executors, editors, and researchers as they do about Keynes himself.

As an example, consider the issue of Keynes's sexuality and its evident "embarrassing" nature for so many people. I suggest that the following questions may be worth exploring.

1. Was the decision to shield this part of Keynes from public view purely a private one by Geoffrey Keynes, or does it reflect a more widespread worry—not to say paranoia? It strikes me, for instance, that the discussion of what to hide and to destroy seems to have involved Keynes's wife very little.

2. What is the role of Roy Harrod in this regard? Jacky cites a 1969 letter from Harrod to Kahn, and the common lore among Keynes scholars is that Harrod consciously suppressed this aspect of Keynes's life. In fact, we know very little that is concrete in this regard. It all seems so mysterious.

For example, Roy Weintraub's memoir, in the recent *HOPE* minisymposium on Keynes, recounting Harrod dodging this issue at his father's table, is tantalizing in its evocation of Harrod's involvement. But it ends, frustratingly, where "the family's conversation ceased and we simply passed the potatoes and gravy in silence" (1994, 98). It was not Weintraub's intention to examine the issue in detail, but we are left wanting to know more. Perhaps Warren Young's forthcoming work using the Harrod papers in Japan will settle the matter.

3. Roy Weintraub's dating of this episode concerned the "outing" of Keynes presented in Holroyd's (1971) biography of Lytton Strachey.[1] It would appear, though, that not many economists read Holroyd's book, as it still caused something of a sensation in the profession (or, more likely, was the source of various jokes among economists) when Hession's (1983) "personal" biography and Skidelsky's (1983) first volume appeared, both of which contained more or less detailed coverage of Keynes's early homosexual relationships. Why should Keynes's sexuality be such a controversial issue? One answer concerns the narrow outlook of the profession as a whole. It has to be admitted that sex is a professionally taboo subject for economists and historians of economics. At least part of this is due to the seemingly inherent social conservatism of the discipline. Also, legitimately, it is often suggested that such personal issues are irrelevant to the scientific validity of anyone's economics. This is fair enough, but not in contradiction with the recent extension of Keynes scholarship into areas that are not so strictly economistic. From the context of modern cultural history, so suffused with gender analysis, gay studies, and so on, the reaction of the economic profession on this head to this day reflects a seriously provincial attitude.

4. To broaden this a bit, it is interesting to speculate on the extent to which history has validated the opinion of Geoffrey Keynes and Harrod on the issue of the dire consequences of Keynes's sexual proclivities for the influence of Keynesianism.

On the one hand, the public image of Keynes was sure to have suffered in the 1950s and 1960s from such exposure. One need only consider the relatively mild sexual content of the Profumo affair and the tragic treatment by the British government of one of Jacky's other Kingsmen, mathematician Alan Turing, to judge the median public opinion on this issue in postwar Britain. David Laidler, in oral discussion after Jacky

1. And why and how did the Keynes-Strachey correspondence get photocopied in the first place—against the wishes of Keynes's executors?

Cox's paper, mentioned that Keynes's sexuality was well known to the academic economics community in Britain in the 1950s, but that it was never mentioned in public. Perhaps the fears of Geoffrey Keynes and Harrod were reasonable. Even so, a more thorough cultural history of this context would be worthwhile.

On the other hand, there is recently accumulating a body of evidence by political scientists and historians on the paths by which Keynesian policies were achieved in various countries in the postwar era that implicitly questions the view of Keynes's executors. Examples include Jim Tomlinson's contribution here (this volume) and Peter Hall's (1989) recent collection, *The Political Power of Economic Ideas: Keynesianism across the Nations*. In a sobering majority of this work—sobering, that is, for specialists in Keynes's ideas—Keynes's own influence and ideas are little in evidence. This should certainly be humbling for what Hall calls in his introduction "economistic" historians of economics, who tend to neglect the details of the process by which economic doctrine influences policy, if at all. One is forced to wonder if Keynes's executors were perhaps overly enamored of the towering figure whose work they were responsible for in thinking that his polemical influence would survive even the grave. Would the worldwide dominance of free market politics today suddenly collapse if a historian were to find new evidence on the "personal" reasons that Adam Smith lived with his mother until her death and found little use for diamond wedding rings?

5. Finally, returning back to the Keynes papers themselves, was Keynes even aware of this issue? Did his choice of his more conventional brother Geoffrey to execute his personal papers implicitly recognize the dangers to his public image that the papers contained? Perhaps he really did mean it when he suggested that the majority of his papers be burned.[2] He did after all have the chance to include the "higher sodomy" as one of his "early beliefs" in his famous retrospective memoir.

No, I think Keynes would really have been above it all. Too old, too busy, too important to really give a damn what others made of the pieces of his life, including his sexuality—though confident the attempt would be made. In fact, Don Moggridge's (1992, 170) recent biography quotes one of Keynes's letters from 1906 that speaks directly to this very issue.

---

2. Skidelsky (1992, 36) claims in his recent volume that the really racy letters in the papers, those between Keynes and his last male lover, Sebastian Sprott—the same flamboyant Sprott who was fond of employing ex-convicts as houseservants while he was a professor of psychology at Nottingham University in the 1920s–were in fact burned by Geoffrey Keynes.

Replying to a friend about the risk of being "found out," Keynes writes: "We don't live in Russia and the police don't raid our drawers even if we've raided other people's. . . . The drawers of the dead are not sacred [though]—that is true."

Finally, two short suggested additions to Jacky's list of unexplored parts of the Keynes papers.

1. Jacky tells us that the rare books in Keynes's library were accounted for and saved, and in a footnote she mentions that his working library of economics books was "disposed of." Speaking from my own experience with the Keynes papers and the still extant copies of Alfred Marshall's books in the Marshall Library, I think it would be a great service to Keynes scholars if some effort were made to collect and catalogue the Keynes Library. Perhaps some effort along the lines of Bonar's Catalogue of the Library of Adam Smith is called for.

2. Besides Don Moggridge's very helpful tables and charts, and the selected documents included in the *Collected Writings*, no comprehensive study has ever been made of the records in the Keynes papers relating to his investment activity. This would appear to be a potentially valuable unexplored territory.

References

Hall, P., ed. 1989. *The Political Power of Economic Ideas: Keynesianism across the Nations.* Princeton: Princeton University Press.

Hession, C. H. 1983. *John Maynard Keynes: A Personal Biography of the Man Who Revolutionized Capitalism and the Way We Live.* New York: Macmillan.

Holroyd, M. 1971. *Lytton Strachey: A Biography.* Harmondsworth: Penguin.

Moggridge, D. E. 1992. *Maynard Keynes: An Economist's Biography.* London and New York: Routledge.

Skidelsky, R. 1983. *Hopes Betrayed, 1883–1920.* Vol. 1 of *John Maynard Keynes.* London: Macmillan.

————. 1992. *The Economist as Saviour, 1920–1937.* Vol. 2 of *John Maynard Keynes.* London: Macmillan.

Weintraub, Roy. 1994. Editor's Introduction, Minisymposium: Keynes's Lives in Several Communities. *HOPE* 26.197–98.

After the Revolution: Paul Samuelson and the Textbook Keynesian Model

Kerry A. Pearce and Kevin D. Hoover

The Keynesian Revolution and Normal Science

Thomas Kuhn's (1962) famous description of the development of science as radical revolutions followed by periods of steady elaboration of the revolutionary paradigm may not be the key to understanding scientific history or epistemology. It is nonetheless a useful heuristic. Revolutions are, of course, exhilarating; and, even in the historian's backward gaze, they command the most attention. Yet they are only half of Kuhn's conjugate pair, and normal science—the development and elaboration of the revolutionary paradigm—itself demands some attention.

The idea of the scientific revolution long predates Kuhn. Keynes sought self-consciously in *The General Theory of Employment, Interest and Money* (1936, v–viii) to stand traditional economics on its head, and early interpreters agreed that that was just what he had done. Lawrence Klein's interpretive book was entitled *The Keynesian Revolution* (1947).[1] Klein represents an excellent example of the other of Kuhn's conjugates. After paying homage to Keynes the revolutionary, Klein embarked on

We thank the participants in the conference on New Perspectives on Keynes, and especially Allin Cottrell, Don Patinkin, and Robert Clower for comments on an earlier draft.

1. Of course, not all commentators on Keynes believed that his work was revolutionary, even if they found it important. Hansen (1936a) initially argued that Keynes provided no new foundation for economics, although he soon altered his view (Hansen 1938). Hicks ([1937] 1967) saw Keynes as a special case of a general theory that nested both the classical and Keynesian models—hardly the stuff of revolution.

a classic career of normal science. He applied the (also new) tools of econometric analysis to the empirical implementation of the Keynesian model; the final results of which were the Federal Reserve–SSRC–Penn econometric model of the United States and Project LINK, which attempts to connect national macroeconomic models into a global macro model. Although Klein won the Nobel Prize for this work, it was not itself a revolution; for, as we tell our students, the beating heart of every major macroeconometric model is a little IS-LM model.

Elaboration of the paradigm is not all there is to normal science, however, just as important is the way in which normal science enforces and maintains its norms. One method of doing this is to establish a canon. The canon, however, comprises original texts that are rooted in the context of lively debate. Their authors may have been giants, but they were fallible nonetheless. To the degree that the canonical texts are seen as the contingent products of people, times, and places, they are subject to fundamental revision. Normal science can keep the student and practitioner on the straight and narrow if there develops an interpretive tradition that makes it unnecessary to consult the canonical texts with all their ambiguity, passion, and contingency. The development of textbooks is a hallmark of that interpretive tradition. Teachers of economics sometimes complain that, pedagogical style apart, current economics textbooks are almost all alike. This should be no surprise, for vis-à-vis normal science, that is exactly the point.

The existence of canonical textbooks is a considerable part of what distinguishes economics from other social sciences. In this article, we offer a preliminary history of the development in economics of the textbook tradition (a key aspect of normal science). Our history is told mostly through the work of Paul Samuelson, in particular through the successive fourteen editions of his *Economics*, first published in 1948. And who better? For among economists, Samuelson is Mr. Science. He is widely credited with establishing the scientific ideal in economics at the graduate and professional level with his 1947 *Foundations of Economic Analysis*.[2] He

---

2. Weintraub 1991, chap. 3 describes the scientific mileau in which *Foundations* was conceived, particularly Samuelson's debts to physicist and statistician E. B. Wilson and population biologist A. J. Lotka. Boland 1989 argues plausibly that it is Samuelson's methodological approach to economics, one dominated by his understanding of the essence of scientific method in the late 1930s and early 1940s, that enjoys the practical allegiance of the economics profession, despite the attention and lip service paid to Milton Friedman's 1953 "Methodology of Positive Economics."

takes pride in being a scientist: much of his life's work is gathered under the title *The Collected* Scientific *Papers of Paul A. Samuelson* (1966–86; emphasis added). The citation for his Nobel prize in Economic Science (to quote its correct title) reads in part: "for scientific work through which he has developed static and dynamic economic theory and actively contributed to raising the level of analysis in economic science" (Lindbeck 1985, 40).

History is about what it was like then and how it became what it is like now. What we offer here is a history of the normal science embodied in the Keynesian economic model in the Principles textbooks since World War II. We emphasize process. It is important to understand at the outset that, in keeping with our theme of normal science, this is the history of the "hydraulic" (Coddington's 1983 [chap. 6, sect. 3] term) or "bastard" (Robinson's 1962 term) Keynesian model; it is (in Leijonhufvud's 1966 famous distinction) Keynesian Economics and not the Economics of Keynes. Futhermore, our concern is exclusively with the American textbook tradition, and not with how things have developed in Britain or elsewhere.

Then and Now

These disclaimers aside, it is easier to understand the story if we know where we are starting from and where we are going. To identify the starting point, it is useful to consider the main points of *The General Theory* as summarized, for example, in its chapter 18 (or in Keynes 1937). The key features are (a) the aggregative framework represented in the $Y = C + I$ or $I = S$ relationships (this was a triumph of rhetoric, avoiding many of the thornier controversies of the early 1930s with carefully chosen definitions; cf. Hansen 1936a); (b) the distinction between the monetary and the barter economy that is embodied in the rejection of Say's law and the existence of independent aggregate supply and aggregate demand curves; which (c) depended in turn on an analysis of labor markets in which, without further market imperfections, workers could be involuntarily unemployed whenever aggregate demand was deficient; and given (d) the marginal propensity to consume less than one, which implies the multiplier, aggregate demand would be deficient in fact, unless other spending, principally investment or government capital expenditure filled the gap; investment depended upon the comparison of (e) the marginal efficiency of capital with the rate of interest, which in turn was

determined by the interaction of monetary policy and (f) liquidity preference; given the state of (g) expectations, upon which both the marginal
efficiency of capital and liquidity preference depended, investment might
be insufficient to hold aggregate demand at a level high enough for full
employment; a deficiency that could be made up for by (h) programs of
government capital expenditure.

It is striking how successful the Keynesian agenda has been in one
form or another in the textbooks. The latest edition of Samuelson's *Economics* (the fourteenth, now coauthored with William Nordhaus) is organized around these key Keynesian points. This is also true of virtually all
macroeconomics textbooks.[3] In addition to the main features of *The General Theory*, Samuelson and most other textbooks on economic principles
and intermediate macroeconomics today also include features unknown
to Keynes, the two most prominent being Okun's law and the Phillips
curve.

It was not always like this, however. The textbooks of 1948 were not
dominantly Keynesian, and even Samuelson's (1948) first edition was
not tightly structured around Keynes's own conceptual framework. How
then did the textbooks of the 1940s evolve into the textbooks of 1994? Our
view is that this process represents a taming of the Keynesian revolution.
While *The General Theory* was a theoretical rather than a policy-oriented
book, its underlying motivation was to bring intellectual coherence to a
family of antidepression policies that had already been widely supported
on pragmatic grounds (see Clarke 1988). The Keynesian revolution in
practice was both a revolution in policy and in theory. By 1994, however,
the policy revolution had essentially been forgotten, and the analytical
framework could be regarded as essentially neutral: it was adequate for
the analysis of any sort of policy. The ubiquity of the Keynesian framework is underlined by the small number of obvious exceptions: Miller
and Upton's (1974) *Macroeconomics: A Neoclassical Introduction* and
Barro's (1993) *Macroeconomics* are true dissenters. The taming of the
Keynesian revolution by the normal science of textbook Keynesianism
begins with Samuelson's first edition in 1948 (S1-1948).[4]

---

3. Baumol and Blinder 1991, Lipsey et al. 1993, McConnell 1987, to name a few of the
principles books; Dornbusch and Fischer 1994, Gordon 1993, Hall and Taylor 1993, to name a
few of the intermediate macroeconomics books.
    4. Hereafter the editions of Samuelson's *Economics* will be indicated by S[edition number]-
[publication date].

The Problem of Keynesian Interpretation: The Search for a Model

Revolutions do not resolve into normal science without a period of turmoil and confusion. The decade after publication of *The General Theory* was such a period. To understand the environment in which Samuelson's first edition was launched, we must briefly consider the history of this period.

Was Keynes a revolutionary? If so, what was the nature of the revolution? These questions animated the debate over *The General Theory* from the beginning. A prior question was the nature of Keynes's contribution: Was it to economic theory or to economic policy? *The General Theory* was widely reviewed in the United States, not only in economics journals but also in serious popular magazines such as the *Saturday Review* and *The Nation*. Reactions were mixed. On the one hand, it received a number of favorable reviews (Franklin 1936; Hardy 1936) that praised its freshness, consistency, and lack of the arrogance typical of the heterodox economist. Other reviewers thought it seriously incomplete (Stewart 1936; Taylor 1936). Writing in *The New Republic*, Taylor opined that "the *General Theory* will not add directly to [Keynes's] popular prestige" because it was written in "a highly abstruse and mathematical fashion" (1936, 349).[5] Alvin Hansen opens his famously negative review by applying to *The General Theory* Keynes's own words from a review of J. A. Hobson's *Gold, Prices and Wages*: "This book is . . . made much worse than a really stupid book could be, by exactly those characteristics of cleverness and intermittent reasonableness which have borne good fruit in the past" (1936a, 667). Later in the review Hansen writes:

> The book under review is not a landmark in the sense that it lays a foundation for a 'new economics.' . . . The book is more a symptom of economic trends than a foundation stone upon which a science can be built. . . . It is reasonably safe to predict that Keynes's new book will, so far as his theoretical apparatus is concerned, fare little better than did the *Treatise on Money*. (686)

Hansen grasps the main lines of *The General Theory* and sees Keynes's as a contributor to economic theory, albeit not a revolutionary one. Indeed, he argues that Keynes's theory "is not tenable except upon

---

5. Would that Mr. Taylor could review, say, the books of Thomas Sargent!

the assumptions of an approach to a rigid economy in which costs are highly inflexible and supplies monopolistically controlled" (Hansen 1936b, 829).

Other commentators saw Keynes as a revolutionary in the matter of economic policy, but were skeptical: "The ideas put forward by Keynes would entail a revolution in power and property, but we can hardly believe that mankind will accept a new economic and social set-up by persuasion" (Lederer 1936, 487).

The dual aspect of Keynes's revolution remained in the American debate for some time. Famous in his rejection of Keynes, Hansen became yet more famous for his Pauline conversion to Keynesianism. By the time his review of Keynes from the *Journal of Political Economy* (Hansen 1936a) was reprinted, he had removed the passages most damning of Keynes's theoretical achievement (Hansen 1938, 34). The Oxford symposium of 1936—which led to the famous interpretive papers of Harrod, Meade, and Hicks (see Young 1987, chap. 1, esp. pp. 12–38)—was critical. Hansen was greatly influenced by Hicks, calling his contribution "brilliant" (Hansen 1949, 71). In Young's (1987, 115) word, his series of proselytizing books (Hansen 1949, 1951, 1953) "institutionalized" Hicks's SI-LL diagram under the now standard name of IS-LM. Hansen effectively joined the theoretical and the policy aspects of the Keynesian revolution, showing how the IS-LM apparatus could be used for policy analysis. While this established a major interpretive tradition eventually to become the core of textbooks in intermediate macroeconomics, it took a long time to become the standard analysis. Hansen's work remained for some time part of revolutionary faction rather than the foundation of normal science.

The interpretive approach, of which the IS-LM model was a part, also formed the basis for another aspect of the development of Keynesian economics. In America, Modigliani 1944 and Klein 1947 (appendix) formalized the Keynesian model in a manner very close to that of Hicks [1937] 1967. As observed above, this was the beginning of the program of Keynesian econometrics. Klein also made a first attempt at deriving the key Keynesian functions from the behavior of individual economic actors—an early contribution to the program of microfoundations for macroeconomics that was developed in the work of Clower 1965, Friedman 1957, Patinkin 1956, Tobin 1958, and others. This program, too, may be seen as ultimately the working out of normal science, but in its beginnings it remained mired in debates over the true meaning of *The*

General Theory and over which assumptions and specifications were necessary to obtain essential Keynesian conclusions such as the existence of involuntary unemployment.

Whereas for Hansen Keynes heralded a theoretical revolution (at least as he was interpreted by Hicks), for Abba Lerner it was the Keynesian policies that were revolutionary. Lerner used his own theoretical insights to promote Keynesian policies. He clarified the paradox of thrift, showing how the sense of paradox arose from a fallacy of composition (Scitovsky 1984, 1556). He pioneered the macroeconomics of rigid wages and prices. He showed that for a decrease in wages to stimulate employment, wages and prices would have to fall instantaneously and to the full extent needed to return the economy to full employment. Lerner points out that this perfect flexibility is incompatible with a monetary economy (Scitovsky 1984, 1558).

Lerner's theory of functional finance met with stiff resistance at first, but it soon became accepted as the clearest representation of Keynesian policy prescriptions (Scitovsky 1984, 1561). David Colander aptly observes:

> What eventually became known as textbook Keynesian policies were in many ways Lerner's interpretations of Keynes's policies, especially those expounded in *The Economics of Control* (1944) and later in *The Economics of Employment* (1951). . . . Textbook expositions of Keynesian policy naturally gravitated to the black and white 'Lernerian' policy of Functional Finance rather than the grayer Keynesian policies. Thus, the vision that monetary and fiscal policy should be used as a balance wheel, which forms a key element in the textbook policy revolution, deserves to be called Lernerian rather than Keynesian. (1984, 1573)

By 1948, the Keynesian revolution in the upper reaches of the economics profession was stabilizing around a rich hydraulic Keynesianism: the IS-LM model on the theoretical side and Lerner's analysis on the policy side. Elementary textbooks did not settle down so easily. Keynesian ideas entered them in bits and pieces.

The attitude of textbook writers before 1948 is summarized in a characteristic remark from one of them:

> Whether we agree fully with the Keynesian theory or not, and regardless of whether we accept the practical measures to meet the prob-

lem of unemployment that are offered by Keynes and Hansen and their followers, we cannot afford to ignore the impact upon traditional economic theory which has been made by the theory of savings and investment.[6] (Meyers 1948, viii)

The "impact" of Keynes is shown in the coverage his ideas receive in texts. In Meyers's last edition of *Elements of Modern Economics* (1948), the chapter on saving, investment, and employment (chap. 25) is based mainly on *The General Theory*, although "many of the statements . . . are not in strictly Keynesian terms" (396n). Meyers's book adopts the Keynesian national accounting scheme, permits equilibrium with underemployment, and uses liquidity preference to help determine the interest rate. Missing, however, are key pieces of the Keynesian model: the marginal propensity to consume, the consumption function, and the multiplier.

The quotation from Meyers's textbook is instructive: Keynes is being absorbed into American textbooks at one remove, and Hansen is a primary transmission mechanism. But just as Hansen's reaction to *The General Theory* in his more advanced work underwent a transformation, so did his treatment of Keynes in his elementary textbook. In the second edition of *Principles of Economics*, Hansen and his coauthor Frederic Garver teach the classical approach of Say's law: "The monetary and credit facilities of a country usually find in the long run reasonably full employment" (Garver and Hansen 1937, 333). The only mention of Keynes is in the chapter on business cycles, and this is just a passing reference: "A long list of writers, including Spiethoff, Wicksell, Robertson, and Keynes, have advanced the view that the essential characteristic of the business cycle is the fluctuation in investment in capital goods" (363).

Garver and Hansen's third edition (1947) is somewhat more Keynesian, but even it is incomplete. It focuses mainly on the Keynesian accounting scheme, mentioning the marginal propensity to consume and the multiplier only briefly. It does, however, completely adopt the Keynesian view that the price level is better explained through "aggregate demand" or "income theory" than through a Fisherine quantity equation (233–36). Nevertheless, it is only in Hansen's later textbooks (1949, 1951, 1953) that a complete Keynesian model is present.

---

6. The earlier, second edition of this text (Meyers 1941) had not contained any discussion of Keynesian theory.

Other textbooks are selective in their use of Keynesian analysis. Benham and Boddy adopt a single Keynesian tool: a liquidity-preference function. They argue that Keynes's (and Hansen's) analysis is, in the main, an "economics of slump," believing themselves "that something approaching full employment can and will be achieved" (1947, 10).

Although borrowing more from the Keynesian toolkit (underemployment equilibrium, the propensity to consume, the paradox of thrift, and liquidity preference), John Ise's *Economics* (1950, 406) also denies the generality of Keynes's analysis, calling Keynes the leader of "depression economists" and confining systematic Keynesian analysis to a single chapter. In contrast, Valdemar Carlson's *An Introduction to Modern Economics* (1946), is more favorable to Keynes, though still incomplete— and still filtered through Hansen. Carlson uses some Keynesian terminology and advocates some Keynesian policies, and he sees effective demand as the key to unemployment policy. He argues that once full employment is achieved, public policy can attempt to increase investment to combine with consumption to maintain full employment. Alvin Hansen is Carlson's main source, not Keynes himself.

While many textbooks found the essence of Keynes in his treatment of aggregate demand, most adopted only selected elements of Keynesian analysis. At the same time, a largely separate struggle to incorporate a Keynesian analysis of aggregate supply into textbooks was under way. King observes that a large part of the reason for debate about aggregate supply was that Keynes

> did not provide a diagrammatic exposition of his argument. . . . Had he done so, however, it would have been in Z,N space, where Z represents aggregate proceeds (realised or expected), and N the level of employment. Keynes's aggregate supply and demand curves clearly would not have been drawn in P,Q (price level-quantity of output) space, as in modern textbooks. But aggregate supply and demand lay at the core of Keynes's analysis. (1993, 4)

Fifteen years after publication of *The General Theory*, confusion still reigned about aggregate supply and demand. The lack of a consensus view on the treatment of aggregate supply is reflected in the differences in diagrammatic presentation. Different articles and monographs mapped on the vertical axis, variously, individual price, the money value of expenditure, the real value of expenditure, and the aggregate price level and on the horizontal axis, variously, individual output, aggregate employment, the real value of aggregate output, and the money value of aggregate output (King 1993, 32). Only relatively late, in Joseph McKenna's *Aggregate Economic Analysis* (1955) does the aggregate supply curve appear in something close to the form common in modern textbooks.

Lorie Tarshis's *Elements of Economics* (1947) is often regarded as the first systematically Keynesian textbook (see Blaug 1991, 74). Tarshis's book was a self-conscious break with the contemporary textbook tradition; it identified *The General Theory* as its major inspiration, placing a greater emphasis on the determination of national income than on the theory of distribution (Tarshis 1947, x, 346). Tarshis includes the essential elements of the Keynes's agenda, but he rejects the view that Keynes provides only the economics of the slump, carefully distinguishing between the beneficial employment effects of aggregate demand expansion below full employment and its inflationary and distributional effects at full employment (475). He also moderates the policy aspects of the Keynesian revolution: "To conclude that an increase in public investment would bring about a rise in employment does not necessarily mean that we should endorse that remedy" (518; cf. 499). Thus, Tarshis's book was a systematic Keynesian textbook, but it did not capture the hearts and minds of the economics teacher. It did not succeed in "normalizing" the new Keynesian science of macroeconomics because it remained too close to Keynes's canonical text. It was more like the exegetical commentaries, main debating tools of the scholastics, that remind the reader that interpretation of the canonical text was up for grabs, than like the pedestrian primer that makes the reader wonder how there could ever have been a passionate debate in the first place.[7]

Another book that was Keynesian in its outlook was the second edition of Kenneth Boulding's *Economic Analysis* (1948). Like Tarshis's textbook, Boulding's book reminds the reader that Keynesian concepts are still elements in debate and are still held tentatively subject to further analysis and discovery. Boulding, for example, uses an aggregate supply and demand diagram in PQ space, *but* he uses it to point out the dangers of aggregative thinking, arguing that if one tries to draw supply and demand diagrams for output as a whole, "no solution is possible" (262).

Textbooks like those of Tarshis and Boulding in some sense repre-

---

7. Elzinga (1992, 864) suggests that Samuelson's textbook had a "second-mover" advantage, Tarshis's book having paved the way for it and having drawn hostile responses that would inevitably meet the first Keynesian textbook.

sented a high-water mark in the influence of Keynes on elementary economics, but they remained part of the Keynesian revolution and were unable to ensure a "return to normalcy." For that, students had to wait for Samuelson's *Economics*.

Samuelson's First Edition: Bastard Keynesianism or Virgin Birth?

Samuelson's *Economics* succeeded in establishing normal science where earlier textbooks had failed in large measure because, unlike the authors of those earlier books, Samuelson did not attempt to explicitly and faithfully reproduce Keynes's ideas. Joan Robinson labeled hydraulic Keynesian models as "bastards," a term that suggests they are the product of an irregular liaison. In the case of Samuelson, however, it may be closer to the mark to absolve Keynes of paternity altogether. In some sense, Samuelson's macroeconomic model is the product of a virgin birth. As with the more famous story of Jesus, the birth of Samuelson's model is more complicated.

Keynes is the Joseph of the story. For just as Jesus was careful to identify himself as a branch of Jesse's tree, as a true member of the House of David, Samuelson's model is called Keynesian, though it bears a highly circumscribed relation to *The General Theory*.[8] In Samuelson's first edition, there are only two references to Keynes—and neither is truly substantial. The connection to Keynes is invoked without the details of Keynes's analysis, and Samuelson's first edition does not make reference to the rich interpretative tradition of the years between 1936 and 1948. He does not mention Hicks, Hansen, Meade, or Harrod; nor does he mention Tarshis, Boulding, or the other textbook writers.

The core of the macroeconomic model of the first edition of *Economics* is the 45-degree diagram frequently known as the "Keynesian cross." This diagram does not appear in *The General Theory*, and Samuelson's

---

8. Our metaphor should not be misunderstood. We do not mean to imply that the content of Samuelson's book is antithetic or contrary to *The General Theory* or that Samuelson was ignorant of Keynes. In calling Samuelson's model a virgin birth, we instead wish to stress that identification with a Keynesian school of thought was a secondary consideration for Samuelson, and that the development of his model was not substantially constrained by considerations of fidelity to Keynes's intentions, exposition, or method. Samuelson serves the god of economics, not the law of Keynes. Don Patinkin has suggested to us that this attitude is an illusion due to the fact that writers of textbooks aim not at scholars but at students, and therefore rarely carefully document their sources. We do not believe this is an adequate explanation because, as we show presently, Samuelson's attitude is similar in his own scholarly work.

use of it derives directly from his two papers on the interaction of the multiplier and the acceleration principle (Samuelson 1939a, 1939b). In these papers, the multiplier is mentioned in connection with Keynes, although the tone of the discussion suggests an idea that is just "in the air."[9] The accelerator principle is also not Samuelson's own invention, but is taken by him to be a commonly accepted tool of the business-cycle literature. Samuelson himself appears to recognize that it is not Keynesian (1939b, 787). His own contribution is to explore the cyclical properties of models containing both multipliers and accelerators.[10]

To begin his analysis, Samuelson first considers "the position of the equilibrium state which, if established, would maintain itself and around which all oscillations take place." Without any induced investment, the stationary level of income must be that which businesses "receive back from consumers the whole amount which they pay out to factors as costs of production" (1939b, 789–90). This is illustrated in the 45-degree diagram as the intersection between the typical consumption function and a 45-degree line. When net investment is included, the level at which income can remain stationary is higher. This is shown in the diagram by raising the consumption function to cross the 45-degree line at a higher level of income. "There is, of course, no reason why the stationary equilibrium level could not be very near the level of full employment" (Samuelson 1939b, 791). The 45-degree diagram occupies a mere two pages in the article and is not used any further there. A decade later, the 45-degree diagram became the analytical core of Samuelson's first edition. To extend the sacred metaphor, we might think of the intervening years as its time in the carpenter's shop.

Samuelson's first edition, to be sure, has some characteristically Keynesian features. The accounting system, $Y = C + I + G$, forms the backbone of the book.[11] As he puts it, "national income provides the central unifying theme of the book" (S1-1948, v). The marginal propensity to con-

9. Whether or not the analysis underlying the 45-degree diagram is to be found in Keynes is hotly debated (see Davidson 1989; Fusfeld 1985; Patinkin 1989). We are inclined to agree with Patinkin and with Allin Cottrell, our discussant at the conference on New Perspectives on Keynes, that the Keynesian cross is a rendering of a simplified analysis of the macroeconomy found in *The General Theory* (especially chap. 3). However, as noted in note 8 above, Samuelson's use of it is detached from its Keynesian roots.

10. Samuelson (1939a, 75) credits the multiplier-accelerator model to Hansen.

11. Don Patinkin has pointed out that it is not to Keynes but to Colin Clark and Simon Kuznets that this accounting system is ultimately due. Nevertheless, it is clearly the system that Keynes adopts in *The General Theory*.

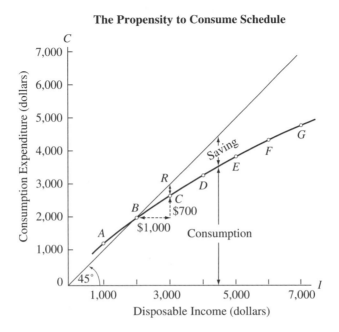

The Propensity to Consume Schedule

Figure 1   The 45-degree diagram for a single family (source: Samuelson's *Economics*, 1st ed., 1948, p. 210). This shows how consumption depends on family income.

sume and the multiplier are fundamental to the analysis of the 45-degree diagram. Samuelson constructs a propensity-to-consume schedule for a single family (see figure 1). The intersection of the propensity to consume (the consumption function) and the 45-degree line is called the "break-even income" where families spend exactly what they make (S1-1948, 210).

From the analysis of the single family, Samuelson aggregates his model to provide the "modern theory of income analysis." He stresses that the level of total spending is determined by the interplay of the forces of saving and investment (S1-1948, 253). The propensity-to-consume schedules were previously developed in relation to "behavior of a typical family as it receives more or less income. Now we want to add up all the different family patterns to get the propensity-to-consume schedule for the whole community" (257). The system converges to equilibrium at the intersection of the propensity-to-consume and the 45-degree line.

**The Consumption and
Saving Schedules**

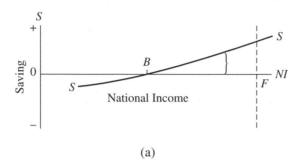

(a)

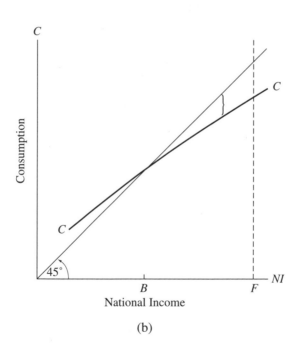

(b)

Figure 2   The 45-degree diagram for the community (source: Samuelson's *Economics*, 1st ed., 1948, p. 258). In these propensity-to-save and propensity-to-consume schedules, the vertical distances shown by brackets are equal.

The analysis is presented graphically (see figure 2) and verbally—but not algebraically.

Samuelson elaborates the basic 45-degree model. The multiplier is introduced verbally, then presented graphically using the diagram. Thereafter Samuelson models investment as dependent on national income and discusses the paradox of thrift, the idea that an increase in thriftiness may cause a deeper depression. To disentangle the paradox, he appeals to two considerations: first, he notes the problem of the fallacy of composition—an individual increases personal savings with greater thrift, but in aggregate this need not be so because income adjusts; second, the paradox is restricted to situations below full employment (S1-1948, 270): "If output could be assumed to be always at its maximum, then the old-fashioned doctrine of thrift would be absolutely correct" (271). In advocating the soundness of the paradox of thrift, Samuelson at the same time underwrites the Keynesian denial of Say's law.

Samuelson faithfully relates Keynes's theory of liquidity preference as part—but only a part—of the determination of interest rates (S1-1948, 304). Samuelson acknowledges that interest rates may be depressed by expansionary monetary policy and that investment may be stimulated by the lower rates, but he puts little store in the mechanism and does not integrate the discussion of money with the discussion of income determination. Money is a fifth wheel in Samuelson's model: "Today . . . we no longer hold out high hopes for effectively maintaining full employment and high production by means of Federal Reserve monetary policy" (338). Perhaps, Samuelson says, monetary policy is ineffective because of the existence of excess reserves. Open-market purchases may serve only to increase excess reserves, with the action ending there. Monetary policy cannot be used to dampen the business cycle: "An expansionary monetary policy may not lower effective interest rates very much but may simply spend itself in making everybody more liquid" (353).

Key features of Keynes's analysis are missing in Samuelson's first edition. While Samuelson acknowledges an underemployment equilibrium and discusses money in the detached manner already noted, he does not seriously consider the difference between the real and the monetary economy. The core 45-degree model is a real one in which monetary factors play no role. Samuelson's investment analysis appeals to the acceleration principle—a non-Keynesian idea—and, even here, the context is his discussion of the theory of business cycles. The acceleration principle is connected to the 45-degree diagram only indirectly: "We may be in a vicious circle whereby the acceleration principle and the multiplier interact so as to produce a cumulative deflationary (or inflationary) spiral" (S1-1948, 407).

A checklist of Keynesian features—present or absent—does not do justice to Samuelson's achievement. His *Economics* is above all a harmonist book. The core model continues in its sanctified role as the Prince of Peace among competing economic doctrines. The foundations of the peaceable kingdom are, above all, in *scientific* economics. Students of economics are encouraged to become scientists: "At every point of our analysis we shall be seeking to shed light on . . . policy problems. But to succeed in this, the student of economics must first cultivate an objective and detached ability to see things as they are, regardless of his likes or dislikes" (S1-1948, 5).

Science, for Samuelson, is not just a matter of naive realism; it also relies on a neutral and generally applicable analytical framework: "The important thing is to provide the analytical machinery that will enable the reader to arrive at, and defend, his own opinion, and, what is hardly less important, to understand the position of those with whom he most disagrees" (S1-1948, vi). With this in mind, Samuelson sets out the course of study: "The first task of modern economic science [is] to describe, to analyze, to explain, to correlate these fluctuations of national income" (4). Once this is done,

> the important hard kernel of truth in the older economics of full employment can then be separated from the chaff of misleading applications. Moreover, as we shall see later, if modern economics does its task well so that widespread unemployment is substantially banished from democratic societies, then its importance will wither away and traditional economics (whose concern is wise allocation of fully employed resources) will really come into its own—almost for the first time. (10)

Samuelson's analysis thus reconciles the competing economics of Keynes and the classics—establishing a heaven of economic analysis on earth by attacking the original sin of slack resources.[12]

---

12. Allin Cottrell reminds us of a passage in *The General Theory* (378–79) that is remarkably like the quotation from Samuelson. As we show in the next two paragraphs, however, the relationship between the Keynesian and classical analysis is much more policy-oriented, and therefore more Lernerian, than Keynes's own analysis.

In the first edition, the harmony that Samuelson establishes is not a harmony of a very general analytical apparatus in which Keynesian and classical economic analysis appear indifferently as special cases. His harmony is one in which positive policy actions must cure the imperfections of the economy, removing the special circumstances in which Keynesian analysis is essential and establishing the special circumstances in which classical analysis is informative. In keeping with our metaphor, a demanding ethics is required of Samuelson's believer. The difficulty that economics must face, in Samuelson's view, is that there is no guarantee "that there will be just exactly the required amount of investment to ensure full employment: not too little so as to cause unemployment, nor too much as to cause inflation" (S1-1948, 255). Samuelson appeals to Abba Lerner's analogy of the economy as "a system without a steering wheel" (S1-1948, 255; cf. 407–9).

Samuelson advocates fiscal policies that aim to supply the missing "governor" or "steering mechanism" for the economy. Fiscal policy has two main goals: countering the business cycle and providing secular stimulus. Samuelson advocates public works, welfare spending, and tax policy as countercyclical measures. He maintains that few people would object to the objects of countercyclical policy (S1-1948, 417). He is, however, frank about the difficulties of implementing it: difficulties of planning, timing, crowding out, and coordination between government bodies (especially coordination of state and local government with federal government). He regards policies for secular stimulus as far more controversial, noting that "many eminent economists are opposed to any policy of continuous deficits" (418).

While Samuelson's peaceable kingdom offers a truth available to advocates of different policy ends, it depends on particular policies itself. These might be described as moderately liberal. From such a standpoint, Samuelson is able to strike a neutral pose between extreme policies. Samuelson credits much of the modern income analysis to Keynes, but adds that "today its broad fundamentals are increasingly accepted by economists of all schools of thought, including, it is important to notice, many writers who do not share Keynes' particular policy viewpoints and who differ on technical details of analysis" (S1-1948, 253). Samuelson is quick to separate this analysis from the narrow definition of "Keynesian": "in the sense of belonging to that narrow band of zealots associated with some of the policy programs that Keynes himself espoused during the Great Depression" (254).

Samuelson's pose of neutrality and detachment from Keynes's own policy positions is perhaps the essential first step in taming the Keynesian revolution and setting macroeconomics on the path of normal science. Samuelson is subsequently able to convert what might have been thought to be disputes about normative ends into technical disputes about scientific economics. He thus stigmatizes various monetary cranks: "Some monetary cranks think that this [leakage of] saving necessarily means unemployment and depression. Such a view is simply incorrect" (S1-1948, 263). "But there is also a second school of monetary cranks: they go to the opposite extreme and insist that saving and investment can never cause income to be too high or too low. . . . It is only in the last few decades that economists have learned how to separate out the truth and falsity of both extreme viewpoints" (264). Keynes himself (1936, chaps. 23–24) found significant insights and inspiration in the imperfect analyses of monetary cranks such as Major Douglas and Silvio Gesell. He appreciated the linkage between their policy concerns and their attempts to formulate adequate understandings of the economy. His joint theoretical/policy revolution aimed in part to perfect the deficiencies of their analysis. Samuelson's technocratic dismissals of the monetary cranks underscores the extent to which he has moved beyond Keynes in normalizing macroeconomics.

Divine figures resolve paradoxes by embracing them. Samuelson's *Economics* presents the neoclassical microeconomics of resource allocation and, simultaneously, the Keynesian economics of underemployment. Samuelson's advocacy of full employment policies may in a practical sense serve his liberal politics, but its analytic goal is to resolve the paradox between Keynes and the (neo-)classics. This is accomplished through studied vagueness. There is no serious attempt to reconcile the macroeconomics of his first edition with microeconomics; resolution of the paradox is then mostly an avoidance of its implications. The 45-degree diagram is helpful in this regard: it is, at best, one piece of an analytical model, not a closed model in itself. The advantage of featuring such a model centrally is that it is easy to justify the need to add verbal qualifications and nuances to the analytical framework—as Samuelson constantly does—to make it speak to a wide range of issues without facing the problem of developing a model that is both internally consistent and informative about the world. The cost of this strategy is that Samuelson's model is not a closed system that could, for example, be developed into a full-scale econometric model, which is the fate of the richer hydraulic Keynesian models from IS-LM on.

The True Church: The Developments of Samuelson's Later Editions

Samuelson's *Economics* went through eleven editions in which he was the sole author; it remains in print (editions twelve to fourteen were coauthored with William Nordhaus). It is among the best-selling textbooks in any field.[13] Principal features of Samuelson's text remain unchanged over a period of forty-six years. We have argued that Samuelson's "son" of Keynes was really the product of a virgin birth; it also appears true that, in common with other products of immaculate conception, the analytical apparatus of Samuelson's *Economics* has remained unsullied by its confrontation with the world. The larger uses of that apparatus have also remained unchanged: Samuelson of the eleventh edition remains the harmonist and neutral scientist of the first edition. Maintaining neutrality is a difficult business that must be actively pursued. Over five decades, Samuelson has had to respond to various challenges, so that subsequent editions are considerably different from the first. The church has history, despite the constancy of its core doctrine.

As we observed already, in the first edition, Samuelson had sought to explicitly identify his macroeconomic analysis with Keynes, while nonetheless distancing it from the particular policies Keynes advocated in the 1930s and the subsequent policy positions of Keynesian "zealots"; at the same time, he argued that proper policies would underwrite the relevance of classical allocation theory. In subsequent editions, Keynes becomes increasingly deemphasized and the harmonist ideal becomes more prominent. In the second edition, Samuelson writes:

> In recent years, 90 per cent of American economists have stopped being "Keynesian economists" or "anti-Keynesian economists." Instead they have worked toward a synthesis of whatever is valuable in older economics and in modern theories of income determination. The result

13. Data in Elzinga (1992, table 3) show that up to 1984 Samuelson's *Economics* had cumulative domestic sales of 3,031,499, just greater than those of the various editions of McConnell (1987). But McConnell's textbook first appeared twelve years after Samuelson's, and outsold it in most of the years after 1966.

might be called neo-classical economics and is accepted in its broad outlines by all but about 5 per cent of extreme left-wing and right-wing writers. (S2-1951, 260)

By the third edition, Samuelson has coined one of the most famous phrases in the history of macroeconomics and underscored his harmonist aim in salvationist terms:[14]

> Repeatedly throughout the book I have set forth what I call a "grand neoclassical synthesis." This is a synthesis of (1) the valid core of modern income determination with (2) the classical economic principles. Its basic tenet is this: Solving the vital problems of monetary and fiscal policy by the tools of income analysis will *validate* and bring back into relevance the classical verities. This neoclassical synthesis does something equally important for the teaching of economics. It heals the breach between aggregative macro-economics and traditional micro-economics and brings them into complementing unity. (S3-1955, vi)[15]

The ornaments of Samuelson's *Economics* shift with the times in complicated ways. In the first edition, he claims—without closely justifying— Keynesian roots, but he refers most frequently to his macroeconomics simply as "modern theories of income determination." In contrast, the chapter on income theory in the seventh edition begins with the quotation from Milton Friedman: "We are all Keynesians now" (S7-1967, 195). Rather than taking partisan satisfaction in Friedman's concession, Samuelson restates his ideal of scientific neutrality: "Modern economists are 'post-Keynesians,' keen to render obsolete any theories that cannot meet the test of experience" (196). Later in this edition, however, he stoops to conquer, adopting "Keynesian income theories" in place of "modern income theories" as his preferred terminology (581). This change was probably driven by the resurgence of the quantity theory

14. The third edition, along with the first and seventh, are the ones that Samuelson himself regards as his "vintage" editions (Samuelson S9-1973, ix).

15. A well-known story attributes Samuelson's coinage to his desire to appear less "pink" during the McCarthy era. Samuelson himself lends credence to the story with his discussion of the effect of McCarthy on the economics profession in his introduction to the fourteenth edition. Furthermore, both Samuelson and Tarshis were among those assailed from the right (see for example, William F. Buckley's attack on the economics department at Yale in his famous *God and Man at Yale* (1951, chap. 2) in which the textbooks of both authors figure prominently).

of money and the need, for the first time in two decades, to distinguish between competing analytical apparatuses. Over time, the terminology "neoclassical synthesis" is deemphasized, although the goal it represents remains central. By the seventh edition, Samuelson instead refers to the "new economics," while noting that it is not new or different, but simply the macroeconomics he has advocated through the previous six editions of *Economics* (S7-1967, vi).[16]

The shifting terminology of the seventh edition suggests that Samuelson's analytical apparatus was, by the mid-1960s, subject to two different pressures. On the one hand, he had sought from the first edition on to reconcile microeconomics and macroeconomics through application of policies that assured full employment and effectively created the conditions under which Say's law would apply. On the other hand, the analytical apparatus itself was subject to challenge from alternative approaches to macroeconomics. These two challenges are, of course, not independent. The policy problem of maintaining full employment originally suggested the neoclassical synthesis. The emerging problem of inflation in the 1960s encouraged the development of alternative analytical frameworks such as Friedman's restatement of the quantity theory. Nevertheless, to the degree that the challenges were analytical, the maintenance of a neutral, scientific, and harmonist macroeconomics required a different tactic. Samuelson had to argue now for the *generality* of his analytical framework, for its ability to nest competing views as special cases. Let us now consider the development of his framework as a response to the challenges of policy on the one side and of competing theoretical frameworks on the other. Like the church, Samuelson's analytic framework had to adapt to modern conditions and to confront the forces of schism and reformation.

In the first edition of *Economics*, the national accounting scheme had been central and the 45-degree diagram was modestly displayed. By the second edition, "the national income approach has been retained, but it has been subordinated to the over-all goal of synthesizing aggregate concepts with economic analysis of the component parts" (S2-1951, vi). The

16. In the eighth edition, Samuelson refers to the "post-Keynesian neoclassical synthesis" (S8-1970, 309). By the ninth edition, Samuelson has begun to treat the neoclassical synthesis as principally a chapter in the history of economic thought: "Just a century ago the tree of economics bifurcated. One branch led through neoclassical economics and Keynesian economics to the present-day era of post-Keynesianism" (S9-1973, 843).

45-degree diagram provides the skeleton upon which these component parts are hung. Its importance is highlighted by the fact that it appears embossed on the cover of the book.

The policy concerns of the second edition are not just the avoidance of depressions. With a return to an economy that is obviously cyclical, an economy with both booms and slumps, Samuelson is more careful to use the model as part of a description of business cycles and as a guide to countercyclical policy. Monetary policy begins to be less of a fifth wheel as Samuelson now illustrates how cheap money lowers interest rates, stimulates investment—shifting the C + I curve upward in the 45-degree diagram—and so produces a multiplied effect on national income (S2-1951, 343).[17] To justify this sequence, Samuelson not only concedes to monetary policy a greater analytical role, but he also must move more in the direction of Keynes's own analysis of investment in terms of a comparison of the "marginal efficiency ('demand') schedule of investment" and an interest rate (S2-1951, chap. 29).

Having conceded the analytical role of money in income determination, the policy concerns of the hour continue to guide Samuelson's emphasis. In the fourth edition, he is careful to state that the investment function is likely to be nearly vertical in a deep depression, robbing monetary policy of its potency (S4-1958, 333). By the eighth edition, he notes that the research of Milton Friedman reinforces that of post-Keynesians such as James Tobin, Franco Modigliani, and himself who agree with Keynes—but not necessarily with some of his followers—that money matters very much (S8-1970, 310).

The shifting emphasis on the role of money is, in part, a response to the reorientation of policy concerns since publication of the first edition toward the problem of inflation. Samuelson's apparatus was not well adapted to the analysis of inflation: aggregate supply plays a very small role in his initial model, and there is no attempt to integrate price and wage determination into the 45-degree diagram. The discussion of the labor market, wages, and factors of production is largely restricted to the microeconomic sections of the book. The level of full-employment GNP is taken to be a datum. Demand insufficient to support full employment is described in terms of a "deflationary gap" that can be filled with additional

---

17. Patinkin 1983 provides a general overview of the development of Samuelson's thinking in monetary economics not restricted to his textbooks.

investment, while demand in excess of full employment is reconciled by rising prices. Samuelson continues to use this analysis across the entire run of *Economics*. Yet, as inflation develops into the principal policy problem, its inadequacies became clearer. One difficulty is that the treatment of inflation and deflation is asymmetrical: deflationary gaps appear to provide definite answers about the level of unemployment and the shortfall of GNP; inflationary gaps result in rising prices and wages, but there is no definiteness about their levels or rates of change. A second difficulty is that Samuelson becomes convinced over time that factor-costs have become an important determinant of inflation. This is clear in the fourth edition where he distinguishes between "demand-pull" and "sellers'" inflation (S4-1958, 335).

The fact that the 45-degree diagram was inadequate to the analysis of inflation probably explains the rapidity with which the Phillips curve was incorporated into Samuelson's *Economics*. Phillips's article on wage inflation and unemployment was published in 1958; Samuelson and Solow extended it to price inflation and used it for policy analysis in an article in the *American Economic Review* in 1960. And it appears in *Economics* for the first time in the fifth edition, published in 1961. Phillips's analysis had featured firms setting rates of change of nominal wages in response to the state of the labor market, the tightness or looseness of which was a product of demand pressures. Samuelson, however, considers the Phillips curve in the context of cost-push inflation in which firms set prices as a mark-up over factor costs. The Phillips curve presents the policy maker with a menu:

> The indicated 'Phillips Curve' shows by its downward slope that increasing the level of unemployment can moderate or wipe out the upward price creep. There is, so to speak, a choice for society between reasonably high employment with maximal growth and a price creep, or reasonably stable prices with considerable unemployment; and it is a difficult social dilemma to decide what compromises to make. (S5-1961, 383)

Despite later criticisms from Phelps 1967, Friedman 1968, Lucas 1976, and Lucas and Sargent 1979, Samuelson did not regard the Phillips curve as immutable. He understood clearly that if the economy were always near full employment there would be something like Friedman's "natural rate of unemployment." In the classical world, the Phillips Curve would be a vertical line at the minimal unemployment level: Q would then always correspond to full employment, and P would float in free labor markets to whatever level that total money spending would determine. In a limiting model of depression unemployment, where wage rates were inflexible against any downward movements but where no costs ever rose until full employment was restored, the Phillips Curve would be the horizontal axis until minimal unemployment was reached, and it would then shoot up vertically. (S5-1961, 383)

Different countries would have different Phillips Curves "depending upon their institutional pattern and psychological outlooks" (383). The nub of the problem is this:

> How can a mixed economy, without relying unduly on inefficient direct wage and price controls, give itself a Phillips Curve in which closer approaches to high employment can be made without engineering a considerable price creep? . . . This is truly an important, but terribly difficult, problem of the 1960s. (384)

By the eighth edition, the Phillips curve, which had been set apart in an appendix in the fifth, sixth, and seventh editions, is integrated fully into the main text. Samuelson acknowledges more clearly the instability of the Phillips curve, evidently acknowledging the turn of the profession toward the expectations-augmented Phillips curve and anticipating the Lucas critique: "We should reemphasize that economics is not an exact science. The data will not really fit any one Phillips Curve perfectly. More important still is the fact that the measured Phillips Curves represent short-term relationships which will shift in the longer run" (S8-1970, 811). A more detailed discussion of the role of expectations and the natural rate hypothesis are confined to a footnote (821n).

Although, as noted here, Samuelson mentions the idea of society giving itself a more favorable Phillips curve already in the fifth edition, the idea is left undeveloped until the ninth edition. Up to that point, the Phillips curve is treated principally as a description of the inflationary dilemma that faces the policy maker, who chooses among the feasible combinations of inflation and unemployment. Stagflation renewed Samuelson's interest in a better Phillips curve. The 45-degree diagram suggested that inflation and unemployment were mutually exclusive possibilities; stagflation suggested that the data did not agree. This meant abandoning parts of the earlier analysis. In the first edition, Samuelson had argued that monetary policy was ineffective; in subsequent editions, he had allowed monetary policy its day; now, in the ninth edition, he argues that both monetary and fiscal policies are effective only against demand-pull inflation and that incomes policy is essential (S9-1973, 363). For Samuelson, the problem became not to understand macroeconomic performance, but to change it: "How can a mixed economy supplement monetary and fiscal macro policy by an incomes policy *designed to give itself a better Phillips Curve?*" (833). Samuelson suggests three policies to improve the trade-off in the Phillips curve and to lower the natural rate of unemployment: (1) manpower training programs and improved labor market mechanisms; (2) reduction of discrimination against particular classes in the labor force, along with increased realism on the part of workers about employment opportunities; and (3) government-sponsored "last resort" employment programs (836).

The other staples of the analysis of aggregate demand in intermediate macroeconomics textbook, Okun's law and the static aggregate-supply curve, do not appear in *Economics* until Samuelson is joined by his coauthor William Nordhaus in the twelfth edition. The introduction to this edition notes that all the major issues in macroeconomics will be analyzed using the aggregate-supply/aggregate-demand apparatus. The twelfth edition therefore marks the decisive break with the established Samuelsonian tradition.

Although the Phillips curve was an innovation relative to the first edition of *Economics*, Samuelson presented it as an extension or supplement to the core analytical apparatus, not as a replacement for it. The shifting policy problem, however, raised analytical challenges as well. Over the course of eleven editions in three decades, Samuelson moved from a confident assertion of the unity of modern economics to the acknowledgment of division and schism: "Solving one kind of problem often leads to emergence of a new kind of problem. The easy Keynesian victories against chronic depression are long behind us. As we shall see, the new phenomenon of 'stagflation' . . . poses grave new challenges for the mixed economy" (S11-1980, 223). As a result of the failure of the "new economics" to solve this problem, "vigorous debates now rage between different schools in macroeconomics" (309).

The bête noire of Samuelson's macroeconomics were the advocates of the quantity theory of money. In the first edition, Samuelson had been able to stigmatize quantity theorists as "monetary cranks." He struck a pose of scientific detachment—but one that presupposed the adequacy of his own account of income determination—and dismissed quantity theory as simply empirically incorrect because prices were not proportional to total spending and total spending was not proportional to the stock of money, as the crudest versions of the quantity theory suggest (S1-1948, 291).

Reacting to the revival of the quantity theory in the wake of Friedman's "Quantity Theory of Money: A Restatement" (1956), Samuelson is no longer so dismissive: "Since there has been something of a revival of interest in the quantity theory by a number of competent American economists [including Milton Friedman] in recent years, it is worth taking an eclectic approach here and reviewing the fundamentals of a sophisticated quantity theory approach" (S5-1961, 315). A sophisticated quantity theorist believes "that controlling the behavior of M[oney] will help much to control N[et]N[ational]P[roduct], for the reason that the resulting changes in V[elocity] will either be so small or so predictable as to make one confident that dollar NNP will still move in the same direction as M" (316). Confident of the neutrality of his framework and harmonist as always, Samuelson dismisses any further discussion of this theory, saying, "qualitatively, this is in agreement with almost any modern theory of income determination" (316).

A decade later, the eighth edition echoes the same position with respect to "monetarism," the nom de guerre of Friedman's quantity theory. Since the Great Depression,

> the majority of experts think that monetary policy must be reinforced by stabilizing fiscal policies. But there is one important minority dissent to this view. A school called the 'monetarists,' originating at the University of Chicago and led by the able economist Professor Milton Friedman, believe [*sic*] that essentially everything that can be done to control macroeconomic aggregates—inflationary gaps and epochs of depression and slow growth—has to be done by control of the money supply alone. (S8-1970, 309)

Although monetarism represents an extreme view, Samuelson the scientist will not dismiss it: "After all, scientific truth could turn out to be on one extreme rather than in the middle" (309). However, "where monetarism differs from this so-called 'post-Keynesian neoclassical synthesis,' it is essentially wrong and indeed an extreme" (309).

Samuelson's treatment of monetarism represents a general strategy of finding the middle ground that goes back to the first edition. But, in the first edition, he regarded the problem largely as one of practical policy:

use macroeconomics to get the economy to full employment and, then, classical microeconomics takes over. This position seemed, however, to confirm the common view that Keynesian economics was the economics of depression. From the beginning, Samuelson opposed this view. At first, he was content to point out that since there was a deflationary gap as well as an inflationary gap, the 45-degree apparatus was sufficiently general to address boom or slump (S3-1955, 241). As the analytical incapacities of the 45-degree diagram became clearer, Samuelson's focus shifted to the individual components of his model, while still appealing to neoclassical synthesis as the instrument of reconciliation.

The theory of interest rates provides a good example. The classical theory was that the interest rate was determined in the market for loanable funds. Changes in the level of real income shift the saving and investment curves, however, making the interest rate indeterminate. The classicals did not see this problem because "they had the comfortable view that chronic unemployment was impossible" (S3-1955, 560). Samuelson notes that the reader may question why such an "ancient (and irrelevant)" theory is still discussed. "Fifteen years ago, the author wouldn't have known quite what to say. But today one can give a confident reply" (569). The neoclassical synthesis allows redrawing the marginal efficiency schedule of investment, drawn up "given factors of expectation and technology and—most important—*at the level of full employment assured by appropriate public tax and fiscal policies*" (570).

As monetarism becomes a more important rival to Keynesian analysis, Samuelson modifies his strategy, stressing less that his post-Keynesian policy prescriptions are the middle ground and more that the analytical apparatus is neutral and general, so that alternative views all represent special cases. In the fifth edition, he writes:

> Classical views that there can never be unemployment and depression versions of the Keynesian system will turn out to be alternative poles of such an analysis; and what most economists would consider to be the most realistic description of how our economy works and what are the potencies of policy weapons will fall somewhere on the continuum between these extreme poles. (S5-1961, 377)

Generality is again seen in the individual components of the model. Those who believe in the ineffectiveness of monetary policy in a depression will make the schedule of liquidity-preference horizontal, while those who believe in an effective monetary policy would make it vertical. Similarly with the schedule of the marginal efficiency of investment:

> A 'deep depression' pessimist will pencil in an almost vertical sched-
> ule: so depressed are investment opportunities believed to be then,
> . . . that lowering *i* practically to zero will have little reviving ef-
> fects. Alternatively, a classical optimist who thinks monetary policy
> has great potency will . . . pencil in an almost horizontal marginal
> efficiency schedule: for him the road to high employment and to zero
> inflationary gap is an easy one. (378)

Instead of the chain Money $\Rightarrow$ Interest Rates $\Rightarrow$ Investment $\Rightarrow$ Net National Product, sophisticated quantity theorists prefer Money $\Rightarrow$ Money
$\times$ Velocity $\Rightarrow$ Net National Product. But this latter chain "asserts that an
increase in M, unless *offset* fully by an induced shift in V of the type that
neither they nor the believers in the four-link chain consider likely, will
serve to increase dollar NNP" (S5-1961, 379). Although "these different
modes of language . . . formally represent the same facts . . . those
who prefer one terminology usually think that certain hypotheses about
the real world are more fruitful than certain other ones" (380). The bulk
of economists "incline toward the [four-link-chain] view, [but] there is
no need to be dogmatic about the matter" (380).

It is in the context of his increasing stress on the generality of the
theoretical framework that Samuelson gradually introduces the IS-LM
model into *Economics* (S3-1955, 580). The diagram is first introduced in
an appendix to the third edition, attributed equally to Hicks and Hansen.
The IS curve is called the BB curve; the LM curve is called the MM
curve. By the seventh edition, the IS-LM diagram, "the Hicks-Hansen"
synthesis, is used in the analysis of inflation (S7-1967, 330). The LM
curve is used to assert the generality of the analytical framework. It is
drawn nearly horizontal at low levels of income (depression model or
"liquidity trap" pole) and nearly vertical at high levels (classical model)
(331). Samuelson notes that the depression model is sometimes called the
Keynesian model, "but most authorities agree that this is bad terminology,
since Keynes' *General Theory* covered all cases from the beginning and
not merely that of the Great Depression" (331n).

The ultimate expression of the neutrality of the IS-LM framework
comes in the ninth edition. Samuelson dismisses the monetarist movement as a minor aside, and no threat to the Keynesian model:

> The Hicks-Hansen diagram [IS-LM] . . . succeeds in synthesizing

fiscal and monetary policy, the theory of income determination, and the theory of macroeconomics by providing a definite and general theory of the velocity of M. Thus the monetarist counterrevolution reduces to debate about the shapes of LM and IS. (S9-1973, 352)[18]

The IS-LM model is never held up as an alternative to the 45-degree diagram. Although he does not provide a derivation of the former from the latter, Samuelson believes that they are alternative ways of presenting the same underlying model. And the IS-LM model is always held to a subordinate role. Over time, it plays a somewhat more important part: first because over the sequence of editions of *Economics* a richer collection of factors is seen to be macroeconomically important; second because the IS-LM model is better adapted to make Samuelson's point about the generality of Keynesian analysis. In adopting it, however, Samuelson adds nothing that was not available to the sophisticated economist of 1948.

In the eleventh edition, Samuelson is forced to concede that even the new wonder-weapon of IS-LM was not enough to convince the profession of the neutrality and unity of the Keynesian model. The persistence of the problem of stagflation presents a theoretical as well as a policy challenge. As a result of the failure of the "new economics" to cure stagflation, "vigorous debates now rage between different schools in macroeconomics" (S11-1980, 309). Macroeconomics had become riven with schism and sects. In the face of these divisions, Samuelson nevertheless stands not just as a voice of orthodoxy, but perpetually as the voice of harmony and scientific neutrality: "To understand the challenges offered by monetarists and believers in 'rational expectations,' you will first need to understand the fundamentals of income analysis" (196).

Reformation and Disestablishment

Our analysis of the Keynesian model in Samuelson's *Economics* ends in 1980 with the eleventh edition, the last one in which Samuelson is

---

18. Milton Friedman (1974, 137–38) argues, correctly, that the main tenets of his monetarism cannot be reduced to assumptions about the slopes of the IS-LM curves. The real issue between the monetarists and the Keynesians come down to two issues. First, the shape of the aggregate supply curve: essentially, is it possible to have prolonged underemployment? The monetarists take the classical view that the natural tendency of the economy is to return to full employment. Second, the causal priority of money over nominal income. Neither the 45-degree diagram nor the IS-LM diagram, since both are comparative static apparatuses, is suited to address this issue.

the sole author.[19] Macroeconomics for the decade before and the decade and a half after that date continues to be in ferment—a period not unlike the 1920s and 1930s before Keynes wrote *The General Theory*. Macroeconomics textbooks continue, by and large, to be Keynesian. Introductory textbooks can be rightly viewed as the progeny of Samuelson's *Economics*, typically stressing the same 45-degree apparatus that *Economics* has featured for over forty years. Intermediate textbooks typically stress the IS-LM presentation, supplemented with an aggregate supply analysis and a Phillips curve. The analytical apparatus of these textbooks is no longer closely associated with any particular policy. The analytical uniformity of American textbooks and the policy neutrality of their analytical machinery is one of Samuelson's central achievements, for, although he always advocated certain policies, his emphasis on scientific economics drove a wedge between those policies and positive economics. Samuelson's work is thus the triumph of normal science.

But four decades of normal science in macroeconomics may well be passed. The current scene is littered with inchoate alternatives and schools that stand in self-conscious opposition to Keynesian analysis on both the policy and the analytical fronts. Some people see the advent of the New Classical Macroeconomics as a revolution parallel to the Keynesian revolution (Hoover 1988, 1993). If that is so, the new revolution awaits its Samuelson. The existing new classical textbooks— Sargent 1987 at the graduate level and Barro 1993 at the undergraduate level—play roles similar to those played by the textbooks of Boulding and Tarshis. The new classical revolution has yet to be formulated in a textbook that could dominate the market and be sincerely flattered with the imitation of most other texts. If the New Classical Macroeconomics is a scientific revolution, its period of normal science has yet to be firmly established.

References

Barro, Robert. 1993. *Macroeconomics*. New York: Wiley.
Baumol, William J., and Alan S. Blinder. 1991. *Economics: Principles and Policy.*

19. It would have been interesting, as Allin Cottrell among others have urged, to consider the editions in which William Nordhaus is Samuelson's coauthor. The first of these editions, the twelfth, is a decisive break with the first eleven editions, joining the analytic tradition of the forty-five-degree diagram firmly with the IS-LM tradition. To do justice to this alternative tradition would require far more than the available space.

New York: Harcourt Brace Jovanovich.

Benham, Frederic, and Francis Boddy. 1947. *Principles of Economics.* New York: Pitman.

Blaug, Mark. 1991. Second Thoughts on the Keynesian Revolution. *HOPE* 23. 2: 171–81.

Boland, Lawrence A. 1989. *The Methodology of Economic Model Building: Methodology after Samuelson.* London: Routledge.

Boulding, Kenneth. 1948. *Economic Analysis.* 2d ed. New York: Harper.

Buckley, William F. 1951. *God and Man at Yale.* Chicago: Henry Regnery.

Carlson, Valdemar. 1946. *An Introduction to Modern Economics.* Philadelphia: Blakiston.

Clarke, Peter. 1988. *The Keynesian Revolution in the Making, 1924–1936.* Oxford: Clarendon.

Clower, Robert. 1965. The Keynesian Counterrevolution. In *The Theory of Interest Rates.* Edited by Frank Hahn and F. P. R. Brechling. London: Macmillan.

Coddington, Alan. 1983. *Keynesian Economics: The Search for First Principles.* London: Allen & Unwin.

Colander, David. 1984. Was Keynes a Keynesian or a Lernerian? *Journal of Economic Literature* 22 (December): 1571–79.

Davidson, Paul. 1989. Patinkin's Interpretation of Keynes and the Keynesian Cross. *HOPE* 21.3:549–53.

Dornbusch, Rudiger, and Stanley Fischer. 1994. *Macroeconomics.* 6th ed. New York: McGraw-Hill.

Elzinga, Kenneth G. 1992. The Eleven Principles of Economics. *Southern Economic Journal* 58 (April): 861–79.

Franklin, Fabian. 1936. Keynes's Economics. *Saturday Review* 13 (April 4): 32–33.

Friedman, Milton. 1953. The Methodology of Positive Economics. In *Essays in Positive Economics.* Chicago: University of Chicago Press.

———. 1956. The Quantity Theory of Money: A Restatement. In *Studies in the Quantity Theory of Money.* Edited by Milton Friedman. Chicago: University of Chicago Press.

———. 1957. *A Theory of the Consumption Function.* Princeton: Princeton University Press.

———. 1968. The Role of Monetary Policy. *American Economic Review* 58 (January): 1–17.

———. 1974. A Theoretical Framework for Monetary Analysis. In *Milton Friedman's Monetary Framework: A Debate with His Critics.* Edited by Robert J. Gordon. Chicago: University of Chicago Press.

Fusfeld, Daniel R. 1985. Keynes and the Keynesian Cross: A Note. *HOPE* 17.3:385–89.

Garver, Frederic, and Alvin H. Hansen. 1937. *Principles Of Economics.* 2d ed. Boston: Ginn.

———. 1947. *Principles Of Economics.* 3d ed. Boston: Ginn.

Gordon, Robert J. 1993. *Macroeconomics.* 6th ed. New York: HarperCollins.

Hall, Robert E., and John B. Taylor. 1993. *Macroeconomics.* 4th ed. New York: Norton.

Hansen, Alvin H. 1936a. Mr. Keynes on Underemployment Equilibrium. *Journal of Political Economy* 44 (December): 667–86.

———. 1936b. Under-employment Equilibrium. *Yale Review* 25 (Summer): 828–30.

———. 1938. Keynes on Underemployment Equilibrium. In *Full Recovery or Stagnation.* London: A. & C. Black.

———. 1949. *Monetary Theory and Fiscal Policy.* New York: McGraw-Hill.

———. 1951. *Business Cycles and National Income.* New York: Norton.

———. 1953. *A Guide to Keynes.* New York: McGraw-Hill.

Hardy, Charles O. 1936. Review of *The General Theory of Employment, Interest and Money*, by John Maynard Keynes. *American Economic Review* 26 (Spring): 490–93.

Hicks, John R. [1937] 1967. Mr. Keynes and the Classics. In *Critical Essays in Monetary Theory.* Oxford: Clarendon.

Hoover, Kevin D. 1988. *The New Classical Macroeconomics: A Sceptical Inquiry.* Oxford: Basil Blackwell.

———. 1993. The Rational Expectations Revolution: An Assessment. *Cato Journal* 121 (Spring/Summer): 81–96.

Ise, John. 1950. *Economics.* New York: Harper.

Keynes, John Maynard. 1936. *The General Theory of Employment, Interest and Money.* London: Macmillan.

———. 1937. The General Theory of Employment. *Quarterly Journal of Economics* 52 (February): 209–23.

King, J. E. 1993. Aggregate Supply and Demand Analysis since Keynes: A Partial History. Paper presented at the Malvern Conference on Political Economy, Great Malvern, England. August.

Klein, Lawrence R. 1947. *The Keynesian Revolution.* New York: Macmillan.

Kuhn, Thomas. 1962. *The Structure of Scientific Revolutions.* Chicago: University of Chicago Press.

Lederer, Emil. 1936. Commentary on Keynes. *Social Research* 3:478–87.

Leijonhufvud, Axel. 1966. *On Keynesian Economics and the Economics of Keynes.* New York: Oxford.

Lindbeck, Assax. 1985. The Prize in Economic Science in Honor of Alfred Nobel. *Journal of Economic Literature* 23 (March): 37–56.

Lipsey, Richard G., Paul N. Courant, Douglas D. Purvis, and Peter O. Steiner. 1993. *Economics.* 10th ed. New York: HarperCollins.

Lucas, R. E. Jr. 1976. Econometric Policy Evaluation: A Critique. In *The Phillips Curve and Labor Markets.* Edited by K. Brunner and A. H. Meltzer. Carnegie-Rochester Conference Series on Public Policy, vol. 1. Amsterdam: North-Holland.

Lucas, Robert E. Jr., and Thomas J. Sargent. [1979] 1981. After Keynesian Macroeconomics. In *Rational Expectations and Econometric Practice.* Edited by Robert E. Lucas Jr. and Thomas J. Sargent. London: Allen & Unwin.

McConnell, Campbell R. 1987. *Economics.* 10th ed. New York: McGraw-Hill.

McKenna, Joseph. 1955. *Aggregate Economic Analysis.* New York: Rinehart-Winston.

Meyers, Albert L. [1941] 1948. *Elements of Modern Economics.* 3d ed. New York: Prentice-Hall.

Miller, Merton H., and Charles W. Upton. 1974. *Macroeconomics: A Neoclassical Introduction.* Homewood, Ill.: Irwin.

Modigliani, Franco. 1944. Liquidity Preference and *The Theory of Interest of Money. Econometrica* 12 (January): 44–88.

Patinkin, Don. 1956. *Money, Interest and Prices.* New York: Harper & Row.

———. 1983. Paul Samuelson's Contribution to Monetary Economics. In *Paul Samuelson and Modern Economic Theory.* Edited by E. Cary Brown and Robert M. Solow. New York: McGraw-Hill.

———. 1989. Keynes and the Keynesian Cross: A Further Note, with a Reply by Daniel R. Fusfeld. *HOPE* 21.3:537–47. Phelps, Edmund S. 1967. Phillips Curves, Expectations of Inflation and Optimal Unemployment over Time. *Economica,* n.s., 34 (August): 254–81.

Phillips, A. W. 1958. The Relation between Unemployment and the Rate of Change of Money Wages in the United Kingdom 1961–1957. *Economica,* n.s., 25 (November): 283–99.

Robinson, Joan. 1962. Review of *Money, Trade and Economic Growth* by H. G. Johnson. *Economic Journal* 72 (September): 690–92.

Samuelson, Paul A. 1939a. Interactions between the Multiplier Analysis and the Principle of Acceleration. *Review of Economic Statistics* 21:75–78.

———. 1939b. A Synthesis of the Principle of Acceleration and the Multiplier. *Journal of Political Economy* 47 (December): 786–97.

———. 1947. *Foundations of Economic Analysis.* Cambridge: Harvard University Press.

———. 1948–80. *Economics.* 1st ed. 1948; 2d ed. 1951; 3d ed. 1955; 4th ed. 1958; 5th ed. 1961; 6th ed. 1964; 7th ed. 1967; 8th ed. 1970; 9th ed. 1973; 10th ed. 1976; 11th ed. 1980. New York: McGraw-Hill. (Cited within text as S[edition no.]-[publication date].)

———. 1966–86. *The Collected Scientific Papers of Paul A. Samuelson.* Cambridge: MIT Press.

Samuelson, Paul A., and William D. Nordhaus. 1985–92. *Economics.* 12th ed. 1985; 14th ed. 1992. New York: McGraw-Hill. (cited within text as S12-1985–92)

Samuelson, Paul A., and Robert M. Solow. 1960. Analytical Aspects of Anti-inflation Policy. *American Economic Review* 50 (May): 177–94.

Sargent, Thomas J. 1987. *Macroeconomic Theory.* 2d ed. Orlando: Academic Press.

Scitovsky, Tibor. 1984. Lerner's Contribution to Economics. *Journal of Economic Literature* 22 (December): 1547–71.

Stewart, Maxwell S. 1936. The Mainsprings Of Capitalism. *Nation* 142 (April 15): 485–86.

Tarshis, Lorie. 1947. *The Elements of Economics.* New York: McGraw-Hill.

Taylor, Horace. 1936. Mr. Keynes's General Theory. *New Republic* 86 (April 29): 349.

Tobin, James. 1958. Liquidity Preference as Behavior towards Risk. *Review of Economic Statistics* 25 (February): 65–86.

Weintraub, E. Roy. 1991. *Stabilizing Dynamics: Constructing Economic Knowledge.* New York: Cambridge University Press.

Young, Warren. 1987. *Interpreting Mr. Keynes.* Cambridge, U.K.: Polity.

Comment

Allin F. Cottrell

First of all, I found this article both highly informative and entertaining. More than that, it is a path-breaking piece, opening to detailed and systematic scrutiny the relatively neglected field of the content (and rhetoric) of the textbook tradition in macroeconomics. This field is obviously important, if one stops to think about it, yet it is often regarded as beneath the notice of economists wearing their researchers' hats.

I will begin by drawing attention to some of the things I like best about the article, before offering a few critical remarks and supplementary comments. (I should point out that the authors have done a very scrupulous job of responding to the comments, including my own, received when their article was first read; nonetheless, I do not think this makes redundant the remarks here since they give context to some of the asides in the present version of the article.)

I like the authors' use of Kuhn's distinction between revolutionary science and normal science as an organizing theme. It plays nicely into their point that, in order to achieve success at the textbook level, new concepts have to be "tamed" and their presentation stabilized, making it unnecessary for the student "to consult the canonical texts with all their ambiguity, passion, and contingency."

I expect Pearce and Hoover are right when they say that the early Keynes-inspired textbooks of Tarshis and Boulding failed to catch on, at least in part, because they remained too close to the "Keynesian revolution" itself, and that Samuelson's particular achievement was to deliver Keynesianism as simply "the modern theory of income analysis"—a theory that everyone but cranks would accept as the proper scientific framework for macroeconomics.

I also found very useful the authors' careful reading of Samuelson's many editions, as well as their tracing of his continual search for a general, neutral theoretical framework, capable of nesting all (or at least all the respectable) macroeconomic views that happened to be current. As Pearce and Hoover point out, this general framework became less contentful, and less specifically Keynesian, over the decades as it stretched to accommodate a newly respectable monetarism.

I would also like to mention a little bonus in the article—the lucid thumbnail sketch of the key features of Keynes's *General Theory*, which is offered for reference, to gauge the degree of adoption of Keynesian ideas in the textbooks. I could go on, but praise is less interesting than criticism; and so to the second part of my comments.

It may be worth presenting a counterweight to the authors' appealing metaphor of the virgin birth in relation to the macroeconomics presented in Samuelson's *Economics*. Yes, Samuelson makes very little reference to the literature—and specifically does not present himself as a partisan supporter of Keynes. He presents his ideas as if they had been developed ex nihilo. Yet in many respects his substantive analysis, as opposed to his tone, is very much that of Keynes. Let me give two examples.

First, Hoover and Pearce give a quotation from Samuelson's first edition, which I will reproduce in part for reference. Once the sources of aggregate macro fluctuations are analyzed and explained, says Samuelson:

> The important hard kernel of truth in the older economics of full employment can then be separated from the chaff of misleading applications. Moreover, . . . if modern economics does its task well so that widespread unemployment is . . . banished from democratic societies, then its importance will wither away and traditional economics (whose concern is wise allocation of fully employed resources) will really come into its own—almost for the first time. (1948, 10)

Pearce and Hoover state that via this move Samuelson is reconciling "the competing economics of Keynes and the classics—establishing a heaven of economic analysis on earth by attacking the original sin of slack resources." This is an example of Samuelson the harmonizer at work. My reaction is that in the passage quoted Samuelson is doing little more than paraphrasing Keynes himself, whether consciously or not.

Compare:

> Our criticism of the accepted classical theory of economics has con-
> sisted not so much in finding logical flaws in its analysis as in pointing
> out that its tacit assumptions are seldom or never satisfied, with the
> result that it cannot solve the economic problems of the actual world.
> But if our central controls succeed in establishing an aggregate volume
> of output corresponding to full employment as nearly as is practicable,
> the classical theory comes into its own from this point onwards. If we
> suppose the volume of output to be given, i.e. to be determined by
> forces outside the classical scheme of thought, then there is no objec-
> tion to be raised against the classical analysis of the manner in which
> private self-interest will determine what in particular is produced, in
> what proportion the factors of production will be combined in order to
> produce it, and how the volume of the final product will be distributed
> between them. (Keynes 1936, 378–79)

And so on in the same vein for the next couple of pages. That Keynesian
and classical theory can be reconciled in practical terms, so long as full
employment is maintained via intelligent macro policy, would seem to be
Keynes's own idea rather than a "harmonization" specifically engineered
by Samuelson.

Second, I have some questions regarding Pearce and Hoover's treatment of Samuelson's famous 45-degree diagram or "Keynesian cross."
Was this a case of virgin birth? Well, clearly the 45-degree diagram is
not to be found in *The General Theory*, but I would suggest that it is a
pedagogically effective representation of some of the core ideas of that
book. Having taught the Keynesian cross for many years, I believe it gets
the basic ideas of the multiplier and saving-investment balance across
very well. The nearest equivalent in *The General Theory* itself is the
aggregate demand price-aggregate supply price (or D-Z) apparatus of
chapter 3.

How do these two pieces of apparatus compare? The Keynesian cross
is much simpler, and it does sweep a number of important issues under the rug, but its simplicity is also a great virtue. By comparison,
Keynes's own D-Z system is tremendously cumbersome. Its precise
status—particularly that of the supply price or Z schedule—has continued to trouble even careful and sympathetic students of Keynes for more
than forty years (see, for instance, Asimakopulos 1991; Chick 1983,
1992; Nevile 1992; Patinkin 1978). And there is some suggestion (in

Keynes's correspondence with Hawtrey in 1937) that Keynes himself would have done things differently if he had *The General Theory* to write over again. Specifically, he said that he would have been tempted to suppress the distinction between short-run expectations and outcomes in the interest of focusing more clearly on the forces determining the location of the "point of effective demand," as opposed to the "higgling" process by which this point is reached. One of the points of distinction between the D-Z apparatus and the Keynesian cross is, of course, the fact that the former is expressed in terms of (short-run) expectations while the latter is not.

In addition, the message of the 45-degree diagram can be put across to students with little or no acquaintance with microeconomics, while Keynes's D-Z setup presupposes familiarity with Marshallian microeconomic ideas. Keynes remarked on at least one occasion that his ideas were basically very simple; that they seemed complicated was the result of his and his contemporaries' being enmeshed in the "classical" mode of thought on which they had been brought up. He hoped that a younger generation would be able to grasp his ideas relatively easily and express them in a less convoluted manner. In one respect, I think Samuelson did just this. Nothing said by Pearce and Hoover expressly contradicts this positive assessment of the Keynesian cross, but neither does their discussion particularly encourage such a judgment.

In the foregoing remarks I have in effect drawn Samuelson rather closer to Keynes than Pearce and Hoover suggest. One more observation along the same general lines: I was struck by the authors' account of Samuelson on the Phillips curve. From the start, they point out, Samuelson was thinking in terms of "how to get the economy a better Phillips curve" rather than simply "playing" the existing curve. This attitude is very much in line with Keynes's characteristic brand of can-do optimism. Keynes would, I think, have rebelled at the idea that policy makers are obliged to choose, from a fixed menu, their preferred combination of two evils.

Switching lines of thought, there is one more point I wish to make. This is not so much a criticism, as simply a comment on the scope Pearce and Hoover have chosen—within constraints, of course!—and what has thereby been omitted. They say that they have deliberately chosen to close their narrative as of the date when Samuelson brought Nordhaus on board as coauthor of *Economics*. I see the rationale for this, but breaking off at this point precludes consideration of the role of the aggregate demand/aggregate supply framework (in P-Y space) in the evolution of textbook macroeconomics—since, as Pearce and Hoover remark, this entered Samuelson's text only with the first collaborative edition of 1985.

To my mind, the switch to AD-AS marks a rather decisive break of the textbook tradition from Keynes himself. I have already claimed that the 45-degree diagram is quite faithful to Keynes. I would also contend that the next step in the typical textbook ascent of the heights of macroeconomic theory, namely the fixed-nominal-wage IS-LM model, is defensible as a simplification of Keynes. There are many passages in *The General Theory* that may be read in terms of IS-LM (although one might argue that IS is more strongly implicit in Keynes than LM, since for at least part of the time Keynes treats the rate of interest as an independent variable rather than tying it into a simultaneous system). But the downward-sloping AD curve in P-Y space is definitely not Keynes. Indeed, chapter 19 of *The General Theory* may be read as a posthumous critique of that curve. It is ironic that the mechanism behind that downward slope is often referred to as the "Keynes effect": when wages fall in response to high unemployment, prices fall, too, which raises the real money supply and hence lowers the rate of interest, which, in turn, stimulates investment, raising output and employment. Yes, Keynes gave this account, but he did not regard the mechanism as one that could be *relied on*, given the various countervailing macroeconomic effects of a fall in wages and prices. He presented the "Keynes effect" as the best hope for a "classical" self-adjusting system, but he set little store by it himself.

The writing of a downward-sloping AD curve into the textbooks—and it is the rare text that offers any critical commentary on this curve—produced a subtle (or maybe not so subtle) shift in the terms of debate. In place of the argument over whether the macroeconomy is self-adjusting at all (or is reliably so), the focus changes to the *speed* of self-adjustment: Is it slow enough to open a space for stabilizing government intervention or sufficiently fast that attempted stabilization is likely to be counterproductive?

But the AD curve is no doubt an issue for another article. I hope that in the future we will see further work on the nature and history of textbook economics along the lines that Pearce and Hoover have so ably opened up.

References

Asimakopulos, A. 1991. *Keynes's General Theory and Accumulation.* Cambridge: Cambridge University Press.

Chick, V. 1983. *Macroeconomics after Keynes.* Deddington: Philip Allan.

————. 1992. A Comment on John Neville's Notes on Aggregate Supply. *Journal of Post Keynesian Economics* 15.2:261–62.

Keynes, John Maynard. 1936. *The General Theory of Employment, Interest and Money.* London: Macmillan.

Nevile, J. 1992. Notes on Keynes's Aggregate Supply Curve. *Journal of Post Keynesian Economics* 15.2:255–60.

Patinkin, D. 1978. Keynes' Aggregate Supply Function: A Plea for Common Sense. *HOPE* 10.4:577–96.

Samuelson, Paul A. 1948. Foundations of Economic Analysis, 2d ed. New York: McGraw-Hill.

The Diffusion of the Keynesian Revolution: The Young and the Graduate Schools

D. E. Moggridge

Experience seems to show that people are divided between the old ones whom nothing will shift and are merely amazed by my attempts to underline the points of transition so vital in my own progress, and the young who have not been properly brought up and believe nothing in particular. . . . I have no companions, it seems, in my own generation, either of earliest teachers or of earliest pupils.—Keynes to Harrod, 30 August 1936

The *General Theory* caught most economists under the age of 35 with the unexpected virulence of a disease first attacking and decimating an isolated tribe of South Sea islanders. Economists beyond 50 turned out to be quite immune to the ailment. With time, most economists in between began to run the fever, often without knowing or admitting their condition.—Paul A. Samuelson, "Lord Keynes and the General Theory"

The division of professional opinion cannot be described in the same terms for every country: in some it amounted to no more than a ripple on the surface. But in England and the United States it went deep, and here a phenomenon asserted itself unmistakably that deserves passing notice. Keynesianism appealed primarily to young theorists whereas a majority of the old stagers were, more or less strongly, anti-Keynesian. One aspect of this is too obvious to detain us and has, in addition often been emphasised: *of course* it is true that part of the resistance which every novel doctrine meets is simply the resistance of arteriosclerosis. But there is another. The old or even mature scholar may be not only the victim but also the beneficiary of habits of thought formed by his past work. . . . And in a field like economics, where training is often defective and where the young scholar very often simply does not know enough, this element in the case counts much more heavily than it does in physics where teaching, even though possibly uninspiring, is always competent.—Joseph A. Schumpeter, *A History of Economic Analysis*

Keynes, Samuelson, and Schumpeter have provided the profession with oft-repeated characterizations of the spread of Keynesian (and other) ideas. They are, however, characterizations that have been followed up only informally. There have been, it is true, "reviews of the reviews" of *The General Theory*, not to mention surveys of the various controversies that the book generated (Klein 1947, chap. 4). There have also been studies of aspects of what followed, such as the invention and adoption of IS-LM and the reactions of various individuals or institutions to the new work (Asso 1990; Collins 1981; Durbin 1985; McCormick 1992; Stein 1968; Young 1987; Young and Lee 1993), and there have been memoirs (Brown 1988; Kregel 1988). The purpose of this article is to add to the existing literature by providing more information about the diffusion of the ideas in question, partially with reference to graduate education in economics.

This last matter is of some interest because in the early 1950s, just after the end of the period under consideration, the notion of a "core" of economic theory "which should bind the profession together and . . . enable economists of all types and persuasions to communicate with one another" entered academic economics (Bowen 1953, 42–43).[1] That core included a widely accepted version of Keynesian economics that had emerged in the years immediately after publication of *The General Theory* (Patinkin 1990).

The core of this paper is a bibliographical and biographical study of the 392 articles that appeared between the beginning of 1936 and the end of 1948 and were recorded either in classes 2.30, 2.31, 2.320, 2.322, and

---

1. As defined by Bowen, the core in economic theory was "the field as it is generally accepted in the profession at the time." The emphasis was to be "fairly conventional but up-to-date and integrated" and "should acquaint the student with some of the important modern literature and with current intellectual issues in the field" (Bowen 1953, 109).

2.325 of the *Index of Economic Journals* or in the surveys of post-*General Theory* developments in the first two revisions of Gottfried Haberler's *Prosperity and Depression* (1946).[2] These 392 articles were by some 180 different authors, for 147 of whom we have biographical data. This bibliographical and biographical information has been supplemented by an examination of *some* graduate prospectuses for some American and British universities. It could be further supplemented by an examination of what actually happened in various classrooms, either through students' or lecturers' notes or of comprehensive examinations and of dissertation titles, but it is probably impossible to recapture the extent of student interaction and mutual stimulation at universities with large graduate programs in economics.[3]

The dates were chosen for straightforward reasons: *The General Theory* appeared in February 1936, while the 1948 appearance of both Don Patinkin's "Price Flexibility and Full Employment" and the first edition of Samuelson's *Economics* could be taken as marking the widespread acceptance of a basic "Keynesian" model and message at both the professional and undergraduate levels. The end date could, of course be extended to encompass more of the postwar period—and incidentally more of the early publishing careers of the postwar Keynesian establishment—but we are not convinced that anything other than perhaps conformity with the dates in the last column of table 3 would be gained thereby.

Let us begin with a discussion of the characteristics of the authors of the articles examined. These are set out in tables 1 and 2. From table 1 it is clear that the authors we are concerned with were more likely than not to have been thirty-five or under when *The General Theory* appeared, for 109 of the 147 have birth years of 1901 or later. They also tended to publish "young," in that the "age" of authors at time of first publication in the field covered in the sample was likely to be under thirty-five.

2. This is a reprint of the third edition. The first edition was published by the League of Nations in 1937. A second edition, with an additional chapter 8, followed in 1939, while the 1943 edition had an additional chapter 13. It is interesting to speculate on the form of what became Haberler's *Prosperity and Depression* and of what, perhaps, the whole process of Keynesian diffusion might have taken had the survey been done by the person to whom it was first offered—Dennis Robertson (Nuffield College, Oxford, Loveday Papers, Box 66, Diary, entry for 2 November 1933).

3. For an indication of such programs in the United States, see table 3. Note that, if one restricted the use of the term "large" to those programs producing an average of ten or more Ph.D.s in economics per annum, the field would be much smaller, including only Columbia and Harvard in the first two periods and adding only Chicago, Wisconsin, Cornell, and Illinois in the third period.

Table 1   Characteristics of Authors

Birth Year	No. of Authors	"Age" at First Article[b]	No. of Authors
Before 1883	4	≤ 25	18
1883–90	11	26–30	34
1891–1900	23	31–35	37
1901–5	27	36–40	22
1906–10	31	41–45	11
1911–15	30	46–50	10
1916–20[a]	18	≥ 51	15

[a]Three individuals were born after 1921.
[b]Difference between the year of birth and the year in which the first article in the sample appeared.

Table 2   Top Ten Sources of Authors' Highest Degrees

University	No. of Authors
Harvard	26[a]
Cambridge	17
London School of Economics	16
Chicago	12
Columbia	9
Oxford	7
Berkeley	4
Berlin	4
Wisconsin	4
Vienna	3

[a]In addition, there were two degrees from Radcliffe.

In terms of their graduate training, tables 2 and 3 set out what we know about the authors and American-trained economists more generally. The authors are likely to have been educated, at least in part, outside the United States: 79 of the 147 individuals for whom we have information have an American degree as their highest degree. If I compare the origins of those whose highest degree was from an American institution with what we know more generally about American Ph.D.s in economics, those in our sample are much more likely to come from Harvard or Chicago than the general run of American-educated economists. The

Table 3 Doctoral Dissertations Accepted in American Universities (those with 3 percent of total dissertations or above named)

Institution	1925/6–1934/5		1935/6–1944/5		1945/6–1950/1	
	No.	%	No.	%	No.	%
Berkeley	59	5.1	57	4.4	. . .	. . .
Brookings	40	3.4	—	—	—	—
Chicago	73	6.5	75	5.8	95	6.3
Columbia	112	9.6	150	11.5	132	8.5
Cornell	82	7.0	94	7.2	68	4.5
Harvard	122	10.5	121	9.3	257	17.1
Illinois	79	6.8	73	5.6	66	4.4
Iowa	. . .	. . .	. . .	. . .	46	3.1
Minnesota	35	3.0	51	3.9	48	3.2
New York	. . .	. . .	56	4.3	46	3.1
Northwestern	. . .	. . .	39	3.0	. . .	. . .
Ohio State	. . .	. . .	51	3.9	47	3.1
Pennsylvania	76	6.5	. . .	. . .	. . .	. . .
Stanford	36	3.1	. . .	. . .	. . .	. . .
Wisconsin	99	8.5	91	7.0	92	6.1
Total for U.S.	1,166		1,317		1,501	

Symbols: — does not have graduate program
    . . . has graduate program but produced less than 3 percent of
    successful Ph.D.s in the period in question
Source: Bowen 1953, 209–10

representation of Columbia and Berkeley is roughly what one would expect, while Wisconsin and the remainder of the top ten universities are underrepresented. Outside the United States, Oxbridge and the London School of Economics (LSE) dominate, although the diaspora of the 1930s is evident in the number of individuals with their highest degrees from Berlin and Vienna.

The ranking of American graduate schools (and, for that matter, LSE) is, however, probably symptomatic of something else. It could be argued that Chicago, Harvard, and LSE, which awarded the highest degrees for 38 percent of those thirty-five or under in 1936, provided graduate students with the best analytical training in economics available in the late 1930s and 1940s. At Harvard, there had been the changing of the guard that brought Schumpeter, Leontief, Haberler, and Hansen to the department. Unusually, none of its 1930s students gained permanent appointments (Mason 1982, 420). At Chicago, the department's existing strength, epitomized by Knight and Viner, was augmented by the arrival in 1939 of Oscar Lange (who provided graduate teaching at the frontier, as it then was) and in 1943 of the Cowles Commission for Research in Economics under Jacob Marschak, which included among its members Trygve Haavelmo, Leo Hurwicz, Lawrence Klein, and Tjalling Koopmans (Patinkin 1981, 8). At LSE, the arrival of Lionel Robbins as professor of economics in fall 1929 and his attempt, over the objections of the director, to make the school a center of economic theory began a period of "creative tension and excitement" that affected both older appointees such as John Hicks and new ones such as R. G. D. Allen, Evan Durbin, F. A. Hayek, Nicholas Kaldor, Abba Lerner, and Ursula Webb (Kaldor, cited in Kregel 1988, 14). There were, as well, links between the younger faculty and the graduate students at LSE and at Cambridge through the joint London and Cambridge Economic Seminar that arose from an attempt by Lerner and some of the other younger LSE people to reduce the intellectual gap between the two institutions. There was also the *Review of Economic Studies* to provide a similar link. Even though LSE was to lose many of those named here to other institutions after 1935, Robbins was able to repeat his exercise of the 1930s after the war and rebuild the economics group, albeit in a different intellectual mold—one created in part by his own change in view which began before the outbreak of and continued during the war (Robbins 1971). Hayek himself left LSE in 1949.

By way of contrast, as far as we can tell, the theoretical training of economists at Columbia left much to be desired. C. P. Kindleberger, who was there as a student, reports that in the 1930s "economics education at Columbia . . . was not exciting" and that "there was no core of economic theory" (1991, 31). A reading of the announcements of the graduate-level offerings of the faculty of political science (which included economics) for the 1930s confirms this. George Stigler, on the faculty from 1947 to 1958, has more to say in its favor. This is perhaps not surprising since the postwar period saw a large infusion of new blood and curricular reforms that swept away many of the traces of institutionalism. However, even Stigler reports: "When I returned to Chicago from Columbia I reckoned it a gain that I was coming to an institution where seniority would not be considered an adequate substitute for research" (1988, 46). He then tellingly compares the Chicago of the 1950s with LSE in the 1930s, of which he had some experience. Wisconsin shared many of Columbia's problems in the period we are discussing.[4]

As yet, we have not mentioned Oxford and Cambridge, largely because they were not well-organized centers of graduate instruction in economics. Both offered doctoral degrees, but the taking of such degrees in economics was a very new phenomenon in the 1930s (and one confined largely to foreigners for several decades), and neither ancient university then offered formal instruction in economics designed specifically for graduates.[5] In these institutions, graduate work really meant learning from the literature, your supervisor, your fellow students, and sympathetic faculty, but it was very much a matter of luck and circumstances, as A. J. Brown's 1988 memoir of his period at Oxford shows. It is true that graduates of overseas universities regularly went to Oxbridge as affiliated students doing a second B.A. In the process, many became quite well-trained economists, as did many of the Oxbridge graduates in our list who left with an undergraduate degree, but the training acquired was a by-product from a system designed for another purpose.[6]

We have briefly considered who the individuals were and where they were educated. We have yet to say anything as to where they published, whom they acknowledged, and whom they cited.

Let us take the matter of acknowledgments first, if only because it was not all that common: only sixty-four (16 percent) of the articles examined contained any acknowledgments; only two individuals[7] published three articles with acknowledgments, and only seven individuals[8] published two articles with acknowledgments. Of those acknowledged,

4. Of course one could do worse. Evsey Domar reports of his undergraduate career at UCLA, which did not produce any Ph.D.s in economics before 1945 (Bowen 1953, 209): "But 1936 was the year of *The General Theory*. It was hotly debated in the journals, and yet all that I learned about Keynes by my graduation in 1939 was that such an economist existed; and even this information came not from my professors but from a fellow student" (quoted in Szenberg 1992, 119).

5. The Oxford B.Phil. was first examined in June 1948, but the small number of candidates (four in 1950) limited the amount of formal teaching provided for some years. The Cambridge M.Phil., which followed almost three decades later, had formal instruction from the beginning.

6. For memoirs of Oxbridge undergraduates during the period surrounding the creation and publication of *The General Theory*, see Brown 1988, esp. 18–31, and Bensusan-Butt [1967] 1980, esp. 26–35; for affiliated students see, for example the notes by Bryce, Salant, and Tarshis in Patinkin and Leith 1977, 39–64.

7. Abba Lerner and Harold Somers.

8. Trygve Haavelmo, Alvin Hansen, Lawrence Klein, H. M. Oliver, Melvin Reder, Paul Samuelson, and Henry Wallich.

only fourteen individuals' names appeared twice or more. The most acknowledged economist was Alvin Hansen with five; Milton Friedman, Abba Lerner, and Dennis Robertson came in with four apiece; and Oscar Lange, Jacob Marschak, and Paul Samuelson came in with three each.[9] All held posts at Cambridge, Chicago, Harvard, LSE, or Oxford during the decade under consideration. Apart from the fact that all of Alvin Hansen's acknowledgments came from Harvard-educated or -employed economists, there is no clear pattern.[10]

Of course, acknowledgments recognize only one possible source of stimulus or assistance. There is also the straightforward citation of the work of oneself and of others. In the articles we examined, there were citations of 897 other individual pieces of literature. The most cited item was Keynes's *General Theory* with 144 mentions. With that number of citations for the one book, it is not surprising that Keynes was the most cited author with 248 citations. Nobody else reached 100, and only five individuals, including Keynes, exceeded 50. The thirty-eight people with ten or more citations appear in table 4; the twenty-six publications with ten or more citations appear in table 5.

It is interesting to note that among the most cited books and articles we get almost all the classic items we would expect from the early years of the discussions of *The General Theory*: Lange's 1938 piece for *Economica*, Haberler's 1946 *Prosperity and Depression*, Hicks's 1937 formulation of IS-LM for *Econometrica*, Hicks's 1939 *Value and Capital*, Robertson's 1940 *Essays in Monetary Theory*, and Hawtrey's 1937 *Capital and Employment*. Perhaps the only oddities arise from the low level of citation of the other papers closely associated with the initial formulation of IS-LM: Meade's 1937 piece for the *Review of Economic Studies* and Harrod's 1937 article for *Econometrica*, both of which received only three citations, two fewer than Modigliani's classic 1944 article for *Econometrica*. But this merely provides an example of the power of a simple diagram in the profession.

The dominance of Oxford, LSE, Harvard, Chicago, and Cambridge continues in the citations. Only four of the twenty most cited living authors did not hold a post at one of those universities at some time between 1936 and 1948. Within the overall rankings, however, the Eu-

---

9. Those with two mentions were W. M. Crum, W. Fellner, R. B. Goode, A. G. Hart, L. R. Klein, W. W. Leontief, and A. C. Pigou.

10. Among those with two acknowledgments, only Crum's and Pigou's were restricted to graduates of or colleagues in their own institutions.

Table 4   Author's Citation Rankings (10 or more citations)

	Name	No. of Citations		Name	No. of Citations
1.	Keynes, J. M.	248	20.	Wicksell, K.	18
2.	Hicks, J. R.	82	21.	Klein, L.	18
3.	Pigou, A. C.	65	22.	Knight, F. H.	17
4.	Robertson, D. H.	64	23.	Dunlop, J. T.	16
5.	Lerner, A.	53	24.	Kuznets, S.	15
6.	Lange, O.	43	25.	Hayek, F.	14
7.	Hansen, A. H.	39	26.	Fisher, I.	13
8.	Robinson, J.	38		Woytinsky, W. S.	13
9.	Haberler, G.	35		Angell, J.	13
10.	Ohlin, B.	32		Smithies, A.	13
11.	Harrod, R. F.	29	30.	Kahn, R. F.	12
	Hawtrey, R. G.	29	31.	Viner, J.	11
13.	Kaldor, N.	27		Frisch, R.	11
14.	Kalecki, M.	26		Tinbergen, J.	11
	Samuelson, P.	26		Shackle, G. L. S.	11
16.	Clark, C.	21	35.	Leontief, W.	10
	Marshall, A.	21		Lutz, F.	10
18.	Schumpeter, J.	20		Myrdal, G.	10
19.	Clark, J. M.	19		Wright, D. M.	10

ropean diaspora prevented those five institutions from dominating the educational experiences of those most frequently cited. Nevertheless, if one considers the "young" within this group,[11] 70 percent took their highest degree at either Oxford, LSE, Harvard, or Cambridge.[12]

The journal citations recorded in tables 4 and 5 also point to another characteristic of the literature: its general supportiveness of the Keynesian position with most of the support coming from the "young." If one goes to the individual publications of living authors recorded in table 5, leaving Keynes himself to one side, fourteen might be considered as supportive of his position and seven as critical. The age factor also comes out clearly in table 5, with eleven of the supportive authors born in 1901 or after, and

11. Because they were both born in 1900, Harrod and Haberler would not count as "young" in Samuelson's sense. Both probably did in Keynes's and Schumpeter's.

12. One other, Lawrence Klein, took his Ph.D. at MIT; Lange had been at LSE and Harvard without taking a degree, while moving toward Chicago. Samuelson, whose undergraduate career included graduate courses, might be said to leave a trace of Chicago on the record (Samuelson 1972).

Table 5   Individual Publication Citation Rankings (10 or more citations)

	Publication	No. of Citations
1.	Keynes, *General Theory*	144
2.	Lange, *Economica* 1938	28
3.	Haberler, *Prosperity and Depression*	27
4.	Hicks, *Value and Capital*	26
5.	Hicks, *Econometrica* 1937	22
6.	Keynes, *Treatise on Money*	21
	Ohlin, *Economic Journal* March & June 1937	21
8.	Keynes, *Economic Journal* June 1937	20
9.	Harrod, *Trade Cycle*	17
	Lerner, *Economic Journal* 1938	17
11.	Robertson, *Economic Journal* September 1937	16
12.	Hicks, *Economic Journal* 1936	15
13.	Robertson, *Essays*	14
14.	Robertson, *Quarterly Journal of Economics* 1936	13
15.	Marshall, *Principles*	12
	Hawtrey, *Capital and Employment*	12
	Hansen, *Fiscal Policy*	12
18.	Pigou, *Industrial Fluctuations*	11
	Kahn, *Economic Journal* 1931	11
	Clark, *National Income*	11
21.	Wicksell, *Interest and Prices*	10
	Lerner, *International Labour Review* 1936	10
23.	Pigou, *Economic Journal* 1937	10
	Dunlop, *Economic Journal* 1938	10
	Kalecki, *Essays*	10
	Klein, *Keynesian Revolution*	10

Note: For full bibliographical details see the bibliography.

all of the critics having been born before 1900. If one goes by the living authors in table 4, again leaving Keynes to one side, the ratio of support to opposition would be much closer. But the same pattern appears: the overwhelming majority of twenty "supporters" were born in 1901 or after, while among the critics, the figures are just as strongly reversed.[13]

13. A rather rough look at the list of all publications by authors for whom we have sufficient biographical data suggests a similar dominance of the young among Keynes's supporters. If one divides the articles into three classes—supportive, opposed, and unknown—for authors born in 1900 or earlier, the numbers are 14:38:11, as compared to 67:27:24 for those born in 1901 or after.

Table 6   Most Cited Journals

	Journal	No. of Citations
1.	Economic Journal	182
2.	Quarterly Journal of Economics	132
3.	Econometrica	100
4.	American Economic Review	95
5.	Review of Economic Statistics	92
6.	Economica	79
7.	Journal of Political Economy	52
8.	Review of Economic Studies	36
9.	International Labour Review	17
10.	Oxford Economic Papers	11

Interestingly enough, the pattern of journal citation differed from that of journal publication, with the *American Economic Review* and *Review of Economic Statistics* less cited than published in and *Economica*, the *Economic Journal, Econometrica*, and the *Quarterly Journal of Economics* more cited. Rankings appear in tables 6 and 7.

It can thus be said that the evidence suggests a strong association between the discussion and diffusion of Keynesian ideas and a limited number of centers of learning. One of these centers, Cambridge, was the source of the ferment as well as of significant criticism. Another, Oxford, had disciples (Harrod and Meade) who had been intimately involved in the creation of the ideas and, in the Institute of Economics and Statistics, an active and a growing research enterprise (Chester 1986, chap. 10; Young and Lee 1993, chap. 5). Neither center provided formal graduate instruction in economics. That was characteristic of the other three centers—Harvard, Chicago, and LSE—of which the last two were also sources of significant criticism as well as of support.

How did the ideas get diffused to particular individuals? Here some notions of Albert Hirschman's might prove useful:

New ideas have two principal intellectual effects: the persuasion effect and the recruitment effect. The persuasion effect is the obvious one of attracting followers from among specialists already labouring in the particular discipline where the idea makes its appearance. The recruitment effect is more important and ambiguous. As a result of

Table 7   Original Journals of Publication

	Journal	No. of Articles
1.	American Economic Review	43
2.	Review of Economic Statistics	37
3.	Quarterly Journal of Economics	34
4.	Economic Journal	32
5.	Econometrica	22
6.	Review of Economic Studies	17
7.	Journal of Political Economy	16
8.	Economic Record	13
9.	Economica	11
10.	Indian Journal of Economics	8
11.	Southern Economic Journal	8

the intellectual excitement generated by the new idea and the ensuing debates, intellectually able and ambitious recruits are newly attracted toward the field where the discovery has been made, where its scientific merits remain to be evaluated, and where its ramifications are yet to be worked out. This phenomenon was extremely important in the United States with its vast university system. (1989, 356)

Good examples of "persuasion" there certainly are. At LSE one need think only of Abba Lerner and Nicholas Kaldor—and, perhaps, Evan Durbin. Before 1936 Lerner had established himself as an active publisher in microeconomics and international trade, but had made no contribution to macroeconomics. However, as the result of persuasion from Joan Robinson and Richard Kahn, he spent some of his Leon Fellowship year in 1934/35 in Cambridge where the ideas were taking their final shape, was persuaded of their utility, and became a prolific and fervent advocate, first at LSE and from 1937 in America.[14] Kaldor started his academic career as a devotee of Robbins and Hayek, yet under the influence of John Hicks, whose reading was more catholic, he was "put on the track of (among others) the younger Swedish economists, particularly Myrdal, who made me realise the shortcomings of the . . . approach of the Austrian school . . . and made me such an easy convert to Keynes after the

14. McCormick (1992, 167) credits Lerner for inviting R. B. Bryce from Cambridge to give a lecture on Keynes's ideas to his LSE seminar. Unfortunately, the paper in question was discussed at four meetings of Hayek's seminar, as Bryce's letter of 5 July 1935 makes clear (CW 29:131). McCormick's study is full of such minor errors, which means it must be used with care.

appearance of the *General Theory*" (Kregel 1988, 14). By that time Hicks had already left LSE for a post in Cambridge, not because he had become a Keynesian "which in a sense I was," but because of an invitation from Pigou and friendship with Dennis Robertson (Hicks, as quoted in Kregel 1988, 4–5). While in Cambridge, of course, he formulated IS-LM. This became an important instrument of persuasion itself. It was first used for such purposes in print by Kaldor in his critique of Pigou's 1937 paper in the *Economic Journal*, which served as a substitute for a presidential address to the Royal Economic Society (Kaldor 1937). Durbin occupied an intermediate position: politically he was more aligned with Labour, but in economic theory he was intellectually influenced by, if critical of, Hayek. Durbin's most important theoretical publications preceded the appearance of *The General Theory*, but from his political views and his correspondence it is clear that he moved part way toward Keynes (Durbin 1985, esp. part 3; McCormick 1992, 71–75).

The classic and by far the most important American case of persuasion was that of Alvin Hansen. The exact dating of the conversion between his two reviews of Keynes's *General Theory* and his first full academic year at Harvard in 1937/38 is uncertain (Barber 1987, 200ff). Gottfried Haberler recalled Hansen's presence at the Geneva seminar organized to discuss the draft of *Prosperity and Depression*, where "he did not take a very Keynesian position" (1976, 11). He called the Hansen conversion "sudden," but does not know how it came about. Neither, it seems, does anyone else. But Haberler suggested that for Hansen, theory was not an end in itself but rather "a means to derive prescriptions for effective policy" (11). In this context he suspects that Hansen was persuaded because Keynesian policies were "the obvious cure for mass unemployment and Keynes provided a rational theoretical justification, while many orthodox economists strongly rejected the obvious remedy" (11). William Barber's discussion of the causes of the conversion, which he dates slightly later, is basically consistent with Haberler's explanation (Barber 1987, 204–5).

Examples such as these were important because they had direct effects in the classroom, as both the LSE calendar list of graduate courses with suggested reading and memoirs of the Hansen/Williams seminar tellingly indicate. *The General Theory* is in the course syllabi of Durbin, Kaldor, and Lerner in the 1936/37 academic year, and it remained there.[15] It

15. The three courses are initially called "The Modern Purchasing Power Controversy," "Problems of the Theory of Economic Dynamics," and "The Theory of Index Numbers." Kaldor's course later became "Advanced Problems of Economic Theory (Statics and Dynamics)," while

even enters the undergraduate curriculum of the school in 1937/38 in
P. B. Whale's course "Theory of Money and Credit" and in 1938/39,
albeit in Hicks's IS-LM form and clearly labeled supplementary and more
advanced reading, it is in Robbins's "General Principles of Economic
Analysis."[16]

There was also the persuasion and recruitment of students by their
peers. The classic case here is R. B. Bryce, the "missionary" to Hayek's
seminar at LSE, who proceeded full of the Keynesian message to Harvard in autumn 1935.[17] This paper, the basis of his LSE seminars, turns
up in Schumpeter's papers as the theoretical justification for Bryce's
"Memorandum of Work Proposed" of 1 October 1935 (Harvard University Archives, Schumpeter Papers, HUG(FP)47, Box 2). Bryce also reported that he used the same notes in discussions with his fellow students
(Bryce, quoted in Patinkin and Leith 1977, 40–41). It is not surprising that
a group of Harvard students around Bryce ensured early access to *The
General Theory* by arranging for the shipment of thirty copies directly
from London. Inevitably, there was a study group, organized at Harvard
by Seymour Harris, to see what the new work contained (Tsuru, cited in
Kregel 1988, 185). Among the students who arrived with Bryce at Harvard in fall 1935 were Paul Samuelson, Robert Triffin, and Shigeto Tsuru.
With Abram Bergson, John Kenneth Galbraith, Richard Musgrave, Paul
Sweezy, and Wolfgang Stolper already in residence and more to follow,
it is not surprising that Triffin recalled, "I learned as much or more, as
an economist, from *student colleagues* of mine in the most brilliant class

---

Durbin's became "Modern Trade Cycle and Monetary Theory." Lerner's departure from the
school meant that he never gave his graduate lectures on "Unemployment in Theory and Practice" advertised in the 1937/38 calendar.

16. In a recent letter to the author, Tom Wilson remembers Robbins's graduate seminar in
the same year: "I was never his pupil at LSE but I used to attend the great graduate seminar
in 1938/39 which he chaired. We watched with fascination the terrific battles between Hayek
and Kaldor which Kaldor usually won. What was particularly interesting was to watch Robbins
himself gradually shift his position towards Keynesianism. He did not move all the way, of
course, but he shifted closer to Keynes than to Hayek." In a sense this is not surprising, since
Robbins's behavior when he joined the Economic Section of the War Cabinet Offices and as
a member and later director provided active support to the campaigns for national income
accounting and employment policy would not make much sense in any other terms (Cairncross
and Watts 1989, chap. 6; CW 22:326–27).

17. Bryce, an engineer by training who had only taken up economics in 1932, was technically
a Ph.D. candidate at Cambridge. His ostensible purpose in going to Harvard was (tellingly in
the light of our earlier discussion) to improve his knowledge of formal economic theory for his
dissertation on business cycles.

that Harvard probably ever had . . . than I did from the professors whose classes I attended" (quoted in Kregel 1988, 151).

The process of recruiting was well under way—and it would continue for no little time.

But let us go back to the beginning and the hypotheses associated with the three quotations from Keynes, Samuelson, and Schumpeter. It is clear that publication of *The General Theory* affected the young more than the old, although, for example, the conversion of Alvin Hansen (born 1887) and the use of IS-LM in *Employment and Equilibrium* (1941) by A. C. Pigou (born 1877) (Solow 1986) show the speed with which the virus could significantly infect the work of scholars over age fifty in varying degrees—in both cases, within five years. The cutoff of thirty-five, with the qualifications about ultimate acceptance, is arbitrary, given that there were a number of people aged just over thirty-five who played an important role in diffusing the ideas—Gottfried Haberler, Roy Harrod, Jacob Marschak, and M. F. Timlin—and a number of people in the thirty-five to fifty age range in 1936 who were *never* reconciled to the ideas: A. W. Marget and J. Rueff, for instance. But the generational emphasis of the hypothesis, which is not new—it is, after all, a part of Thomas Kuhn's (1962, chap. 12) discussion[18] of the process in which scientific revolutions are resolved—is well borne out. However, at least in the context of this body of literature, what might be called the Keynes/Schumpeter hypothesis of "the young who have not been properly brought up" or have been defectively trained does not seem to be well sustained. If it were as likely as not that those involved in the discussion of *The General Theory* and its implications for economics, especially the young, were more likely than normal to have been the recipients of the best training available at the time, including that in Schumpeter's own department, then one must think again. Such training, with its renewed openness to Continental influences, might for Keynes, a Marshallian to the end, have seemed like a less than "proper" upbringing. But it should have hardly been such to Schumpeter, the champion of Walras and almost all things Continental.

Finally, it is clear that in an important sense, as Nathan Rosenberg (1975, 475–76) has emphasized, the decade following publication of *The General Theory* saw the ideas in the book refined, elaborated, and modified so that the profession could make them operationally useful.

18. See also Feuer 1982, 308–11.

This process of "critical revision," which aided the diffusion of the ideas themselves, was itself helped by complementarities between Keynes's ideas, the development of econometrics, and the development of national income accounting.

All of this might only echo David Bensusan-Butt's comment that "the *General Theory* fell among the economists of the day with a very big bang indeed. Nothing, *for any of them*, was ever quite the same again" ([1967] 1980, 35; emphasis added).

References

Asso, Pier Francesco. 1990. *The Economist behind the Model: The Keynesian Revolution in Historical Perspective. A Study of Some Unpublished Evidence of How Keynes Went to America.* Rome: Quaderni di Richerche, 18, Ente per Gli Studi Monetari, Bancari e Finanziari Luigi Einaudi.

Barber, William J. 1987. The Career of Alvin H. Hansen in the 1920s and 1930s: A Study in Intellectual Transformation. *HOPE* 19.2:191–206.

Bensusan-Butt, David M. [1967] 1980. Keynes's General Theory: Then and Now. In *On Economic Knowledge: A Sceptical Legacy.* Edited by D. M. Bensusan-Butt. Canberra: Australian National University.

Bowen, Howard R. 1953. Graduate Education in Economics. *American Economic Review* Supplement 43.4:i–xvi, 1–223.

Brown, A. J. 1988. A Worm's Eye View of the Keynesian Revolution. In *J. M. Keynes in Retrospect: The Legacy of the Keynesian Revolution.* Edited by J. Hillard. Aldershot: Edward Elgar.

Cairncross, Alec, and Nita Watts. 1989. *The Economic Section, 1939–1961: A Study in Economic Advising.* London: Routledge.

Chester, Norman. 1986. *Economics, Politics and Social Studies in Oxford, 1900–85.* London: Macmillan.

Clark, Colin. 1937. *National Income and Outlay.* London: Macmillan.

Collins, Robert M. 1981. *The Business Response to Keynes, 1929–1964.* New York: Columbia University Press.

Dunlop, J. T. 1938. The Movement of Real and Money Wage Rates. *Economic Journal* 48.3:430–54.

Durbin, Elizabeth. 1985. *New Jerusalems: The Labour Party and the Economics of Democratic Socialism.* London: Routledge.

Feuer, Lewis S. 1982. *Einstein and the Generations of Science.* 2d ed. New Brunswick, New Jersey: Transaction Books.

Haberler, G. 1946. *Prosperity and Depression: A Theoretical Analysis of Cyclical Movements.* Lake Success: United Nations.

———. 1976. Alvin H. Hansen: Some Reminiscences. *Quarterly Journal of Economics* 90.1:9–13.

Hansen, Alvin H. 1941. *Fiscal Policy and Business Cycles*. New York: Norton.

Harrod, R. F. 1936. *The Trade Cycle*. Oxford: Clarendon.

―――. 1937. Mr. Keynes and Traditional Theory. *Econometrica* 5.1:74–86.

Hawtrey, R. G. 1937. *Capital and Employment*. London: Longmans Green.

Hicks, J. R. 1936. Mr Keynes' Theory of Employment. *Economic Journal* 46.2:238–53.

―――. 1937. Mr. Keynes and the Classics: A Suggested Interpretation. *Econometrica* 5.2:147–59.

―――. 1939. *Value and Capital*. Oxford: Clarendon.

Hirschman, Albert O. 1989. How the Keynesian Revolution Was Exported from the United States and Other Comments. In *The Political Power of Economic Ideas: Keynesianism across Nations*. Edited by Peter A. Hall. Princeton: Princeton University Press.

Kahn, R. F. 1931. The Relation of Home Investment to Unemployment. *Economic Journal* 41.2:173–98.

Kaldor, N. 1937. Professor Pigou on Money Wages in Relation to Unemployment. *Economic Journal* 47.4:745–53.

Kalecki, M. 1939. *Essays in the Theory of Economic Fluctuations*. London: Allen & Unwin.

Keynes, J. M. 1930. *A Treatise on Money*. London: Macmillan.

―――. 1936. *The General Theory of Employment, Interest and Money*. London: Macmillan.

―――. 1937. Alternative Theories of the Rate of Interest. *Economic Journal* 47.2:241–52.

―――. 1971–1989. *The Collected Writings of John Maynard Keynes*. 30 vols. Edited by D. E. Moggridge. London: Macmillan. (CW)

Kindleberger, C. P. 1991. *The Life of an Economist: An Autobiography*. Oxford: Basil Blackwell.

Klein, Lawrence R. 1947. *The Keynesian Revolution*. New York: Macmillan.

Kregel, J. A., ed. 1988. *Memoirs of Eminent Economists*. London: Macmillan.

Kuhn, Thomas S. 1962. *The Structure of Scientific Revolutions*. Chicago: University of Chicago Press.

Lange, Oscar. 1938. The Rate of Interest and the Optimum Propensity to Consume. *Economica* 5.1:12–32.

Lerner, A. P. 1936. Mr. Keynes' General Theory of Employment, Interest and Money. *International Labour Review* 34.3:435–54.

―――. 1938. Alternative Explanations of the Theory of Interest. *Economic Journal* 48.2:211–30.

Marshall, Alfred. 1890–1920. *Principles of Economics*, 1st–8th eds. London: Macmillan.

Mason, Edward S. 1982. The Harvard Department of Economics from the Beginning to World War II. *Quarterly Journal of Economics* 97.3:383–434.

McCormick, Brian. 1992. *Hayek and the Keynesian Challenge*. London: Harvester-Wheatsheaf.

Meade, J. E. [1937] 1988. A Simplified Model of Mr Keynes' System. *Review of Economic Studies* 4.1:98–107. Reprinted in *Employment and Inflation*, vol. 1 of *The Collected Papers of James Meade*. Edited by Susan Howson. London: Allen & Unwin.

Modigliani, Franco. 1944. Liquidity Preference and the Theory of Interest. *Econometrica* 12.1:45–88.

Ohlin, Bertil. 1937. Some Notes on the Stockholm Theory of Savings and Investment. Parts I and II. *Economic Journal* 47.1:53–69 and 2:221–40.

Patinkin, Don. 1948. Price Flexibility and Full Employment. *American Economic Review* 38.4:543–64.

———. 1981. *Essays on and in the Chicago Tradition*. Durham: Duke University Press.

———. 1990. On Different Interpretations of the *General Theory*. *Journal of Monetary Economics* 26.2:205–43.

Patinkin, Don, and J. Clark Leith, eds. 1977. *Keynes, Cambridge and* The General Theory. London: Macmillan.

Pigou, A. C. 1927. *Industrial Fluctuations*. London: Macmillan.

———. 1937. Real and Money Wages in Relation to Unemployment. *Economic Journal* 47.3:405–22.

———. 1941. *Employment and Equilibrium*. London: Macmillan. Robbins, Lionel. 1971. *Autobiography of an Economist*. London: Macmillan.

Robertson, D. H. 1936. Some Notes on Mr Keynes' General Theory of Employment. *Quarterly Journal of Economics* 51.1:168–91.

———. 1937. Alternative Theories of the Rate of Interest. *Economic Journal* 47.3:4

———. 1940. *Essays in Monetary Theory*. London: P. S. King. Rosenberg, Nathan. 1975. Problems in the Economist's Conceptualization of Technological Innovation. *HOPE* 7.4:456–81.

Samuelson, Paul A. [1946] 1983. Lord Keynes and The General Theory. In Wood 1983.

———. 1948. *Economics*. New York: McGraw-Hill.

———. 1972. Jacob Viner 1892–1970. *Journal of Political Economy* 80.1:5–11.

Schumpeter, Joseph A. 1954. *A History of Economic Analysis*. New York: Oxford University Press.

Solow, Robert M. 1986. What Is a Nice Girl Like You Doing in a Place Like This? Macroeconomics after Fifty Years. *Eastern Economic Journal* 12.3:191–98.

Stein, Herbert S. 1968. *The Fiscal Revolution in America*. Chicago: University of Chicago Press.

Stigler, George J. 1988. *Memoirs of an Unregulated Economist*. New York: Basic Books.

Szenberg, Michael, ed. 1992. *Eminent Economists: Their Life Philosophies*. Cambridge: Cambridge University Press.

Wicksell, K. [1898] 1936. *Interest and Prices*. London: Macmillan.

Wood, John Cunningham, ed. 1983. *John Maynard Keynes: Critical Assessments*. 4 vols. London: Croom-Helm.

Young, Warren. 1987. *Interpreting Mr Keynes: The IS/LM Enigma*. Oxford: Polity.
Young, Warren, and Lee Frederic. 1993. *Oxford Economics and Oxford Economists*. London: Macmillan.

Comment

William A. Darity Jr.

Unfortunately, Donald Moggridge has written a passionless paper about the most exciting phase of theoretical transition in twentieth-century economics: the emergence and spread of Keynesian economics. Asserting that the "core" of his paper is an enumeration of "a bibliographical and biographical study of . . . 392 articles that appeared between the beginning of 1936 and the end of 1948 . . . recorded either in classes 2.30, 2.31, 2.320, 2.322, or 2.325 of the *Index of Economic Journals* or in the surveys of post–*General Theory* developments in the first two revisions of Gottfried Haberler's *Prosperity and Depression*," Moggridge addresses neither the content of these papers nor their significance or impact in promoting the acceptance of Keynesian doctrines across the economics profession. Moggridge's leavings are a tedious accountant's exercise serving, at best, as a supportive appendix to a hopefully more interesting study of how the Keynesian revolution developed in the economics profession.

Given the vast effort methodologists have devoted to the question of the emergence of new theoretical approaches (or, dare I say, paradigms) in science, it is odd that Moggridge does not attempt to connect the pattern of the spread of Keynesian economics to Thomas Kuhn's characterization of scientific revolutions, Imre Lakatos's characterization of the development of new research programs, or Donald McCloskey's characterization of rhetorical persuasion as the mechanism for propagation of new theoretical approaches. The absence of attention to the latter is particularly surprising, given Keynes's self-professed intention in the preface of *The General Theory* of speaking to his professional colleagues with the goal of persuading them of the correctness of the "general" theory as an alternative to the "classical" theory.

Even the late Harry G. Johnson (1978, 183–203), no particular enthusiast for Keynesian doctrine, offered a provocative analysis of the juxtaposition of the Keynesian revolution vis-à-vis a subsequent Monetarist counterrevolution. Neither are Johnson's insights, some presented with tongue in cheek, about the ingredients for a successful revolution in economics confronted by Moggridge in his essay.

We are treated to homilies, derived from a famous quotation by Paul Samuelson presented as an epigram at the start of the article about the greater receptiveness of younger economists than older economists to the new ideas. No substantive attempt is made to explore why this was the case. Certainly the numbers of today's younger economists who find nonmainstream approaches to economics appealing are comparatively small; most aspiring Ph.D.s simply attach themselves to the marginalist-inspired research agendas of the senior professors who supervise their dissertation research as the path of minimal professional resistance.

What made circumstances different in the 1930s through 1950s? Was a certain intellectual impatience and freedom to explore a different approach fostered by the unsettled global conditions created by the Great Depression and World War II? Was economics in a sufficiently early phase of professionalization that rigid indoctrination of the new recruits was less compulsively pursued at the time *The General Theory* was published than it is today?

With respect to the latter question, in a section of the article that had potential for richer development, Moggridge quotes Charles Kindleberger as saying at Columbia in the 1930s "there was no core of economic theory." The notion of a micro-macro core uniformly taught to all first-year graduate students was still embryonic, but by the 1960s the scope of professionalization and homogenization in economics had led to virtual standardization of the basic curriculum for graduate students. Perhaps it was fortuitous for the rising Keynesians that they came on the scene before a standard core of economic theory had become a norm; it was possible for macroeconomics—predominantly a product of Keynesian economics—successfully to become included in the core. Similarly, I find myself nostalgic for a time when economics departments were scrambling to ensure that their faculties included researchers who understood the Keynesian ideas, particularly in contrast with the recent 1970s and

1980s where departments, anxious to keep "up to date" were bent on hiring Ph.D.s schooled in rational expectations, New Classicism, and game theory.

Economics tends to spawn developments that come into vogue, leading to a surfeit of researchers of that type being overrepresented in departments until a new approach gains cachet. At this moment, the hot new areas seem to be the "new" growth theory, the "new" trade theory, and the "new" theory of technical change. But, with the exception of Keynesian economics, none of these new approaches has made the claim that it stands in opposition to received theory. Instead, they all constitute subfield developments self-consciously intended to extend or embellish on the scope and reach of neoclassical/marginalist economics. Keynesian economics promised, at least in Keynes's own rhetoric, to reconstruct the way in which all economics is to be done. That did not occur. Even with macroeconomics firmly ensconced in the standard core, microeconomics (neoclassical/marginalist) took equal standing. Consequently, great intellectual resources have been devoted to preventing intellectual schizophrenia in the attempt to reconcile macroeconomics with microeconomics (the enduring search for microfoundations for macroeconomics). Keynes explicitly envisioned his general theory as a substitute, not a companion, for what he termed the "real exchange economics" of Marshall and Pigou. Moggridge's paper tells us nothing about what in the nature of the diffusion of the Keynesian revolution made it possible for orthodoxy to preserve its authority and proceed to subsume Keynesian economics under the marginalist umbrella.

Furthermore, Moggridge tells us little about the depth of the rupture felt by those who experienced the Keynesian revolution. What was it they felt decisively separated Keynesian economics from pre-Keynesian economics? Indeed, how are we to tell who were the Keynesians and who were not? For the purposes of his accounting exercises, Moggridge seems to know from on high who to place in the Keynesian camp, but he never tells the reader what is the basis for his selection. Are economists Keynesian simply because they made a public confession that they are, even though they possess a grossly superficial understanding of *The General Theory*, like Alvin Hansen? Or, are they Keynesian because Keynes himself did not break with them even though they never embraced *The General Theory*, like Ralph Hawtrey?

And what were the extent and consequences, both professional and personal, of ideological conflict and departmental warfare surrounding the propagation of Keynes's economics? We know that Keynes's own propagandizing on behalf of *The General Theory* contributed to a degeneration in his personal relationships with some of his colleagues at Cambridge, most notably Dennis Robertson. There is evidence to suggest that other nonmainstream approaches, particularly Schumpeter's economics, got shunted into comparative obscurity because of the onslaught of the Keynesian revolution (while Schumpeter himself is quite famous, his theory of economic development and the business cycle did not ascend into the standard "core of economic theory"); Schumpeter's animosity toward Keynes and Keynesian economics was probably attributable to his awareness that his analysis of the economics of unemployment and the depression was overshadowed by the profession's response to Keynes's ideas.

There was a tide that swept the economics profession in the era surrounding World War II. It was a tide that affected professional fortunes, inspired entirely different patterns of research, and ultimately crested and fell into conformity with the tenets of the tide that had gone before. That is the story of the diffusion of the Keynesian revolution that I would have hoped to have explored and illuminated. Moggridge's essay simply does not do it. It is a shame it does not.

References

Johnson, Harry G. 1978. The Keynesian Revolution and the Monetarist Counter-Revolution. In *The Shadow of Keynes: Understanding Keynes, Cambridge and Keynesian Economics*. Edited by Elizabeth S. Johnson and Harry G. Johnson. Chicago: University of Chicago Press.

Irving Fisher, J. M. Keynes, and the Transition to Modern Macroeconomics

Robert W. Dimand

The agenda and form of modern macroeconomics were shaped by Maynard Keynes in *The General Theory* (1936), with the terminology, concerns, and even the name of the new discipline of macroeconomics indicating a break with the older study of business cycles and the quantity theory of money. This change was reflected in the shift of the economics profession's attention from Irving Fisher to Maynard Keynes. Patrick Deutscher calculates that Fisher was the most cited macroeconomist between 1920 and 1930, cited in thirty articles on macroeconomic topics in English in those years, compared to nine articles that cited the tenth-ranked Keynes (of *A Tract on Monetary Reform*) (1990, 189–94). Keynes's *Treatise on Money* (1930) boosted him to first place in 1931–35, with Fisher tied with R. G. Hawtrey for fourth place behind Robertson and Hayek. Fisher dropped to a four-way tie with Frisch, Kuznets, and Myrdal for sixteenth most-cited macroeconomist in 1936–39, with barely a tenth as many citations as Keynes, and he vanished entirely from Deutscher's list for 1940–44.

The secondary literature shares this shift of attention. John Cunningham Wood reprinted 110 journal articles written on Keynes between 1946 and 1981 in the four volumes of *John Maynard Keynes: Critical Assessments*, while Mark Blaug included another 73 published from 1981 to 1989 in the Keynes volumes of *Pioneers of Economics*. By contrast, one volume of *Pioneers of Economics* comprising nine articles suffices for Irving Fisher, Arthur Hadley, Ragnar Frisch, Friedrich Hayek, Allyn Young, and Ugo Mazzola.

Despite this disparity in attention, modern macroeconomics displays affinities to Fisher as well as to Keynes. Empirical research in macroeconomics builds on Fisher's work on distributed lags and index numbers and has more in common with the Fisher article of 1926 (reprinted in 1973 as "I Discovered the Phillips Curve") than with Keynes's severely skeptical 1939 review of Jan Tinbergen's *Statistical Testing of Business Cycle Theories*. Since the 1970s, many macroeconomists have turned to new versions of the quantity theory of money used by Fisher and by the Keynes of the *Tract* but rejected by the later Keynes: between 1981 and 1985 Keynes was cited more than 2,000 times, but Milton Friedman more than 3,500 times (Dogan and Pahre 1990, 424).

There are also interesting affinities between Fisher's monetary economics and that of Keynes. Keynes wrote in 1937 that "I find, looking back, that it was Professor Irving Fisher who was the great-grandparent who first influenced me strongly towards regarding money as a 'real' factor" (CW 14:203n). Keynes wrote to Fisher from Bretton Woods in 1944 that "you were one of my earliest teachers on these matters and nothing is more satisfactory to any of us than to satisfy one of those from whom we have learned" (Keynes to Fisher, 7 July 1944, quoted in Fisher 1956, 326). These affinities were accompanied by equally emphatic divergences: Keynes's 1944 accolade to Fisher from Bretton Woods occurs in a letter declining to be persuaded by Fisher's proposal for 100 percent reserve banking.

This article examines two related questions: What did Keynes's macroeconomics owe to Fisher? What features of the messages of Fisher and Keynes accounted for the displacement of Fisher by Keynes in the profession's attention?

Keynes on Fisher's *Purchasing Power of Money*

Fisher, drawing on Simon Newcomb's "equation of societary circulation," organized *The Purchasing Power of Money* ([1911, 1913] 1985) around a version of the quantity theory of money with a different emphasis from the Cambridge cash balance approach of Keynes 1923, Pigou 1917, and Marshall 1923 (see Patinkin 1990). The Marshallian economists at Cambridge considered the cash balances desired at a given level of nominal income (and, in some formulations, wealth), $M = kPY$, while Fisher stressed the transactions velocity of circulation and allowed for currency and bank deposits having different velocities,

$MV + M'V' = PT$. Use of such forms of the equation of exchange rather than explicit functional notation for the demand for money often led monetary economists of the period to forget that Marshall's verbal discussion included wealth as well as income as an influence on money holding. Similarly, Keynes, in the chapter of the *Tract* on the value of money, forgot that the analysis elsewhere in the book of the social cost of an inflation-induced reduction in real money balances implied the rate of change of prices as an influence on money demand. Fisher recognized foregone interest as a cost of holding money, yet he did not write the velocity of circulation as a function of the nominal interest rate. Only with liquidity preference in *The General Theory* was money demand written as an explicit function of income and interest rate.

Keynes reviewed Fisher 1911 for the *Economic Journal* in September 1911 (CW 11:375–81), judging that "Professor Fisher's book is marked, as all his books are, by extreme lucidity and brilliance of statement. It is original, suggestive, and, on the whole, accurate; and it supplies a better exposition of monetary theory than is available elsewhere" (376). He complained, however, that

> Professor Fisher never explains clearly *how* new gold raises prices *in the first instance*, and is content with showing by the quantity theory that new gold *must* raise them somehow. There is, of course, no single explanation suited to all times and places, but the general outlines of the theory have been indicated by Dr Marshall in his evidence before the Gold and Silver Commission in 1887, and before the Indian Currency Committee in 1898. (377)

It was at the latter that Marshall explained how increased bank reserves due to new gold supplies lead to increased lending at lower interest rates, stimulating spending. Keynes added in a footnote that "Professor Fisher's book contains no reference to this evidence, which constitutes the most important contribution to monetary theory published in England since the time of Ricardo, and there seems good reason to suppose that he is not acquainted with it" (377n).

Keynes's review of Fisher asserted the existence of a Cambridge oral tradition in monetary theory, passed on in lectures and tutorials and published only in Marshall's answers to questions of official commissions. This testimony was largely inaccessible until Keynes edited Marshall's *Official Papers* for the Royal Economic Society in 1926. The octogenarian Marshall's *Money, Credit and Commerce* (1923) incorporated decades-old official testimony and manuscripts from half a century before. In his 1924 memorial article on Marshall, Keynes repeated his claim:

> Since *Money* was from the early seventies onwards one of his favourite topics for lectures, his main ideas became known to pupils in a general way, with the result that there grew up at Cambridge an oral tradition, first from Marshall's own lectures and after his retirement from those of Professor Pigou, different from, and (I think it may be claimed) superior to, anything that could be found in printed books until recently. (cited in Pigou 1925, 27)

He added in a footnote that "Professor Irving Fisher has been the first, in several instances, to publish in book-form ideas analogous to those which had been worked out by Marshall at much earlier dates" (27n). Fisher accepted Keynes's claim of priority for Marshall and quoted this footnote in a talk at a dinner given by Harvard's economics department for Fisher's seventy-fifth birthday in 1942 (Fisher 1956, 339). Keynes's claim for a Cambridge oral tradition was weakened by his immediately preceding footnote, observing that Marshall's "unsystematic method of lecturing prevented the average, and even the superior, student from getting down in his notes anything very consecutive or complete" (Pigou 1925, 27n).

Keynes claimed priority for Marshall on the distinction between the real and money interest rates on the basis of the concluding note of book 6, chapter 6 of the *Principles* without mentioning Fisher's attribution of the distinction to Marshall (Pigou 1925, 30). Keynes added in a footnote that "in repeating the substance of this Note to the Indian Currency Committee (1899), [Marshall] refers in generous terms to the then-recent elaboration of the idea in Professor Irving Fisher's *Appreciation and Interest* (1896). See also for some analogous ideas Marshall's [and Mary Paley Marshall's] first *Economics of Industry* (1879), Book III, chap.i" (30n). Keynes was more concerned with questions of priority between Marshall and Fisher than were either of the principals.

Keynes may have been mistaken in his review about Fisher's ignorance of Marshall's testimony. In *Appreciation and Interest*, Fisher ([1896] 1991, 78n, 86n, 90n) cited Marshall's testimony on bimetallism and a multiple standard in the 1886 Report on Depression of Trade, and he quoted Marshall's *Principles*, crediting Marshall with understanding the distinction between money and commodity interest (Fisher [1896] 1991, 79; cf. Fisher [1911] 1985, 71–72). The first footnote on page 79 of Fisher

[1896] 1991 referred to the Report of the Gold and Silver Commission of 1888 along with the Report on Depression of Trade, and was between two footnotes citing Marshall, but it did not mention Marshall's evidence contained in the Gold and Silver Commission report.

In the preface to the second edition of *The Purchasing Power of Money*, Fisher stated that, were it not for his desire to disturb the plates of the first edition as little as possible, he would wish to make some changes

> to meet a criticism of Mr. Keynes's to the effect that, while my book shows *that* the changes in the quantity of money do affect the price level, it does not show *how* they do so. To those who feel the need of a more definite picture of *how* the price level is affected by a change in the quantity of money I refer the reader to my *Elementary Principles of Economics*, pages 242–247, and to other writers on this subject, particularly Cairnes. ([1913] 1985, xiii)

Fisher's reference was to the second edition of *Elementary Principles of Economics* published in 1912 (the first edition in 1910), after Keynes's review, so that exposition might be regarded as a response to Keynes.

A striking feature of Keynes's review, in light of his later interests, is the absence of discussion of Fisher's chapter 4 on transition periods during which monetary changes have real effects, the source of Fisher's monetary theory of economic fluctuations (see Dimand 1993; Patinkin 1972). Instead, Keynes, who had in 1909 won the Adam Smith Prize with an essay on "The Method of Index Numbers with Special Reference to the Measurement of General Exchange Value" (CW 11:49–156), preferred to examine Fisher's index number calculations. Keynes complained that

> when Professor Fisher comes to the separate determination of P and T, he is content to publish what seem to the present reviewer to be unscientific guesses of the wildest character. . . . This choice of weights seems to be founded on little evidence. . . . Professor Fisher's theory, that the weights employed in compiling an index number seldom affect the result, naturally leads him to think that an index number made for one purpose is equally suitable for another, and that the method of compilation can be safely determined by considerations of taste and convenience. (CW 11:379–80)

He also objected that "in the long appendix on index numbers, in which marks for different kinds of merit are given to 44 different formulae, it seems a waste of time to have demonstrated the unsuitability of numerous expressions which have never previously been suggested, far less advocated, by anyone" (381).

Keynes concluded with a brief notice of "Professor Fisher's admirable proposal for an international currency, based on a combination of a tabular standard and a gold-exchange standard. The main outlines of his scheme do deserve very careful consideration, and if he can revive general interest in such proposals he will have done a great service to the progress of monetary reform" (CW 11:381). Keynes's advocacy of a central bank and gold-exchange standard for India culminated in his first book, *Indian Currency and Finance* (1913). Under such a gold-exchange standard, as with Ricardo's ingot plan, only paper would circulate domestically, with gold reserved for international payments to maintain the fixed gold parity of the currency. This would economize on the use of real resources to produce gold and give the central bank some leeway to vary the internal note issue in response to seasonal and other fluctuations (see Dimand 1991b). Such interests led Keynes to see more of the gold exchange standard in Fisher's compensated dollar proposal than was there. Fisher advocated varying the gold value of the dollar to stabilize the dollar value of a basket of commodities, while Keynes 1913 proposed a fixed value for the rupee in gold-convertible sterling.

After World War I brought floating exchange rates, Keynes shifted in the *Tract on Monetary Reform* (1923) to domestic currency management to maintain internal price stability in place of a fixed gold value of the currency, but with inconvertible paper currency, not Fisher's notion of gold convertibility at a varying parity. In *A Treatise on Money* (1930), Keynes turned from the nationally managed currency of the *Tract* to endorse an international currency based on a tabular standard of the sort advocated by Fisher and Marshall, stabilizing the price of a basket of sixty commodities, not just the price of the single commodity gold. National currencies would be convertible into supranational bank money issued by an international central bank.

Keynes cited Fisher's *Purchasing Power of Money* in both his elementary and more advanced lectures on money at Cambridge from 1912 to 1914. Apart from listing that book, *The Rate of Interest* (1907), and *Appreciation and Interest* among the general references, Keynes referred only to Fisher's attempts at inductive verification of the quantity theory of money (CW 12:702, 771) and, at greater length, to Fisher's discussion of influences on the velocity of circulation and his attempt to directly measure the velocity of circulation of money held by Yale students (700,

760–64). He remarked again that in America "Prof. Marshall's evidence before G. and S. Commission is not generally known there (not even by Prof. Fisher)" (730).

Keynes on Fisher and the Credit Cycle, 1913

Keynes first met Fisher in London in 1912 and, according to Robert Skidelsky (1992, 168), "the two men got on well and remained in touch for the rest of Keynes's life," despite differences in temperament between the economist whose great regret in life was not drinking enough champagne and the teetotaling, nonsmoking, near vegetarian who wrote three books opposing the repeal of Prohibition. Bloomsbury might have shocked Fisher even more than the sight of Mrs. Pareto smoking a cigarette (Fisher 1956, 65; "Mrs." is the title that Fisher accorded the marchioness).

Whether because of their conversation in London in 1912 or because of further reflection, Keynes's interpretation of Fisher's economics changed substantially. In his 1911 review, Keynes criticized Fisher for not explaining how an augmented gold stock would increase credit, spending, and prices, and ignored his chapter on real fluctuations due to monetary disturbances. On 3 December 1913, Keynes addressed the Political Economy Club at the Hotel Cecil in London on "How Far Are Bankers Responsible for the Alternations of Crisis and Depression?":

> The most ordinary theory of the way in which banking considerations come in, chiefly associated perhaps with the name of Professor Irving Fisher, is roughly as follows: Bankers find themselves with a higher ratio of cash reserves than in their opinion caution really requires. Accordingly they give more credit. This raises prices. Producers generally have a bigger volume of trade at better prices than they ever expected. They are, therefore, very ready to borrow. Bankers now raise the rate they charge for accommodation. But they do not, in general, raise it fast enough to keep pace with the growing profitableness of buying something now, with money borrowed for three months, which is going to be worth more three months hence. Gradually or suddenly bankers discover that their cash reserves have sunk to a lower ratio than is safe. Credit is sharply curtailed. Those, who have bought on the expectation of prices rising yet higher or of trade expanding yet further, find themselves out in their calculations. And a crisis or depression has arrived. (CW 13:2)

Keynes said of this theory that "for my own part I have always felt it clever, rather than satisfactory. It does not seem to be laying bare fundamental things. It strikes one as diagnosing symptoms rather than causes" (CW 13:3). Influenced by Dennis Robertson's forthcoming *A Study of Industrial Fluctuation* (1915) (see Keynes to Robertson, 28 September 1913, CW 13:1), Keynes offered instead the argument that "what precipitates a reduction of banking facilities and a crisis is not lack of money, that is to say of gold coin, but lack of free, uninvested capital. It is not so much the proportion of [a] bank's commitments to its cash reserves, as the *character* of its commitments" (CW 13:9). Keynes stressed the relation of investment to saving rather than the amount of bank reserves.

In light of his review of Fisher two years before, it is noteworthy that Keynes associated Fisher with a theory of how a change in the monetary base changes credit and affects economic activity. It is also notable that Keynes considered this monetary theory of fluctuations so recently formulated in Fisher (1911) and Ralph Hawtrey's *Good and Bad Trade* ([1913] 1970), anticipated by some remarks by Marshall, to be the approach "most in vogue in academic circles today." Fisher was the only economist named in Keynes's paper (and the only economist cited in Hawtrey's book). Keynes did not refer to his fellow Cambridge wrangler and Apostle Hawtrey, perhaps tactfully since that was the first meeting of the Political Economy Club attended by Hawtrey (Deutscher 1990, 16). In his 1961 foreword to a reissue of *Good and Bad Trade*, Hawtrey recalled concluding that "a falling price level makes a given market rate of interest more onerous, and a rising price level less so. Here, I thought, was a discovery, but I was disillusioned when I learnt from an economist friend that the principle was one already recognised, and had been expounded in Irving Fisher's work, *The Rate of Interest*" ([1913] 1970, vii). Perhaps Keynes was the economist friend. The economist friend evidently did not mention chapter 4 of Fisher 1911, since Hawtrey "was not discouraged, for at any rate its application to the explanation of the trade cycle would be new" (vii).

Monetary Reform

In the *Tract on Monetary Reform*, Keynes wrote that his exposition of the quantity theory of money followed the general lines of Pigou (1917) and Marshall (1923) rather than the perhaps more familiar analysis of Professor Irving Fisher. Instead of starting with the amount of cash held by the public, Professor Fisher begins with the volume of business transacted by means of money and the frequency with which each unit of money changes hands. It comes to the same thing in the end and it is easy to pass from the above formula to Professor Fisher's; but the above method of approach seems less artificial than Professor Fisher's and nearer to the observed facts. (CW 4:63n)

Keynes's writings of this period, within the quantity theory tradition of Marshall and Fisher, are well thought of by new classical macroeconomists such as Thomas Sargent (1992, 51n, 239n, 251n), with the silent omission of the *Tract*'s account of the unpleasant consequences of deflation.

The *Tract* was based on articles by Keynes in the series of twelve supplements on "Reconstruction in Europe" that he edited for the *Manchester Guardian Commercial* in 1922. Discussing "The Stabilisation of the European Exchanges" in the eleventh supplement (7 December 1922), Keynes warned that deflation would depress business and cause unemployment, citing an article on "Devaluation versus Deflation" making that case in the same issue, "written with overwhelming force and lucidity" by Irving Fisher. According to Roy Harrod, "this article by Keynes was his first to sound a clear warning against the evils of deflation and may therefore be regarded as the preface to the work which was to absorb his interests for the next fifteen years and to lead him far from his original starting-point" (1951, 314).

Keynes pointed out that "the proposals of Professor Irving Fisher for a compensated dollar amounted, unless all countries adopted the same plan, to putting into practice a preference for stability of internal price level over stability of external exchange" (CW 4:126), just as Keynes wished.

We shall look on Edward III's debasements of sterling money with a more tolerant eye if we regard them as a method of carrying into effect a preference for stability of internal prices over stability of external exchanges, celebrating that monarch as an enlightened forerunner of Professor Irving Fisher in advocacy of the 'compensated dollar,' only more happy than the latter in his opportunities to carry theory into practice. (131)

Keynes went on to remark that "the pioneer of price stability as against exchange stability, Professor Irving Fisher, advocated the former in the shape of his 'compensated dollar,' which was to be automatically adjusted by reference to an index number of prices without any play of judgement or discretion" (CW 4:147). Keynes opposed such a mechanical rule, quoting Hawtrey to the effect that monetary policy should counteract expected future price changes, not past price changes. Accordingly, Keynes envisioned a greater role for discretionary monetary management since "Professor Fisher's method may be adapted to deal with long-period trends in the value of gold but not with the, often more injurious, short-period oscillations of the credit cycle" (148).

In 1925, Keynes wrote to Fisher that "all students of Monetary Theory and advocates of Monetary Reform will always recognise you as the true leader and pioneer of this movement" (Keynes to Fisher, 14 May 1925, quoted in Skidelsky 1992, 168). The price stabilizer who wrote the *Tract* was in close sympathy with Fisher.

Fisher, as a pioneer in index numbers, received extensive mention in Keynes's *Treatise on Money* (1930). Book 2 dealt with index numbers, drawing on Keynes's Adam Smith Prize essay of 1909. The index to the *Treatise* listed ten references to Fisher, all but one in the first volume, two of them to passages from the *Treatise* that were six or seven pages long. Fisher was cited on index numbers in book 2 (CW 1:55, 56n, 78, 111–16), on the distinction between real and money interest rates (CW 1:197n, 2:202), and for the equation of exchange (CW 1:78, 150, 233–39). Keynes moved in the *Treatise* toward Fisher's proposed international tabular standard. The theoretical heart of the *Treatise*, however, was where Keynes parted from Fisher. He cited Fisher for the equation of exchange used to illustrate the quantity theory of money, and then he replaced this with his own so-called fundamental equations for the value of money which would coincide with Fisher's equation only when (planned) investment equalled (planned) saving, so that windfall profits would be zero (see Dimand 1988, chap. 2). Keynes presented these fundamental equations (which did not hold up well in critical discussion) within an apparent quantity theory framework, but he was in fact switching to a saving-investment analysis.

Great-Grandparent of *The General Theory*?

In 1937, Keynes wrote:

> The meaning of 'marginal efficiency of capital' of which I make use—
> and which is, in my opinion, the only definition of the term which
> makes good sense—was first introduced into economic theory by Irv-
> ing Fisher in his *Theory of Interest* (1930), under the designation 'the
> rate of return over cost.' This conception of his is, I think, the most
> important and fruitful of his recent original suggestions. (CW 14:101n)

This was written, however, in a volume of essays in honor of Irving
Fisher, and contributors to a festschrift are not under oath concerning
the recipient of the volume. In Robert Bryce's notes on Keynes's lecture
on 26 November 1934 on the marginal efficiency of capital, the statement that "Fisher's solution is just nonsense" is underlined and is set
off by blank lines before and after (Rymes 1989, 150). Stephen LeRoy
(1983) argues that, despite Keynes's careful avoidance of controversy
with Fisher on the issue in *The General Theory*, Keynes's marginal efficiency of capital is the discount rate that would equate the present value
of the stream of expected proceeds from a capital asset to the supply price
of the capital asset, while Fisher's rate of return over cost would equate
it to the demand price of the capital asset (cf. Dimand 1988, 184–87).
This is consistent with Bryce's notes for 26 November 1934, according
to which Keynes held that Fisher "confuses m.e.c. with r. of i." by having
expected inflation act directly on the rate of interest rather than marginal
efficiency of capital (in Rymes 1987, paraphrased in Rymes 1989, 150).
   Keynes wrote to Harrod on 27 August 1935 that "my definition of
marginal efficiency of capital is quite different from anything to be found
in [Marshall's] work or in that of any other classical economist (except
for a passage which he makes little subsequent use of in Irving Fisher's
latest book)" (CW 13:549). Replying on 20 February 1935 to comments
from Robertson, Keynes wrote:

> I agree that in other contexts Fisher in effect assumes that an expecta-
> tion of higher prices causes the marginal efficiency of capital to rise.
> And this, of course, I agree with. My point is that it has been very com-
> mon hitherto to confuse the proposition that the marginal efficiency of
> capital is greater with the proposition that the rate of interest is greater.
> It looks to me as if *you* may still be holding that an increase in the
> marginal efficiency of capital, whilst not quite the same thing as a rise
> in the rate of interest, necessarily involves it. For otherwise you must
> agree with me in accepting one half of the Fisher doctrine and denying
> the other half. (518)

Keynes's letters to Harrod and Robertson, and Bryce's notes on Keynes's lecture, clarify Keynes's attitude toward Fisher on the marginal efficiency of capital. Keynes accepted that Fisher 1930 contained a passage defining rate of return over costs in the manner that Keynes defined marginal efficiency of capital, but he regarded Fisher as usually mistaking the direct effect of expected inflation as acting on the rate of interest rather than on the marginal efficiency of capital (expected rate of return over cost). Jan Kregel (1988, 65) points out that Keynes's acknowledgment of Fisher's definition in *The General Theory* (1936, 140–41) immediately precedes his criticism of the confusion that in his lecture and letters he attributed to Fisher (141–42).

Kregel further finds "no available evidence to indicate that Keynes had read the 1930 book by Fisher or that his development of marginal efficiency was influenced by it" (1988, 65). The similarity of the two definitions was noted by Redvers Opie and communicated to Keynes by way of Claude Guillebaud and Richard Kahn after Keynes had formulated the marginal efficiency of capital (see the note appended to the discussion of Donald Moggridge's paper in Patinkin and Leith 1977, 89n).

In a 1937 journal exchange with Ohlin, Hawtrey, and Robertson, Keynes wrote that he did not regard Hawtrey and Robertson as classical economists:

> On the contrary, they strayed from the fold sooner than I did. I regard Mr Hawtrey as my grandparent and Mr Robertson as my parent in the paths of errancy, and I have been greatly influenced by them. I might also meet Professor Ohlin's complaint by adopting Wicksell as my great-grandparent, if I had known his works in more detail at an earlier stage in my own thought and also if I did not have the thought that Wicksell was *trying* to be 'classical.' As it is, so far as I am concerned, I find, looking back, that it was Professor Irving Fisher who was the great-grandparent who first influenced me strongly towards regarding money as a 'real' factor. (CW 14:202–3n)

Thus, while other economists were closer relations of the Keynes of *The General Theory*, Fisher's work had, in an earlier period, helped Keynes think about the role of money in real fluctuations and to consider what difference it made that real output and employment are determined in a monetary economy rather than a barter one.

Keynes's Influence on Fisher

While Keynes carefully studied Fisher's monetary economics, Fisher's references to Keynes reveal no comparable scrutiny. In *The Money Illusion*, Fisher cited Keynes as proposing a managed currency rather than varying the gold weight of the currency (1928, 169), and he quoted a *New Republic* article by Keynes on the objects of currency reform (223). Keynes was not among the seventy-two people thanked by Fisher for comments on a mimeographed draft of the book. Fisher's *After Reflation, What?* (1933a) opened with two quotations, each dated 3 July 1933, in lieu of a dedication: President Roosevelt's radiogram to the London Economic Conference that "the United States of America seeks the kind of dollar which a generation hence will have the same purchasing power and debt-paying power as the dollar we hope to attain in the near future" and Keynes's comment that "Mr. Roosevelt . . . is magnificently right." In *100% Money*, Fisher quoted a former vice-governor of the Federal Reserve as quoting Keynes to the effect that it is "most unfortunate that depositors should be able to take the initiative in changing the volume of the community's money" ([1935] 1945, 44) and remarked that Keynes and Cassell were among those who had observed that bankers had sometimes opposed changes that turned out to be in their interest (171). Keynes's name did not appear on any of Fisher's five pages of acknowledgments to those who commented on drafts of *100% Money*, nor does his name appear in the index of *The Theory of Interest* (1930). Keynes sent Fisher a complimentary copy of *The General Theory* on its publication (CW 29:207), but it is not clear that Fisher ever read it. Keynes's advocacy of expansionary fiscal policy in the late 1920s and early 1930s differed from Fisher's continued exclusive emphasis on monetary policy, but it did not inspire a published critique.

Fisher referred to Keynes in a fifteen-page letter on 9 July 1945 to Philip Cortney, president of Coty and a gold standard hardliner who disapproved of both Keynes's *General Theory* and Fisher's compensated dollar. Fisher wrote that

> I'm assuming that you earnestly wish to discover any errors you have committed, and are willing to change your mind on evidence, just as Keynes has, and I have, and many other earnest truth seekers.
>
> As to Keynes' views, I have no desire to defend them all; for, as I understand them, I differ in some ways, though not, I think, much in the sphere of money. Incidentally, he told me that my *Purchasing*

Power of Money was the first book on money which "made sense" to him and on the basis of which all his future work was done. . . .

No permanent and satisfactory solution of the money problem is possible unless, and until, it is international. The Bretton Woods proposal is our opportunity and ought not to be missed. . . .

Keynes has, I think, always been a stabilizer, though the criterion of absolute stability has shifted with him just as to some extent, it has with me. (Fisher 1956, 328–30)

This letter epitomizes Fisher's attitude toward Keynes and his very Fisher-centered view of economics. He regarded Keynes as a responsible scholar who would change his mind given sufficient evidence, thought well of Keynes's commitment to internal stability, and approved of the Bretton Woods agreement. At the same time, he made no mention of the substance of Keynes's contributions to macroeconomic theory, and he exaggerated the role of Fisher 1911 as a foundation for Keynes's later work. Fisher did not specify in which decade Keynes made his statement about the Fisherian basis of his later work, which sounds compatible in tone with the *Tract* and Keynes's May 1925 letter to Fisher. Indeed, the lack of discussion of the substance of *The General Theory*, and earlier of the *Treatise on Money*, was typical of Fisher.

Fisher's reaction to Keynes's *Treatise on Money* and *General Theory* is extraordinary for a monetary economist of his generation. Responses to Keynes differed widely among monetary economists and business cycle theorists. Joseph Schumpeter and Friedrich Hayek, who had admired Keynes's stand against the Versailles Peace Treaty and the blockade of Germany and Austria, turned sharply against his later books. Jacques Rueff and Etienne Mantoux, critical of the early Keynes for letting the Germans off on reparations, also rejected *The General Theory*. Alvin Hansen criticized the "fundamental equations" of the *Treatise* and wrote two hostile reviews of *The General Theory* but then became Keynes's American apostle and interpreter. William Beveridge used his final address as director of the London School of Economics in 1937 to denounce *The General Theory* for abstract theorizing, and then became an advocate of interventionist fiscal policy to stabilize unemployment at a level lower than even Keynes thought attainable. Knight and Simons, Hawtrey and Robertson, Viner and Leontief, Williams and Cole, Adarkar and Shenoy, Dobb, Haberler, Henderson, Loria, Pigou, Taussig, Kalecki and Zawadski, Shibata and Takata—all wrote major reviews and review articles on the *Treatise* and *General Theory*. Irving Fisher remained amiably disposed toward Keynes as a person, but he was not moved to take a stand on Keynes's economics or to reconsider his approach to macroeconomic theory. Irving Norton Fisher's 1961 bibliography of his father's voluminous writings lists no reviews of books by Keynes. Instead, Fisher drifted to other interests. The only new books he published after the appearance of Keynes's *General Theory* were *Constructive Income Taxation* (1942), with his brother Herbert W. Fisher, criticizing double taxation and tax disincentives to saving, and *World Maps and Globes* (1944), with O. M. Miller, proposing a new world map to avoid the distortions of the Mercator projection. He brought out a new edition of *100% Money* in 1945 and wrote to Keynes in 1944 to try to enlist his support for 100 percent reserve banking, but this was unrelated to the macroeconomic debates ignited by Keynes.

Why Didn't We All Become Fisherians?

Keynes's *Tract on Monetary Reform*, written within the Marshallian tradition of the quantity theory of money, and the index number analysis of book 2 of *A Treatise on Money* were strongly compatible with such Fisher works as *Stabilizing the Dollar* (1920) and *The Making of Index Numbers* (1922). The later revival of the quantity theory of money as monetarism drew on the innovations of these theorists of the 1920s as much as on a continuing older tradition, and it owed much to Keynes (1923) on interest rate parity and on inflation as a tax, to Fisher (1923) on correlation of an output series with a distributed lag of past price level changes, and to Fisher ([1896] 1991, 1907, 1930) on money interest as the sum of real interest and expected inflation, with the latter represented by a distributed lag of past price changes. However, the *Tract* and book 2 of the *Treatise on Money* were not the works of Keynes that captured the interest and imagination of the economics profession. It is notable that Keynes claimed Fisher as a great-grandparent of *The General Theory* but no closer relation.

   The General Theory tackled a problem not considered by Fisher which the Depression had forced to the profession's attention: the possibility of lasting, massive involuntary unemployment arising from a coordination failure in a decentralized market economy in the absence of deliberate government intervention to restore full employment. Friedrich Hayek, an emphatic critic of Keynes, stressed this problem, investigating how a decentralized market economy could produce spontaneous order and co-ordination. Keynesians and neo-Austrians reached opposite conclusions, but on the same coordination problem (Garretsen 1992; O'Driscoll 1975). Irving Fisher had nothing to say on this question. He presented empirical evidence that monetary changes affected real output and employment, and he proposed a variety of measures to neutralize the effects of these monetary shocks: the compensated dollar, 100 percent reserve banking, index-linked bonds, and educating the public against money illusion. As in *The Purchasing Power of Money*, however, he separated such issues from general economic theory, defining them as problems of the transition from one full employment equilibrium to another, with eventual convergence to the new equilibrium price level and to potential output inevitable.

Fisher's one great, potentially fruitful contribution to macroeconomic theory in the 1930s, the debt-deflation theory of depressions (Dimand 1994; Fisher 1932, 1933b), was largely ignored by reviewers in scholarly journals, appearing after his public reputation was battered by his insistent pre-1929 denials of the possibility of a stock market crash. Fisher (1932) received only a single dismissive paragraph when it was reviewed jointly with another book in the *Economic Journal*, where a more insightful review might have attracted Keynes's attention to the book. Keynes, as a Fellow of the Econometric Society and a member of the editorial advisory board of *Econometrica*, received the issue containing Fisher 1933b, but he did not give *Econometrica* anything like the careful attention he devoted to the *Economic Journal*, which he edited. Keynes thus lacked a powerful support when responding to Pigou's claim that the real balance effect guaranteed that price deflation could restore full employment by increasing wealth and thus real consumption. Keynes and Kalecki argued that the Pigou effect applied only to outside money, not government bonds or other inside debt (see Dimand 1991a). They did not, however, cite Fisher's case that unanticipated price deflation, in the presence of inside debt denominated in money, could depress real aggregate demand through redistribution and risk of bankruptcy (Tobin 1980, chap. 1). Keynes also failed to cite in that context a similar argument in two paragraphs in his 1931 Harris Foundation lectures in Chicago (CW 13:360–61).

Most surprisingly, Fisher's monetary economics was out of place in the macroeconomic debates of the 1930s and later because it was not cast in terms of saving, investment, and effective demand. This seems at first utterly paradoxical. Modern theories of saving and consumption build on the "Fisher separation theorem" between earning and spending decisions of Fisher 1930, with its two-period example of optimization of the intertemporal consumption stream subject to the budget constraint that the present value of lifetime consumption not exceed the present value of expected lifetime income (given efficient credit markets), rather than on the simple current-income consumption function of *The General Theory*. As for investment, when Fisher was discussed in such works as Alvin Hansen's *Business Cycles and National Income* (1951, 329–34), it was to identify the rate of return over cost of Fisher 1930, using Keynes's marginal efficiency of capital. But Fisher developed the capital theory of 1907 and 1930, in which impatience (time preference) and the productivity of capital determined the rate of interest, in sharp separation from his monetary theory of economic fluctuations and his debt-deflation theory of depressions. In his capital theory and his long-run quantity theory of money, he abstracted from transition periods, so that monetary changes (and implicitly any aggregate demand shift) affected only prices and nominal interest, not output, employment, or real interest. His monetary theory of the level of economic activity did not draw on what *The Rate of Interest* had to offer about saving and investment, just as his monetary economics as a whole was not cast in the general equilibrium framework of his doctoral dissertation (Fisher 1892): "In his neoclassical writings on capital and interest Fisher had laid the basis for the investment and saving equations central to modern macroeconomic models. Had Fisher pulled these strands together into a coherent theory, he could have been an American Keynes" (Tobin 1985, 36–37).

Fisher contributed many important things to macroeconomics, but Keynes provided in *The General Theory* a grand synthesis and a framework in which to think about output, employment, and coordination. In Aesop's terms, macroeconomics heeded the hedgehog who knew one big thing, not the fox who knew many things. Modern macroeconomics owes many technical innovations to Fisher, more innovations perhaps than to anyone except Keynes and possibly the pioneering econometricians. Despite this, Fisher's monetary economics did not meet the needs of the post-1930 generations of macroeconomists concerned with saving, investment, the level of effective demand, and the questions of why unemployment occurs and whether it will disappear by itself without activist government demand management.

I am grateful for helpful comments to William Barber, James Tobin, and other participants in the Yale workshop on economic history and the history of economic thought, and to David Laidler and other participants in the *HOPE* conference at Wake Forest on "New Perspectives on Keynes."

References

Blaug, M. 1991. *John Maynard Keynes (1883–1946)*. 2 vols. Aldershot: Edward Elgar.

Deutscher, P. 1990. R. G. Hawtrey and the *Development of Macroeconomics*. Ann Arbor: University of Michigan Press.

Dimand, R. 1988. *The Origins of the Keynesian Revolution*. Aldershot: Edward Elgar, and Stanford, CA: Stanford University Press.

———. 1991a. Keynes, Kalecki, Ricardian Equivalence, and the Real Balance Effect. *Bulletin of Economic Research* 43:289–92.

———. 1991b. "A Prodigy of Constructive Work": J. M. Keynes on *Indian Currency and Finance*. In *Perspectives on the History of Economic Thought*. Vol. 6: *Themes in Keynesian Criticism*. Edited by W. J. Barber. Aldershot and Brookfield, Vt.: Edward Elgar.

———. 1993. The Dance of the Dollar: Irving Fisher's Monetary Theory of Economic Fluctuations. *History of Economics Review* 20:161–72.

———. 1994. Irving Fisher's Debt-Deflation Theory of Great Depressions. *Review of Social Economy* 52:92–107.

Dogan, M., and R. Pahre. 1990. Scholarly Reputation and Obsolescence in the Social Sciences: Innovation as a Team Sport. *International Social Science Journal* 125:417–27.

Fisher, I. [1892] [1925] 1991. *Mathematical Investigations in the Theory of Value and Prices: Transactions of the Connecticut Academy* 9. Fairfield, N.J.: A. M. Kelley.

———. [1896] 1991. *Appreciation and Interest*. New York: Macmillan for the American Economic Association. Fairfield, N.J.: A. M. Kelley.

———. 1907. *The Rate of Interest*. New York: Macmillan.

———. [1910] 1912. *Elementary Principles of Economics*. 2d ed. New York: Macmillan.

Fisher, I., assisted by H. G. Brown. [1911] 1985. *The Purchasing Power of Money*. Fairfield, N.J.: A. M. Kelley.

———. 1920. *Stabilizing the Dollar*. New York: Macmillan.

———. 1922. *The Making of Index Numbers*. Cambridge, Mass.: Houghton Mifflin for the Pollak Foundation for Economic Research.

———. 1923. Business Cycle Largely a "Dance of the Dollar." *Quarterly Publications of the American Statistical Association*, n.s., 18:1024–28.

———. 1926. A Statistical Relation between Unemployment and Price Changes. *International Labour Review* 13:785–92. Reprinted 1973 as "I Discovered the Phillips Curve," *Journal of Political Economy*

81:496–502.

———. 1928. *The Money Illusion*. New York: Adelphi, and London: Allen & Unwin.

———. 1930. *The Theory of Interest*. New York: Macmillan.

———. 1932. *Booms and Depressions*. New York: Adelphi.

———. 1933a. *After Reflation, What?* New York: Adelphi.

———. 1933b. The Debt-Deflation Theory of Great Depressions. *Econometrica* 1:337–57.

———. [1935] 1945. *100% Money*. 3d ed. New Haven, Conn.: City Printing.

———. 1956. *My Father Irving Fisher*. New York: Comet.

———. 1961. *A Bibliography of the Writings of Irving Fisher*. New Haven, Conn.: Yale University Library.

Fisher, I., and H. W. Fisher. 1942. *Constructive Income Taxation*. New York: Harper.

Fisher, I., and O. M. Miller. 1944. *World Maps and Globes*. New York: Essential.

Garretsen, H. 1992. *Keynes, Coordination and Beyond*. Aldershot: Edward Elgar.

Hansen, A. H. 1951. *Business Cycles and National Income*. New York: Norton.

Harrod, R. F. 1951. *The Life of John Maynard Keynes*. London: Macmillan.

Hawtrey, R. G. [1913] 1970. *Good and Bad Trade*. London: Constable. Reprinted, New York: A. M. Kelley.

Keynes, John Maynard. 1913. *Indian Currency and Finance*. London: Macmillan.

———. 1923. *A Tract on Monetary Reform*. London: Macmillan.

———. 1930. *A Treatise on Money*. London: Macmillan.

———. 1936. *The General Theory of Employment, Interest and Money*. London: Macmillan.

———. 1939. Professor Tinbergen's Method. *Economic Journal* 249:558–78.

———. 1971–89. *The Collected Writings of John Maynard Keynes*. 30 vols. Edited by D. E. Moggridge. London: Macmillan. (CW)

Kregel, J. A. 1988. Irving Fisher, Great-Grandparent of the *General Theory*: Money, Rate of Return over Cost and Efficiency of Capital. *Cahiers d'Economie Politique* 14–15:59–68.

LeRoy, S. 1983. Keynes' Theory of Investment. *HOPE* 15:397–421.

Marshall, A. 1923. *Money, Credit and Commerce*. London: Macmillan.

———. 1926. *Official Papers*. Edited by J. M. Keynes. London: Macmillan.

Marshall, A., and M. P. Marshall. 1879. *Economics of Industry*. London: Macmillan.

Moggridge, D. E. 1992. *Maynard Keynes: An Economist's Biography*. London and New York: Routledge.

O'Driscoll, G. 1975. *Economics as a Coordination Problem: The Contribution of Friedrich Hayek*. Kansas City, Mo.: Sheed, Andrews & McMeel.

Patinkin, D. 1972. On the Short-Run Non-Neutrality of Money in the Quantity Theory. *Banca Nazionale del Lavoro Quarterly Review* 100:3–22.

———. 1990. *Irving Fisher, the Cambridge School, and the Quantity Theory*. Seoul: Korea Development Institute.

Patinkin, D., and J. C. Leith, eds. 1977. *Keynes, Cambridge and the General Theory*. London: Macmillan.

Pigou, A. C. 1917. The Value of Money. *Quarterly Journal of Economics* 32:38–65.

————, ed. 1925. *Memorials of Alfred Marshall*. London: Macmillan.

Robertson, D. H. 1915. *A Study of Industrial Fluctuation*. London: P. S. King.

Rymes, T. K., ed. 1987. *Keynes's Lectures, 1932–35: Notes of Students*. Ottawa: Department of Economics, Carleton University.

————. 1989. *Keynes's Lectures, 1932–35: Notes of a Representative Student*. London: Macmillan, and Ann Arbor: University of Michigan Press.

Sargent, T. J. 1992. *Rational Expectations and Inflation*. 2d ed. New York: Harper-Collins.

Skidelsky, R. 1992. *John Maynard Keynes*. Vol. 2: *The Economist as Saviour, 1920–1937*. London: Macmillan.

Tobin, J. 1980. *Asset Accumulation and Economic Activity*. Chicago: University of Chicago Press.

————. 1985. Neoclassical Theory in America: J. B. Clark and Fisher. *American Economic Review* 75.6:28–38.

Wood, J. C. 1983. *John Maynard Keynes: Critical Assessments*. 4 vols. London: Croom-Helm.

Comment

David Laidler

At a conference dedicated to Keynes and Keynesian economics, it is salutary to be reminded that modern macroeconomics was by no means the creation of one man. Keynes did, after all, have important predecessors and contemporaries who made significant contributions of their own, which Keynes then often developed and synthesized, not always for the better. Irving Fisher would have to be high on anyone's list of Keynes's important contemporaries, and Robert Dimand's article is, therefore, extremely welcome. It is also extremely well informed. I very much doubt if there is any detail of the material to which I shall refer in these comments that is not already well known to Dimand, but my view of how some of those details fit into the story of the development of modern macroeconomics is a little different from his.

Let me begin with an early point of contact between Fisher and Keynes to which Dimand draws our attention: namely, the fact that both of them, if forced to make a choice, gave pride of place among policy goals to domestic stability over the maintenance of a fixed exchange rate. In noting this similarity, Dimand is surely right, as he is in drawing attention to Fisher's priority here; but it is also the case that both of them regarded international monetary stability as extremely valuable. Thus, in Fisher 1911, we find extensive discussions of how what he was later to call his "compensated dollar" scheme could be combined with the gold exchange standard to produce price level and exchange-rate stability in the international economy; specifically, Fisher noted that any gold exchange standard country acting in isolation could achieve price stability by varying its exchange rate, but that exchange rate stability could be obtained for the whole system by the central country varying the gold price of its own currency. In the *Treatise on Money* we find Keynes advocating public works expenditure as a second-best policy for Britain around 1930, where adherence to the gold standard inhibited the aggressive pursuit of cheap money.

It should be noted, nevertheless, that recognition of a potential conflict between domestic and exchange rate stability, combined with a preference for domestic stability if a choice had to be made, was not unique to these two. In particular, the same features are to be found in Alfred Marshall's evidence to the Gold and Silver Commission, not least in his well-known paper on "Remedies for Fluctuations in General Prices," ([1887] 1925) which formed part of that evidence. In that paper Marshall advocated what we now call "symetallism," a system based on Ricardo's 1816 ingot scheme under which paper money would be convertible into a fixed weight combination of gold and silver. Under such a scheme, money would, said Marshall, "vary in value with the mean of the values of gold and silver, . . . [The scheme] could be begun at once and without risk by any one nation. . . . If adopted by several nations it would constitute at once a perfect international basis of currency and prices" ([1887] 1925, 206). It seems to me that in this paper, in which, incidentally, he also canvased but did not advocate both a version of the "compensated dollar" and managed inconvertible paper (cf. pp. 206–7, n. 2), Marshall displayed exactly the same priorities vis-à-vis the goals of monetary policy, eventually embodied in the Bretton Woods Agreement, that we nowadays associate with Keynes, and which, as Dimand tells us, were also shared by Fisher. Those priorities, as I have argued elsewhere (Laidler 1991), seem to have been a product of the encounter between neoclassical monetary theory and the bimetallic controversy that took place in the 1880s, rather than of post–World War I monetary instability, though they took on much greater importance in this later period.

A second point of contact between Fisher and Keynes to which Dimand draws our attention is the essential similarity between Fisher's 1930 "rate of return over cost" and Keynes's 1936 "marginal efficiency of capital." Here I have been particularly struck by Keynes's reluctance, as documented by Dimand, to recognize the extent of this similarity lest he also have to accept Fisher's proposition that inflation affects the (nominal) rate of interest. I would be inclined to make more than Dimand of Keynes's resistance to Fisher on this second point, and also to argue that the resistance in question was hardly to Keynes's credit. It was his view (1936, 141–43, 167–68) that the interest rate was determined on the margin between money and bonds. Both were nominal assets, so inflation could not directly affect that variable. Instead, it shifted the marginal efficiency of capital schedule outward, and hence might drive down the real rate of interest. This conclusion was in due course developed by a number of influential British economists, for example Roy Harrod, who concluded unequivocally that "in the Keynes scheme the prospect of inflation has no tendency to raise the rate of interest" (1970, 179), and John Hicks, too, who in his final book still argued that "it is commonly thought that . . . high rates of interest [since 1950] are a consequence of inflation. . . . It is true that inflation makes these high rates of interest bearable, so that their consequences are not so desperate as they would have been in the past. But to make those consequences into causes surely takes things the wrong way round" (1989, 79).

What we nowadays call the "Fisher effect" was another of those ideas earlier developed by Marshall (as Fisher 1896 acknowledged). And if Keynes had not been so fascinated with the idea of money as a store of value—as "*a link between the present and the future*" (1936, 293, italics in original) he would not have lost sight of the proposition, well known to neoclassical monetary economists, particularly Marshall, but Fisher too, that it was also possible to substitute real capital assets of one sort or another for nominal assets, including what Keynes would have called transactions and precautionary balances. It is, of course, precisely substitution on this margin that creates the Fisher effect. Here is surely an instance in which Keynes's economics would have been much improved by a little more Fisherian influence, and the course that post–World War II British economic policy was to take under the influence of his disciples might have been a little smoother, too. In this case, however, Fisher has in the long run proved more influential than Keynes, and—ironically in the light of Keynes's (1911) invocation of the Cambridge oral tradition—as the transmitter of a Marshallian idea into the bargain.

There is another area in which Fisher seems to have outlasted Keynes, to which Dimand also alludes, but of which I wish he had made more. I refer to Fisher's 1930 analysis of the saving decision as the outcome of an intertemporal utility maximization process. This was to become the starting point of Milton Friedman's 1957 permanent income hypothesis of the consumption function. Now I am not here blaming Keynes for failing to see, in 1936, the implications of an argument of which he was probably unaware, and which were not in any event to become apparent for another two decades. This case is very different from his rejection of the Fisher effect. But the fact remains that no less an authority than Alvin Hansen characterized the consumption function as "Keynes's greatest contribution" ([1947] 1966, 18), pointing out that the analysis of the *Treatise* "leaves out the multiplier. The missing link is supplied by the consumption function. This . . . reveals one of the great advances of the *General Theory*" (19). Now, it is well known that the permanent income hypothesis denies a key proposition of Hansen's version of Keynesian economics, namely that "consumption is a function of income in the short run" (18) and hence establishes the multiplier as an unstable magnitude, dependent on the division of current income into permanent and transitory components, and hence inherently unpredictable. If one regards Hansen's version of Keynes's contribution as the true one—a big "if" to be sure, but a defensible one—then Fisher's influence seems, eventually, to have done Keynes's work serious, even fatal, damage.

Let us now sum up these comments, whose brevity prevents them from doing anything but very rough justice to Dimand's thoughtful and carefully nuanced paper. It is beyond question that Keynes was aware of at least some of Fisher's work throughout his professional life, but I suspect that the common elements among their ideas owe more to a common origin in neoclassical, and more specifically Marshallian, monetary economics than to an influence running from Fisher to Keynes. Moreover, in at least one instance where Keynes failed to follow Fisher's lead, that was an error on his part. From the standpoint of modern macroeconomics, Fisher's influence has proven far more durable than anyone might have guessed in the 1930s, and Keynes's less so. Perhaps this too reflects the durability of a broader neoclassical tradition within which Fisher was content to work, and to which Keynes ended up contributing, despite his self-conscious efforts to produce a framework that would supersede it.

The financial support of the Bradley Foundation is gratefully acknowledged.

References

Fisher, I. 1896. Appreciation and Interest. *AEA Publications* 3.11 (August): 331–442.
——— . 1911. *The Purchasing Power of Money*. New York: Macmillan.
——— . 1930. *The Theory of Interest*. New York: Macmillan.

Friedman, M. 1957. *A Theory of the Consumption Function*. Princeton, N.J.: Princeton University Press.

Hansen, A. H. [1947] 1966. The General Theory. In *Readings in Economics*. Edited by M. G. Mueller. New York: Holt, Rinehart, & Winston.

Harrod, R. F. 1970. *Money*. London: Macmillan.

Hicks, J. R. 1989. *A Market Theory of Money*. London: Oxford University Press.

Keynes, J. M. 1911. Review of Irving Fisher: *The Purchasing Power of Money*. *Economic Journal* 21:393–98.

———. 1930. *A Treatise on Money*. 2 Vols. London: Macmillan.

———. 1936. *The General Theory of Employment, Interest and Money*. London: Macmillan.

Laidler, D. 1991. *The Golden Age of the Quantity Theory*. Princeton, N.J.: Princeton University Press.

Marshall, A. [1887] 1925. Remedies for Fluctuations in General Prices. In *Memorials of Alfred Marshall*. Edited by A. C. Pigou. London: Macmillan.

Index

Contributors

A. W. (Bob) Coats is professor emeritus of economic and social history at the University of Nottingham and formerly research professor of economics at Duke University. He is a founding author, member of the editorial board, and one-time associate editor of *HOPE*.

Allin Cottrell is associate professor of economics at Wake Forest University. His research concerns the history of macroeconomic thought, the theory of socialism, and philosophical issues in economics.

Jacqueline Cox is modern archivist at King's College, Cambridge. She is custodian, among other literary, fine art, and economics collections of former members of the college, of the papers of J. M. Keynes and of his disciples Richard Kahn, Nicholas Kaldor, and Joan Robinson.

William Darity Jr. is Cary C. Boshamer Professor of Economics at the University of North Carolina at Chapel Hill. His current research interests include the historical development of expectations in economics, North-South trade models, the social-psychological effects of unemployment exposure, racial and ethnic economic inequality, and Keynes's economics.

John Davis is associate professor of economics at Marquette University. He has recently published *Keynes's Philosophical Development* (1994). He is also coeditor of the forthcoming *Handbook of Economic Methodology*, with Wade Hands and Uskali Maki.

Robert W. Dimand is professor of economics at Brock University, St. Catharines, Ontario, and visiting fellow at Yale University. He is author of *The Origins of the*

Keynesian Revolution (1988) and is currently finishing *Irving Fisher and Modern Macroeconomics.*

Peter Groenewegen is professor of economics and director of the Centre for the Study of the History of Economic Thought at the University of Sydney.

Kevin D. Hoover is professor of economics at the University of California, Davis. He was formerly a research associate and visiting economist at the Federal Reserve Bank of San Francisco. He is author of *The New Classical Macroeconomics: A Sceptical Inquiry* (1988) and an editor of the *Journal of Economic Methodology*. Professor Hoover's research focuses on causality in macroeconomics, especially with respect to monetary and fiscal policy; on the history of macroeconomic and monetary thought; and on the methodology of empirical economics.

Henry Kyburg is Burbank Professor of Philosophy and Computer Science at the University of Rochester. His research has focused on the foundations of statistics and probability, as well as on measurement theory and the philosophy of science. He is the author of a number of books in these areas.

David Laidler has been professor of economics at the University of Western Ontario since 1975. Earlier he held appointments at the Universities of Manchester, Essex, and California, Berkeley. He obtained his Ph.D. from the University of Chicago in 1964.

Michael S. Lawlor is associate professor of economics at Wake Forest University. He is currently at work on a book on the historical context of Keynes's *General Theory.*

Gregory Lilly is a member of the Department of Economics at Elon College. His research interests include bounded rationality, experimental economics, and economic philosophy. Recent publications include "Recursiveness and Preference Orderings," *Journal of Economic Dynamics and Control* 17 (1993), and "Bounded Rationality: A Simon-Like Explication," *Journal of Economic Dynamics and Control* 18 (1994).

D. E. Moggridge is professor of economics at the University of Toronto. He has been (with Elizabeth Johnson) editor of *The Collected Writings of John Maynard Keynes* (1981–1993) for the Royal Economic Society, (with Susan Howson) editor of the diaries of James Meade and Lionel Robbins, and author of *Maynard Keynes: An Economist's Biography* (1992).

Rod O'Donnell is professor of economics at Macquarie University, Sydney. A graduate in economics and philosophy, he received his doctorate from Cambridge University for research into Keynes's philosophy and its links with his economic thought. He has written *Keynes: Philosophy, Economics, and Politics* (1989), edited *Keynes as Philosopher-Economist* (1991), and contributed articles to journals in economics and philosophy. He is currently editing *The Further Collected Writings of J. M. Keynes*, a nine-volume edition of Keynes's remaining unpublished writings of academic significance.

Kerry A. Pearce is a graduate student in the Department of Economics at the University of California, Davis.

Jochen Runde is fellow and director of studies at Girton College, Cambridge. He has published on Keynes, probability, methodology, and Austrian economics. His current research is on small firm credit risk assessment procedures employed by U.K. banks.

Teddy Seidenfeld is professor of philosophy and statistics at Carnegie Mellon University. His research interests include foundational studies in probability, statistics, and decision theory.

Jim Tomlinson is reader in economic history at Brunel University, Uxbridge, Middlesex, England. He is author of *Government and the Enterprise since 1900: The Changing Problem of Efficiency* (1994) and *Democratic Socialism and Economic Policy: The Attlee Years* (forthcoming).